TALKING OF BOOKS

FOR HER

WHO HAS KEPT THEM, AND ME,

DUSTED

OLIVER EDWARDS

TALKING OF BOOKS

HEINEMANN

LONDON MELBOURNE TORONTO

William Heinemann Ltd

LONDON MELBOURNE TORONTO

CAPE TOWN AUCKLAND

THE HAGUE

First published 1957

Printed in Great Britain

at The Windmill Press

Kingswood, Surrey

CONTENTS

Oliver Edwards and
William Heinemann Ltd
are grateful to the Editor of *The Times*
for permission to republish these pieces
which first appeared in
The Times

UNLICENSED READING

This is an age of direct responsibility. Not only are we far away from the time when society could leave living to its valets; the nannies, governesses, school-dames, tutors have in most cases also departed. And the influence of the vicar and the schoolmaster is not what it was. As parents wrestle with the resultant problems, the question of what children should be allowed to read becomes daunting for some of them.

To base any argument on personal experience is to run the risk of narrowing its force. But what seems to be individual often turns out to be common. During all the talk about horror comics, I found my mind going back to a small boot-repairer's shop which was the Mecca of my childhood days. For in addition to his craft of heeling and soleing, and hammering in iron studs and tips, the shoemaker carried on a steady trade in second-hand penny dreadfuls. It was not the fact that for a penny one could choose four of them that was the chief attraction. Once they had been read they could be returned and two more obtained in exchange. Then those two could be bartered for a seventh. At which stage, admittedly, another penny was necessary to keep the process going. How many hundreds of these things I must have read, and also of undesirable periodicals too adult for me really to understand, does not bear estimating. Of course, it will be said that the penny dreadfuls of those days were Simon-pure compared with some of the recent horror comics. But there are climates in crime and sadism as there are in opinion, and I doubt if for their day those productions of the Edwardian age were any less deleterious to their particular readers than those of to-day are to our own children.

I was twelve when I read my first Hardy. It was *Tess of the d'Urbervilles.* I can remember the thrill of the whole new world of emotion and experience it opened up to me. I went day by day to the public library to read other Hardys till I got stuck half-way through *Jude the Obscure.* That was the end of Hardy for me at that time. Did this intensive dose of what G. K. Chesterton called "the village atheist brooding over the village idiot" turn me into a pessimist? Far from it. I am not going to say those were the sunniest days of my life because I have mercifully been blessed so far with a life composed mostly of sunny days. But no matter what I read, and lived in while I was reading, they remained carefree days, full of happiness and wonder, and excitement and serenity.

It is worth remembering that it was not the generation who read Kipling as children that grew up to be imperialists. Thanks to two remarkable talks by Mr. Noël Annan on the B.B.C. three years ago, and to my own experience, I am more in sympathy with Kipling's philosophy now than ever I was in childhood or early manhood. The truth is, I think, that we want to equip children with our own adult reactions, our mature emotions of which they know nothing. The dangers we fear pass them by. We are not even consistent in our fears. G. K. Chesterton put the point well when he said:

> Among these stories there are a certain number which deal sympathetically with the adventures of robbers, outlaws, and pirates, which present in a dignified and romantic light thieves and murderers like Dick Turpin and Claude Duval. That is to say, they do precisely the same thing as Scott's *Ivanhoe*, Scott's *Rob Roy*, Scott's *Lady of the Lake*, Byron's *Corsair*, Wordsworth's *Rob Roy's Grave*, Stevenson's *Macaire*, Mr. Max Pemberton's *Iron Pirate*, and a thousand more works distributed systematically as prizes and Christmas presents. Nobody imagines that an admiration of Locksley in *Ivanhoe* will lead a boy to shoot Japanese arrows at the deer in Richmond Park; no one thinks that the incautious opening of Wordsworth at the poem on Rob Roy will set him up for life as a blackmailer.

The only danger, it seems to me, that a parent should fear is that his or her child will grow up without a taste for reading.

Because reading is an adventure it cannot be successfully confined to chosen tracks. The more areas are roped off as dangerous the more they will acquire a quite unnecessary fascination and significance. The number of children who have come to harm or grief through being let loose in libraries cannot, of course, be known. But I am certain it is microscopic compared with the number who have been hurt through being kept away from them.

If the child's reading should not be censored can it be guided? This is a more difficult question. A child or an adolescent can be helped in its reading, but only provided any advice it is given has the one purpose of causing it to read more by being led to certain things, and not to read less by avoiding certain things. I am not suggesting that "awkward" or so-called "undesirable" books should be put in the young reader's way. There will be a sufficient quota of these provided by chance, anyway. The young can be safely left to cope with them, often without knowing they are doing so. But help can be given, particularly with some authors' works, by suggesting that "B" will be understood and enjoyed more if "A" is read first. The idea has been put forward that "orders of reading" should be established for such writers as Meredith and Conrad, and I think it is a good one. Even Thackeray can benefit from such a guided approach.

But, above all, no effort should be made to restrict children to "children's books". As Anatole France pointed out, being written by adults they are an invasion of the child's own territory, which it knows, moreover, better than any grown-up. What the child is anxious to do is to explore the vast, exciting world beyond its ken. And in the world of letters the good, the true, and the beautiful things are so many that little harm is likely to come from the few blemishes met along the way.

NOR CUSTOM STALE

The new Arden Shakespeare creeps slowly along the shelf, pushing farther apart the Marlowes and the Mermaid Series. An appropriate figure of speech for the process is hard to find. The colour of the newcomers is gay, though scarcely sylvan. Shakespeare knew nothing of delphiniums. But what matters more is that the contents are both physically and textually sturdy. The latest arrival, Mr. J. M. Nosworthy's edition of *Cymbeline*, complete with introduction, appendices, and notes, is an admirable example.

I cannot say I have a liking for notes, unless they are—as in Aulus Gellius, Burton's *Anatomy of Melancholy*, and Cecil Torr's *Small Talk at Wreyland*—the whole volume. Admittedly it is the notes which make the Birkbeck Hill-Powell *Boswell* such a joy. It is the notes which breathe life into Dr. Chapman's fine edition of Johnson's letters. And, with such examples in mind, it is never possible to open a volume of Welby's *Landor* without considering his "usual asceticism" a grievously lost opportunity. But all these are special cases. In general, notes are intrusive and tedious. They are the Oliver Goldsmiths of literature. Distracted by them, one longs to repeat George Michael Moser's "Stay, stay,—Toctor Shonson is going to say something." That is, until we come to Shakespeare.

What is it that makes Shakespeare impervious to all the sense and nonsense that has been written about him? It is not only the plays themselves that cannot be spoilt; in spite of the scores of books, lectures, essays, and annotations of Shakespeare one has read, the appetite remains unsatiated. Ruskin, perhaps, provided a clue when writing about one of the tombs in Santa Croce. "It is the crowning virtue of all great art that, however little is left of it by the injuries of time, that little will be lovely. As long as you can see anything, you can see—almost all;—so much the hand of the master will suggest of his soul." So alive is Shakespeare still, that it is living tissue the annotators bid us look at beneath their eighteenth, nineteenth, and twentieth century microscopes, no matter how minute a quibble they seek to dissect. Each generation comes to him afresh, with its own particular touchstones, complexes, and 'isms. He has withstood the stern common sense of Johnson, the lightning flashes of Coleridge, and the rhapsodies of Carlyle. For another sign of Shakespeare's vitality is that it is the most vigorous minds which take up his challenge. To-day they seem more numerous than ever. Their works pour out. Yet when the evening comes on which there is no longer a quickening of expectation at the sight of a new book about Shakespeare, then indeed must a man know that he has at last grown old.

All the same, even Shakespeare suffers *peine forte et dure* at times and so do Shakespeare's editors. "The numerous conjectural emendations" says Mr. Nosworthy in a note on the words "Whose mother was her painting" in Act 3, Scene IV, "are as distressing as they are superfluous, and there is not the slightest reason for questioning the F reading. . . ." To which most people will gratefully say "Hear, hear". For it must be confessed that Shakespearian emendation often seems a game played for the sake of the ingenuity of which the players are ultimately capable. The Stratford Irregulars can make rings around their Baker Street rivals. Many a time it is possible to read some passage of Shakespeare, see clearly what he meant, and become confused only when the eye strays willy-nilly to the "clarification" at the foot of the page. The effect is rather the same as taking a dose of the higher philosophy. How can sane, and presumably wise, men make such heavy weather out of a clear sky?

In all this, moreover, there is one man—whatever the evidence, I like to think of him as one man; all grievances are strongest when they are individual—who suffers even more than Shakespeare. If only it were possible to conduct libel actions from the Elysian case-room Shakespeare's compositor might be as rich as the Sheik of

Kuwait. Never can a worker's professional skill have been more constantly impugned. For over a century now, clever people have been making brilliant, inspired, and sometimes breath-taking guesses at the things he did wrong. Cortez's men cannot hold a candle to the Shakespearian commentators when it comes to wild surmise. (They, moreover, had the wisdom to keep silent.) That the typesetter made some mistakes must be admitted, for he was human and, even though a compositor, therefore prone to error. But there is no crime of his craft this bemused, incompetent, wretched dunderhead is not presumed to have committed. His fingers were all thumbs. He mistook the characters' names for part of their speeches at the beginning of lines. He left odd letters or whole words off the end of lines. He dropped sentences; he could not read; he had a system of punctuation all his own; occasionally he turned up for work straight from the Mad Hatter's tea party. How he escaped the sack, Heaven knows. Maybe Heaven, in sweet revenge, keeps him happily employed in St. Peter's printing office, setting up his critics' *curricula vitae* for future reference. They, at least, will know what to expect.

But, in all truth, we wish them no harm. Long may they cerebrate and their books about Shakespeare continue. And if there be anyone coming newly to the reading of them, let him not begin with Maurice Morgann's famous essay on Falstaff, which is overrated, but with Ivor Brown's *Shakespeare*, with Bradley's *Shakespearian Tragedy*, and with Frank Harris's *The Man Shakespeare*; after which there will be *Shakespeare's Imagery* by Caroline Spurgeon to carry him into the realms of gold.

ADOLPHUS CROSBIE

Few people, I think, would name *The Small House at Allington* as their favourite Trollope. It has neither the skill of *The Claverings*, the suspense of *Orley Farm*, the charm of *Dr. Thorne*, nor the power of *The Way We Live Now*. Last but one in the Barchester series, it has the disadvantage of all penultimate notes; one is waiting for the close. The fates of four of its main characters are left to be settled in *The Last Chronicle of Barset*. Trollope, who was as shrewd a judge of his own books as any Posterity has yet produced, thought it a good work. It is. But it is revealing that he singled out as its best features the De Courcy family and Sir Raffle Buffle, neither of whom is a main protagonist. His attitude to Lily Dale was rather equivocal, and Quiller-Couch thought Johnny Eames cheap. But I am surprised that so few people, not even Trollope himself, have sung the praises of its most superbly drawn character, the "villain of the piece", Adolphus Crosbie.

It seems to me that the case for *The Small House at Allington* can best be fought on the ground where, for some ninety years, its critics have said it was weakest. They have never understood how Crosbie could go down to Allington, fall in love with the poor but enchanting Lily Dale, announce his engagement to her, and then go straight on to Courcy Castle and become engaged to Lady Alexandrina De Courcy. But Trollope brought his whole power, and a good deal more care in details than he usually worried about, to make it credible. It is true Trollope rushes the first engagement through in his opening fifty pages. That is not only a tribute to Lily's charm but an essential part of the study of Crosbie's character. He had been bowled over. No sooner is the deed done than his doubts begin to sprout. He was very much in love, and life was very pleasant, but "there were moments in which cold fits of a melancholy nature came upon him. He was doing the very thing which throughout all the years of his manhood he had declared to himself he would not do."

For Crosbie was both a social climber and an ambitious careerist. As Trollope says later on, when Crosbie is writing his first letter to Lily from Courcy Castle, he "was not altogether a villain . . . He was an ungenerous, worldly, inconstant man." He was also a mass of indecision. Lily had undoubtedly won his heart. But no sooner does he begin to feel he has destroyed his freedom than he starts to worry about the money question. Squire Dale makes it clear he will settle nothing on his niece. Crosbie will not give up Lily. He begins to assert to himself, "perhaps too frequently", that he has not the slightest intention of breaking off the engagement. All the same, the marriage will have to be postponed. And he will go on feeling aggrieved.

That great drawback of money leads to minor blemishes in his paragon being discovered. On his strolls with Lily he lectures her. She adores him so blindly that she takes it all meekly. He thinks himself free to go on to talk openly of his past life. "He had no fear of losing her. Alas! might it not be possible that he had some such hope!" Yet in the great scene when Lily, just before he leaves Allington, unreservedly offers him his freedom, he cannot bring himself to accept it. His fears are not dissipated. His doubts do not vanish. But the innocence of both daughter and mother is too much for him. "As he walked back alone, he swore to himself, binding himself to the oath with all his heart, that he would be true to those women."

Well in keeping with such a character is the fact that Lady Julia de Guest's vehement harping on his engagement from the moment he arrives at Courcy Castle should have forced him to equivocate. Living with such people intensified all his hankerings after freedom to climb. He cannot have it. He realizes that once married to Lily he will no longer be able to call on the De Courcys. But he could perhaps make an exception of Lady Alexandrina. What a friend she would be for Lily.

> What an advantage would such an alliance confer upon that dear little girl;—for, after all, though the dear little girl's attractions were very great, he could not but admit to himself that she wanted a something—a way of holding herself and of speaking, which some people call style.

From that moment Lady Alexandrina's battle is half-won. The scene in which she clinches her victory is one of Trollope's best.

Yet no sooner is the die cast, Lily thrown over, and the engagement to Lady Alexandrina proclaimed, than Crosbie is again a prey to doubts and regret.

> He felt that he would have given all that he had in the world to have back the last four and twenty hours of his existence. But he had no hope. To jilt Lily Dale would, no doubt, be within his power, but he knew that he could not jilt Lady Alexandrina De Courcy.

So they are married. Promotion and success come. But everything —not merely the thrashing from Johnny Eames—is ashes in his mouth. And, although we are well short of half-way in the book when the issue of Crosbie is settled, the interest in *The Small House at Allington*, for me at any rate, is done. But I doubt if Trollope ever wrote a better 250 consecutive pages than those opening ones in which Crosbie is under the microscope.

Why then the general sense of bafflement and discontent among so many readers? It is, I think, because they get no good picture of Crosbie in the round before he does go under the microscope. He is a clerk; he is an Apollo; he is a swell. But we are never quite sure what he really is. Most of Trollope's characters you can at once see foursquare. But Hugh Walpole was right to complain that Crosbie's social position is amorphous. Even Millais's original illustrations do not help much. They are not among his best. After a number of readings of *The Small House* and *The Last Chronicle*, however, some idea of the Crosbie before it all started does begin to grow. Given that, I will yield to none in my admiration for the way his character spins the plot. Most people bring forward *Cousin Henry* as Trollope's masterpiece in weakness and avarice. For me Adolphus Crosbie is a finer study.

FADED HIBISCUS

If the French ever get tired of hearing that they have no equivalent for the English word "home" they might reply that we could do with a publisher's maid-of-all-work like "cahiers". Exercise books just will not do. Who would dare to put out "The Exercise Books of George Bernard Shaw"? Notebooks is too narrow. The Notebooks of Samuel Butler, of Matthew Arnold, of Henry James have all led us to expect a definite kind of publication. But cahiers can be anything, and when I saw a reference the other day to *Les Cahiers Pierre Loti*, I wondered what treasure from the "master" could still be hauled up 34 years after his death.

I gather the answer is "quite a lot". There is a body called the Association Internationale des Amis de Pierre Loti and they bring out in the *Cahiers* unpublished papers and fragments of Loti's work which still exist in good supply in Loti's old home at Rochefort. And, of course, like all good French literary societies, the Association is devout in appreciations and studies of its *raison d'être*. I must confess I have not read any of them. I have no great inclination to do so. But the knowledge that the Association existed led me to spend the better part of a week browsing once again through Loti's works.

The result was not exhilarating. But then, who would expect it to be? If anyone was *fin de siècle* it was Loti. He has been called the last Romantic. With him existence is one long sigh. What colour there could be in life if it did not always fade. But the sun is setting. "Au crépuscule disparut l'Arabie." Sombre dreams and dark visions came to him in the night. All is *morne* and melancholy. "Je vais continuer à promener mon ennui par le monde." Persia, Baluchistan, the Levant; the Irriwaddy, the Sahara; Japan and the blest islands of the Pacific—all are far away. The kissing and the telling are done. Here speak lips from which all the ends of the world are gone and the moustache is a little weary.

To read Loti is to be led to murmur to oneself Villon's *Ballade des Dames du Temps Jadis.*

> Dictes moy où, n'en quel pays,
> Est Flora, la belle Rommaine . . . .

And Rarahu from Tahiti? And Aziyadé the Circassian? And Pasquala Ivanovitch, the Herzegovinian shepherdess? "Où sont les neiges d'antan!" indeed. Best of all I like the Polynesian girl whose memory he conjured up out of his ditty-box. There, among so many other relics, he found the faded and desiccated hibiscus garland, or *lei.* And once again he was on the sea-shore—at twilight, of course—and the beautiful young maiden was coming towards him, moving exquisitely, savagely entrancing, perfectly formed. "Her hair fell straight to her waist like heavy streams of black lava." (All Loti's women are Rapunzels; blonde or brown, golden or raven, their hair streams about them on the least provocation.) But back to the hibiscus! Naturally she gave it to him. Children they were; the hour was sad; all around them was nature, indifferent and *fatale.* They had their moment of bliss; the next day it rained too hard for them to meet; the day after that, Loti sailed away.

The astonishing thing to-day is that all this once had the power to entrance not only the multitude but good critics as well. That Loti became *académicien* may have meant little. But did not even Anatole France sing his praises? And was he not in England, even in *The Times,* variously compared with Chateaubriand, with Byron, with Conrad? It makes one hot and bothered to think of it. He has neither the genius of his fellow-countryman, the fire of the Englishman, nor the brooding integrity of the Pole. If a better comparison were wanted it might be found in d'Annunzio. But Loti wrote no *La Città Morte,* and d'Annunzio did take Fiume.

How did it all come about? What was Loti's secret? He was no great master of French prose. He wrote simply and well, but he had relatively few stops to pull out; his vocabulary is undistinguished. Admittedly he was of the era of Ella Wheeler Wilcox and Ouida and can therefore be said to have been in tune with his age. They, however, never aroused the same critical enthusiasm. In France it may have been due to the fact that Loti was the first author to open up the world for the Frenchman in action—for one of the key points in almost all his books is the fact that he was a naval officer—after the 1870 débâcle. But in England? Well, Loti was always anti-English. He wrote *L'Inde sans les Anglais* and dedicated it to President Kruger. He regarded the British as "the eternal enemy of our race". He paraded the delicious absurdity that Loti was a Yorkshireman. He also wrote a good sea story in *Pêcheur d'Islande* (though not so good as *Captains Courageous*). What more was needed to make us take him to our hearts?

But one must not altogether make fun of Loti. In at least one thing he was justified. His faith in Turkey's resurgence has been magnificently translated into fact. Lesley Blanch, in a pleasantly evocative article in the *Cornhill* a year ago, wrote of Istanbul as "Loti-land", and when the French Government issued a commemorative stamp of Loti just before the War, they placed him against a background of the Bosporus. At present, so I read in a French newspaper, that tale of the harems, *Les Désenchantées*, is his best-selling novel. Miss Blanch says that to the Turkish people themselves Loti is still a legend. All this should please his shade if it rests quietly in the Ile d'Oléron. But if it wanders farther afield, still looking for the wraith of Aziyadé, I doubt if he will really like her smart and shorn sisters of to-day.

TALK ON THE TERRACE

Tradition has established—probably it is that experience has confirmed—that a fiftieth anniversary is an inappropriate occasion to commemorate a great man. One should, however, seize upon any excuse to recall a good one. So when, as I was reading Goldsworthy Lowes Dickinson's *A Modern Symposium* for the nth time the other day, I noticed that the title page said 1905, I felt a desire to write about him. How much he is read by anyone to-day, which of his books are still in print, and whether the younger generation are aware of him I know not. Maybe some of his arguments have been overtaken by events, the more practical parts of his message outmoded. But the best of his books, his simple and limpid prose, the principles and enthusiasms which drove his life, the sweetness and light of the man himself—these surely still have a meaning.

When he was alive Dickinson's greatest influence was with the young—whom he loved—and I think he will always be essentially a young man's author. It is not without significance that although he died as recently as 1932, and lived to be seventy, his best works were all written before the First World War, and before he was fifty. If I were asked to name them I would list *The Greek View of Life*, *The Meaning of Good*, *Justice and Liberty*, and *A Modern Symposium.* It may seem a small freight with which to voyage into Posterity. But concerned, as they essentially are, with goodness of one kind or another, they are a kind of cargo of which the total bulk in English literature is small. The poets, moreover, have never needed bulk to be remembered. Lowes Dickinson was at heart a poet.

A Modern Symposium exactly describes itself. A body of men prominent in politics or the professions meet at a country house on the North Downs. They include Alfred Remenham, the Liberal Prime Minister of the day, and his "great antagonist" Reuben Mendoza; Lord Cantilupe, a Tory who has just retired from public life; George Allison, a business-man socialist; Angus MacCarthy, an anarchist (later to be killed in St. Petersburg); a journalist, a professor, a biologist, a poet, a writer, a gentleman of leisure, and a Quaker.

After dinner, the time of year being June, and the weather unusually warm, we adjourned to the terrace for our coffee and cigars. The air was so pleasant and the prospect so beautiful, the whole weald of Sussex lying before us in the evening light, that it was suggested we should hold our meeting there rather than indoors. This was agreed.

And so the symposium begins. Cantilupe is supposed to open the proceedings by reading a paper. He has forgotten it. He is asked instead to make a personal confession. Why is he a Tory? Why has he been a politician? Why is he retiring in the prime of life? Cantilupe proclaims, and explains, his Toryism. His is both a eulogy and an epitaph. Remenham follows, to express the mission of Liberalism both at home and abroad. By the end of the night everyone has spoken.

I do not propose to summarize the talk. Rather I hope that some may have their curiosity sharpened enough to get the book for themselves. The interesting thing to remember is that the year is really (although the evening is supposed to have been spent some time earlier) 1905. It was in many ways a pivotal year in English politics. Salisbury, Kimberley, and Harcourt were dead. Spencer was paralysed. Rosebery had had his day. The brief but pregnant reign of Campbell-Bannerman was about to begin. It was the year of the end of the Russo-Japanese War and of the Unemployed Workmen Act. The nations of the world were slowly regrouping themselves and a new social stirring was in the air. Impatience was abroad. It was a time of ardour and hope.

With the spirit of the time, Lowes Dickinson's speakers range far beyond politics. Not merely the generations-old duel of Conservatism and Liberalism, but Socialism, anarchy, the collectivist state, the promise and threat of the American way of life, the claims of aristocracy and democracy, the place of the artist in society, Christianity and Paganism, are all canvassed. And Dickinson does not caricature or parody. He gives a fair hearing to each. The last speaker of all is Geoffry Vivian, a man of letters, who finally invokes "the principles of life, and about them crystallizes the universe. For will is more than knowledge, since will creates what knowledge records. Science hangs in a void of nescience, a planet turning in the dark. But across that void Faith builds the road that leads to Olympus and the eternal Gods."

By the time he had finished speaking the sun had risen, and the glamour of dawn was passing into the light of common day. The birds sang loud, the fountain sparkled, and the trees rustled softly in the early breeze. Our party broke up quietly. Some went away to bed; others strolled down the gardens; and Audubon went off by appointment to bathe with my young nephew, as gay and happy, it would seem, as a man could be. I was left to pace the terrace alone, watching the day grow brighter, and wondering at the divers fates of men. An early bell rang in the little church at the park-gate; a motor-car hooted along the highway. And I thought of Cantilupe and Harington, of Allison and Wilson, and beyond them of the vision of the dawn and the daybreak, of Woodman, the soul, and Vivian, the spirit. I paused for a last look down the line of bright statues that bordered the long walk below me. I fancied them stretching away to the foot of Olympus; and without elation or excitement, but with the calm of an assured hope, I prepared to begin the new day.

I have said Lowes Dickinson was a poet at heart. He was also one in words.

"LOVE IN THE VALLEY"

When Mr. Jack Lindsay, in his new study of George Meredith's life and work, comes to *Love in the Valley*, he remarks that on its first appearance "no one noted the debt of its lingering clashing melody to Darley's *Serenade of a Loyal Martyr*." All one can say is that everyone has done so since. Indeed it is possible to doubt whether the stammering Irish poet-mathematician would be read or remembered at all to-day if it were not for this attribution. If Meredith was in fact indebted to him he has repaid the debt many times over.

When this Darley-Meredith business started I do not know. A memory of Sir John Squire pointing it out in one of his *Observer* articles some thirty-four or five years ago stays with me. Nor do I propose to try to demolish the theory. Even though Darley did once rhyme "use 'em" with "bosom" there are one or two things of his worth, even vicariously, keeping alive. Granting that Meredith did know Darley's work—Darley died when Meredith was 18 and the first version of *Love in the Valley* was published in 1851, five years later—there are, I think, two points worth making. The first is that Darley's particular attitude to Earth and to Nature may have been more influential than one individual metrical exercise. Secondly, the metrical debt has been overrated. Some people mention Darley as if that explained the whole of Meredith's magic away.

Darley-Meredith being one of those easy pieces of literary knowingness that can speak multitudes although they say little, it is worth while putting two individual stanzas side by side and seeing what the debt amounts to. Darley's *Serenade of a Loyal Martyr* opens

> Sweet in her green cell the Flower of Beauty slumbers,
> Lulled by the faint breezes sighing thro' her hair;
> Sleeps she, and hears not the melancholy numbers
> Breathed to my sad lute amid the lonely air?

Here is Meredith

> Under yonder beech-tree single on the green-sward,
> Couched with her arms behind her golden head,
> Knees and tresses folded to slip and ripple idly,
> Lies my young love sleeping in the shade.
> Had I the heart to slide an arm beneath her,
> Press her parting lips as her waist I gather slow,
> Waking in amazement she could not but embrace me;
> Then would she hold me and never let me go?

At once it can be seen that the metre is not identical. What is common is the strong use of the caesura; and Meredith's handling of the pause, the subtlety with which he varies it throughout the poem, were, even in his earlier effort, far beyond anything Darley could manage.

There is a much more fascinating mystery in the writing of *Love in the Valley* which I have never seen convincingly solved. I have spoken of "the first version" and Meredith's "earlier effort". Even some of those who know large stretches of *Love in the Valley* by heart do not realize there are two versions. (G. M. Trevelyan gave them both in his fine, complete edition of Meredith's poetical works in one volume in 1912.) The first was written before Meredith was 23. As he was then passionately in love with Mary Peacock, whom he had married when he was 21, the presumption is that she inspired the poem. Professor Lionel Stevenson in *The Ordeal of George Meredith* denies this on the ground that "Meredith's bride was a widow with a five-year-old daughter, whereas the keynote of the poem was the youth and virginity of the girl." But even though Mary Peacock, or Nicolls as she had become, was seven years older than Meredith, is it likely he saw her in that light? But whether he did or not, whether he sang Mary's wayward graces or those of some other, earlier passion, whether he was only in love with love, the fact remains that he was young, he was ardent, he was enamoured, and he wrote a poem which was only a pale forerunner of the beauty that was to come. Siegfried Sassoon has described it as "eleven immature stanzas". Certainly it would not have lived on if there had never been another version.

If it was merely maturity Meredith had put into *Love in the Valley* as we know it now, and if he had lived a placid domestic life, there would perhaps be little cause to wonder. Instead, Mary and George Meredith grew farther and farther apart with tragic speed. Arthur was born in 1853 and was undoubtedly Meredith's child, but Mary's next child was not. She deserted him in 1858 and went off to Capri with the painter, Wallis. Wallis in turn deserted her. She became mortally ill, distraught, and more or less derelict; dying in 1861. In her last days she wished to see both Meredith and Arthur. At first Meredith was adamant. Neither husband nor son should she set eyes on. He relented, or was forced to give in, so far as Arthur was concerned. But he himself never saw Mary again. In anguish after her death he wrote *Modern Love*. In 1864 he married once more. A new life with Marie Vulliamy began. The great series of novels broke upon the world one by one. The past seemed closed. The pattern of the Meredith we know to-day was set.

And then in 1878, at the age of 50, and 27 years after *Love in the Valley* was first published, he took up this relic of his young, eager, passionate period with Mary again, threw away some of its 11 stanzas, added many others till the finished poem had 26, and left few lines of those he had retained unaltered. He poured into the poem ecstasy, beauty, immortality. He made it a veritable paean of young love. Whether intentionally or not he fixed a picture of Mary Peacock for ever. Why he did it, how he could perform such a miracle, no one has ever been able to explain. Every human heart has its mysteries. For me this is one of the most profound of them.

READING ALOUD

Happily there are still people who read aloud. I do not mean the highly skilled and beguiling performers who broadcast "A Book at Bedtime", but those who, often haltingly and with wildly fluctuating degrees of success in expression, read to each other in the quiet of their own homes.

It takes two to read aloud. I did recently come across a man who was engaged in reading *Guy Mannering* aloud to himself, but he was doing this to prove a theory (and ultimately to write a learned book about it). In general, however, a listener is needed as well as a reader. It should, moreover, be one listener rather than two or three. Numbers usually bring lack of communication somewhere; some sensed, even though unspoken, criticism. And the whole joy of reading aloud comes from the act of sharing; the known reactions of both parties in the undertaking; the mingling of emotions as the work slowly unfolds. For this reason the best books to read aloud are those neither party has read before. If there is acquaintance on the part of the listener then there is not much point in the work being read. In such circumstances attention will be concentrated on the delivery rather than on the content, a course liable to lead to trouble. If the reader knows what is coming on the next page then he or she will be hard put to remain natural. Expression will degenerate into histrionics.

What are the best kind of books to read aloud? One immediate answer is Jane Austen. A woman told me the other day she and her husband had been trying Virginia Woolf's *The Common Reader* as a change and had found it a great success. Most people prefer novels, if only for the story. Character and plot ensure that interest does not flag. (There is nothing more disconcerting for the reader than to suspect he has "lost" his audience.) If there is too much dialogue, however, (especially with a number of characters involved) pitfalls open up. The ordinary reader has not the skill to get his voice inside different characters. Attempts to do so can prove unintentionally funny. Yet a flat, monotonous delivery distributed equally among all the author's creations is unconvincing. There are other pitfalls. I had to abandon reading George Moore's *Héloise and Abélard* aloud when Blois entered the tale.

Many people like best for reading aloud biographies and books of travel. They have obvious advantages. The story of a life has continuity. It must be ill-written if one does not know precisely where one is all the time. Even when the main outline is known—perhaps all the more interesting because of that—there are all manner of new and revealing complications or embellishments. The narrative is bound to have form, to progress to some sort of climax; thereafter, as often as not, to decline towards its inevitable close. No man's life can be contemplated with complete detachment. At some point some emotion—liking, dislike, admiration, scorn, pleasure, or pity—must be stirred. Not the least of all the reasons why Boswell's *Life of Johnson* is the greatest of all biographies is that it is one of the most moving of all books to read aloud. And as the end approaches, and day by day we revisit the dear old man, good, pious, ailing, and so terribly afraid of death, we are so inexpressibly moved that we do manage to express it. With this kind of book the slow deliberateness of reading aloud, the fact that we get through it only in comparatively small doses and that therefore the book spreads out through our days as the man's own life spreads out in time, heightens the emotion. Even though it is all of 35 years ago, and we are only just setting out together, and the end seemed so incredibly remote as to be non-existent, we were in tears.

Travel books rarely stir the depths. They stimulate the imagination. The first time I ever read Kinglake's *Eothen* it was aloud. From the very first sentence, when we meet our author in the streets of Semlin at the furthermost point of "this wheel-going Europe" and on the threshold of "the Splendour and Havoc of the East", we are in thrall. *Eothen* is one of the most splendid of all books to read aloud. It can be argued, of course, that no matter how you read it the effect is tremendous. That is true; but I believe that travel books gain more than most other kinds of literature from being read aloud. The worst of all books for oral reading are humorous books. If the reader does not collapse in laughter how can the hearer? If he does, he is generally a sentence ahead of his audience and goes off into peals of mirth leaving his hearer in suspense, indignant.

But of all leisure activities, there must be fewer rules for reading aloud than for any other. It is so intensely personal an affair. And I have, inevitably, been concerned here far too much with the books and far too little with the people. Any book will affect every couple differently. A husband and wife told me the other day that they had read alternate chapters of *Moonfleet* to each other, and had been so overcome that the only way they could get through the last chapter was silently and separately. Two others to whom I had recommended it had vertigo on the cliff climb but found themselves merely more and more excited as the tale went on. In both cases they had had a memorable and happy experience. That, perhaps, is the ultimate joy of reading aloud. The sense of communion lives on long after the book itself may have been almost forgotten.

DINER CHEZ MAGNY

I see that the French courts have decided that there is no reason why we should not have a fuller and less expurgated version of the Goncourts' journals, although I doubt whether by now there is anything very exciting left to reveal to the world. Personally, I would be willing to forgo all other disclosures for just one newly found sheet giving us a full picture of one of the Magny dinners.

At their best they cannot have had their equal in the world's history as entertainment for our generation. (The Greek *symposia*, as decorously left to us, are nobler, but the number of people they entertain to-day is limited.) Yet the Magny dinners started unobtrusively. The Goncourts' journal—the fullest record of them I know—notes that the first one took place on November 22, 1862. The Goncourts attribute the organization of the affair jointly to Gavarni and Sainte-Beuve. But I recall that Mr. Palache in his book *Gautier and the Romantics* some 30 years ago said the real originator was Dr. Veyne; one of those amiable figures so often to be found in the background of any literary scene. Gavarni was entering what proved to be his last illness (although he was not to die till four years later), and needed taking out of himself. Dr. Veyne suggested a regular party. Sainte-Beuve took up the idea enthusiastically and chose the Café Magny because it was then his favourite restaurant.

The company at the first dinner was small: Gavarni, Sainte-Beuve, the Goncourts, de Chennevieres, and of course Dr. Veyne. They decided they would meet every other Saturday, and add other members to their circle. The first recorded addition was the Comte de Nieuwerkerke, who can hardly have enlivened the company (though he took them back to smoke a cigar with him in his apartments in the Louvre). But on February 23, 1863, they landed their first big fish. Turgenev joined them for the first time. He was given a great reception and won all their hearts. There was talk of the state of Russian literature and of Heine. The story was told of Heine's deathbed remark that forgiving was God's profession. Others joined thick and fast. Taine was at the next dinner; soon Gautier, and Renan, and Flaubert are regularly of the company, which also includes such lesser lights as Soulié, Scherer, Neftzer (hardly a light at all), and Saint-Victor. The Saturday was changed to Monday for Sainte-Beuve's benefit. The stage was set; the cast assembled; it remained only for the performers to perform.

That they did so brilliantly is certain. It can be said to be almost a matter of history. One has to say "almost" because it is at this point the Goncourts' journal becomes so exasperating. We are given so many illuminating flashes. Then, just as things become absorbing, the curtain descends. The Goncourts were interested in too many things, had too many other irons in the fire, to be true Boswells of these conversations. Now and again there is an extended discussion, but it is never rounded. And all too often we are given only the headings of what was talked about.

It was wide enough and catholic enough in all conscience. We have Sainte-Beuve explaining why he would like to be an Englishman, the discussion moving on, as only after-dinner talk can, to About, and to religion, to God, and to Taine's conviction that musical natures tend towards Protestantism. March 28, 1863, saw something of a battle royal. It was Renan's first appearance, so they started off with religion. Soon Voltaire was brought in and the Goncourts, perhaps to put the cat among the pigeons, declared that *Candide* was the only work he deserved to be remembered by, and what was *Candide* but "La Fontaine in prose"? Abuse of Voltaire leads to abuse and praise of Rousseau. Soon the feathers are flying. Poor Renan is shocked into silence. But slowly they calm down and come back to religion. "It's curious," says de Goncourt, "how at dessert one always talks about the immortality of the soul." "Yes," replies Sainte-Beuve, "when one no longer knows what one is saying." At other times they discuss Confucius, Joubert's letters, the nature of love, are the planets inhabited?, the behaviour of decapitated bodies, the slow freezing of the world, and the political significance of whether Gautier's waistcoat at the first night of *Hernani* was red or pink. A favourite topic was George Sand, until the historic dinner when the lady actually joined them.

The dinners were great fun while their freshness lasted. By June, 1864, they had become the subject of a newspaper article; in October, 1866, an American journalist was present. At their height the Goncourts were prepared to come back from the country not to miss one of them. But five years covered their best span. Death, the coming of the Franco-German War, and the fact that the geniuses of the Second Empire left no generation to replace them took their toll. The entries get fewer and fewer in the journal. The dinners are moved to Tuesdays. On December 1, 1874, Edmond de Goncourt records that "the old Magny dinners become really wearisome." Jules de Goncourt was dead; so was Sainte-Beuve; so was Gautier. On November 3, 1885, there was an effort to get the dinners going again and to recapture the Magny spirit. Among the talkers recorded are Pouchet, Hébrard, Paul Bert, and Ribot. The rest is silence.

A. J. RAFFLES

Thirty-five is a number of no particular significance, and the fact that E. W. Hornung died at St. Jean de Luz 35 years ago to-day* is therefore likely to go unnoticed. But I have felt more than once that the creator of Raffles has had less than justice done to him. For some reason I have never fathomed, Guy Boothby is in the *Dictionary of National Biography* and Hornung is not. I have nothing against Boothby. Dr. Nikola was, and is, one of my favourite characters in fiction; the years have made him only more endearing as they have made him more absurd. But if Boothby can enter our national Valhalla why not Hornung? Both wrote innumerable novels, and in both cases fewer than a handful are remembered. Hornung also wrote a few patriotic poems during 1914–18, and did some useful war work. And if these things are hardly credentials for Posterity, then I believe Raffles to be a better, more believable, and more enduring character than Nikola.

What the young generation of to-day think of either I do not know. Mr. Eric Gillett, in an interesting talk to the English-Speaking Union a few weeks ago, asserted that this is not an age of literary characters. He could think of only Jeeves, Poirot, and, perhaps, Hornblower as likely to endure. Personally, I should put in one or two others with a question mark, and Biggles without one. But, generally speaking, Mr. Gillett is right. We have no fictional characters with the force and conviction of Holmes, Raffles, Captain Kettle, or even Convict 99 to-day. And at the head of them all, even at the risk of incurring the wrath of Mr. Christopher Morley, Mr. S. C. Roberts, Mr. Bernard Darwin, and the whole host of Baker Street irregulars great and small, I would place A. J. Raffles.

*March 22, 1956

What pictures the name conjures up! First of all, that of the man himself. The dare-devil figure in the Zingari blazer, the batsman at the nets with his pocket full of sovereigns which he put on the stumps instead of bails, the England slow bowler who believed that "if you can bowl a bit your low cunning won't get rusty, and always looking for the weak spot's just the kind of mental exercise one wants." Cricket, however, was not the only attribute on the respectable side. There was also the Raffles who could quote Virgil, read the lessons in church, play in the Old Boys' match, relish Steinberg 1868 and *jambon du Westphalie au champagne*, and smoke, except in the course of duty, nothing but Sullivans. (The only part of this Raffles I have become dubious about in later years is the man Lord Thornaby thought he might get into the Athenaeum under Rule II. But then, maybe Lord Thornaby himself was rather hazy about the Athenaeum.)

It may seem to be standing Raffles on his head to present this guise of him first. For, as the worshipping Bunny himself saw clearly, Raffles was a villain. He was first an amateur cracksman and later a professional one. Not only did he steal; on occasion he used violence. It is true that Bunny averred that the bullet he sent across the roof tops at the "sporting oafs" who were hunting him in *A Thief in the Night* was "the only shot that Raffles ever fired in his whole career as a midnight marauder." But one never knew quite how far he would, at a pinch, go. A thrill came into his voice more than once when he spoke of the possibility of committing a murder. Alongside the more elegant tools in the Raffles relics, the thin steel ladder, the silk rope, the black mask, there was also the far from elegant life-preserver. But there was more to Raffles than the fact that he was a contrast. Gentleman crooks had probably existed before—and, alas, have been legion since. The point is that while the respectable Raffles is as firmly fixed in the mind's eye, as certain in every detail, as the most conventional of our friends, the other Raffles forever remains a completely uncertain quantity. What *would* he do or not do? How far *would* he go? Bunny never knew to his last day. Raffles's strange morality, or rather a-morality (how well Gerald du Maurier used to bring out this side of him) keeps us constantly guessing. He will not hesitate to rob his host because he is outraged at being invited to a country-house party for his cricketing prowess ("engaged like the waiters and the band" is his indignant comment). But he will not smuggle Bunny into the Lord's pavilion for the University match. Most of the time he was affectionately meticulous and quixotically ready to hazard himself in his protection of Bunny. Yet the two tricks he played on his companion at the outset of their career together were both pretty outrageous and void of any honour.

Bunny forgave him and we forgive him, precisely because of this very incalculability. It was so with every hero we had at school. Part of our education is to find exactly where each man's feet of clay begin. Hornung understood that queer mixture called schoolboy honour as few writers have done. The longer we read of Raffles the greater are the number of episodes from our own boyhood tragedies and comedies that come back to us. There comes back, too, the London of Atlas buses, of the hansom cab, of the sulphurous fogs, of the lazy country-house life, of the long, lovely decade of the Edwardian age. (Chronologically, of course, Raffles was Victorian, but in spirit he was Edwardian.) No one, I think, has given us in fewer words so true a feeling of all that we lost when that life vanished. They were, moreover, words of one syllable. For not the least attractive part of the Raffles books is the simple, plain, unaffected language in which each one of them is written.

FOOLISH FANNY

I have often wondered what it must be like to live with a silly woman. Now I know. For I have been reading, very slowly and in daily doses spread out over some weeks, *The Diary and Letters of Madame d'Arblay*, better known, perhaps, as "Fanny Burney's Diary".

One starts it with every possible prepossession. There is, first in point of time, Macaulay's essay. Although among his last, it is far from one of his best. But Macaulay is read in boyhood. He sweeps you whither he wills and certainly off your feet. His recital of her girlhood, her success, her immurement at Court, the indignities she suffered at the hands of Madame Schwellenberg, makes a lasting impress. One even swallows the idea that her style was ruined by Dr. Johnson. Later, when one reads *Evelina* and *Cecilia*, it is impossible not to feel some surprise at the furore they created. But *Evelina* is an attractive book none the less. Finally, there is the whole charmed Streatham circle to give young Fanny Burney a setting. How many times as the years go by do we not glimpse her, sitting with Johnson, chatting with Windham or Burke, corresponding with Mrs. Thrale. It is true that, if we pause to think about it, she never seems to be making quite the impact her fame would lead one to expect. The *Diary* explains why.

The Burneys were a rather irresponsible and light-hearted lot. They did not lack piety or respectability, especially by the time they had got to "the great Dr. Charles". Fanny was undoubtedly a good, devoted, earnest, and upright woman. Unfortunately virtue and sense are by no means automatic companions. Sensibility and sensitiveness she certainly had. She is always in a flutter about something or other. The early "embarrassments" over the success of

Evelina and the "mystery" surrounding its authorship can be forgiven, although their constant reiteration in the *Diary* becomes tedious. After all, she was a young authoress suddenly rocketed to fame (though not so young as she later thought she had been). But it is when she gets to Court that her essential silliness comes out. One can share the indignation against her father for being so unthinking, and perhaps selfish, as to send her there. But if there is any pity at all evoked by the absurd and at times farcical (for it is farce and not tragedy) recital of all her ups and downs, ecstasies and mortifications, shiverings and twitterings during her five years as a royal servant, it is for her masters rather than for herself. They shine with goodness. Who but two naturally forbearing souls would have put up with the ineffable Mrs. Delany? (Fanny's inherent lack of balance is shown in her immoderate references to the old lady.)

George III was an essentially kindly man, and though Queen Charlotte, as her portrait shows, had a much harder streak in her, she did not ever, according to her lights or the lights of those days, treat her Keeper of the Robes with any great lack of consideration. Quite the reverse. She put up with a good deal. In fairness to Fanny it must be said her *Diary* never implies otherwise. But thanks to Macaulay and others an absurd legend has grown up that "royal slavery" not only robbed the world of a great genius but added harshness to the process. Neither assumption is true. All the evidence is there to suggest that Miss Burney had, when she entered the royal service, written just about all she was capable of writing, and that the "immurement" was in effect a blessing.

It gave her to all eternity an excuse for not having developed, and for never equalling the output of Miss Austen. Her later unreadable efforts are all forgotten. Her complete failure with *The Witlings* is ignored. How marked a decline *Cecilia*, her second work, was from *Evelina* is slurred over. The fact that she lived close on 50 years after her resignation from the Court and in all that time published not a line worth considering then or now is hardly taken into account. Even the uncomfortable truth that the roundly abused and harshly treated Mrs. Piozzi was worth, in brains, in personality, in attractiveness, and in character, half a dozen Fanny Burneys is never admitted. Mid-Victorian literary uppishness plus perhaps the then unpopularity of the occupant of the throne confirmed a generation in the belief that a great genius had been cruelly stifled in youth and the world robbed of masterpieces that would otherwise have appeared. After all, had not Dr. Johnson made nice noises to her and even kissed her hand?

Are we to take it then that the *Diary* is of no consequence? Of course it has value. But diaries fall into two classes: those that are personal revelations of a character which, however odd or even ignoble, is none the less worth knowing, and those which relate at first hand, or throw new light on, great events. Fanny Burney sought to do both. But so far as she herself is concerned there is little worth knowing. All one can say is that she was good, and let it go at that. At the same time, she lived in stirring years and was thrown into the company of some famous men and women. One readable volume could be got out of her seven, concentrating on the Johnsonian years, the madness of George III, the trial of Warren Hastings, and her life in Paris and Brussels during the Hundred Days. For, as *Evelina* showed, Fanny Burney had an eye. She was an excellent reporter. And what she has to say of these experiences is of great interest and still vividly alive to-day. Nicely illustrated and with a proper period flavour it would make an excellent Christmas book. Progress in printing and publishing being what it is, I offer it as a suggestion to some book maker for, say, three Christmases after next.

CRAS AMET

Living, just over a hundred years ago, in the pleasant surroundings of Bear Wood, the Rev. Robert Aris Willmott clearly did not find his labours as Rector of St. Catherine's fully disposed of his time. So he set to work to bring the poems of Thomas Gray, Thomas Parnell, William Collins, Matthew Green, and Thomas Warton within the compass of one volume. As he also included biographical notices on each, preliminary essays to the longer poems, a running commentary in footnotes on the nicer points of elegance and taste, to say nothing of illustrations by Birket Foster and Edward Corbould, a very thick, squat, dumpy, unhandy volume it is. Yet it has accompanied me on many a holiday. For there was something in the Rector's idea. These poets are all of a piece. They divert and please without demanding too much. They each have one or two poems worth all the attention one can give. As the years pass, one finds one's favour moving from one poet to another. For some time I have had a weakness for Thomas Parnell.

The friend of Pope and Swift, he was the only likeable member of that trio. Goldsmith wrote his biography, which enabled Dr. Johnson to make "Parnell" one of the most perfunctory of the *Lives of the Poets*. That Parnell died from drink is fairly certain; but whether he took to it because of the loss of his wife, or his son, or his hopes of preferment no one has been able to determine. In our own day Earle Welby has called him "the last confidant of the fairies". Johnson thought "An Allegory on Man" the happiest of Parnell's works; others have given first place to "The Hermit" or "A Nightpiece on Death". But the poem of Parnell's which interests me most is "The Vigil of Venus". In his other works Parnell may be said to be competing with himself. In attempting to make an

English version of *Pervigilium Veneris* he invited comparison with many others.

Pervigilium Veneris has been variously ascribed to Catullus, to Sidonius Apollinaris, Tiberianus. The truth is that no one knows by whom, where, or when it was written. Sir Cecil Clementi, who devoted a lifetime of study to the poem, could come to no conclusion. One guess is as good as another and the most attractive of all is Walter Pater's, in *Marius the Epicurean*, that Marius's friend, Flavian, wrote it after hearing the refrain of a popular song sung by young men on the sacred day in March when the "Ship of Isis" was launched as a tribute to the Great Goddess, the patroness of sailors.

Cras amet qui nunquam amavit;
Quique amavit cras amet

they sang, and the words have lured, enchanted, and baffled poets ever since.

I am no scholar to dissertate on the innumerable versions of the *Pervigilium Veneris* as a whole, and it is indeed a rather dull subject. But the attempts of men in different countries through four centuries to render effectively these nine simple words are fascinating. The thing was summed up almost at the outset, perhaps, by Michel de Marolles, who in 1653 produced eleven different versions in French, all of them inadequate. Four years earlier, in 1649, Thomas Stanley had led the English team on to the field with

Love he to-morrow, who lov'd never;
To-morrow, who hath lov'd, persever.

Since then, the efforts have been endless. R. W. Postgate, who himself translated *Pervigilium Veneris* in 1924, referred to "at least twenty-five attempts", but this was of the whole poem. The score of published and unpublished tries at *Cras amet* alone must run into hundreds. Among the few I have collected are:

Let those, who never yet have lov'd,
  Tomorrow feel love's pain,
Let those, who have the passion prov'd,
  Tomorrow love again.

Anon, 1795.

Tomorrow let those love, who have never loved; let those who have loved, love to-morrow.

Walter Kelly, 1854.

They that have never loved before, let them love ere tomorrow's o'er!
They that once have loved before, let them tomorrow love once more!

F. G. Fleay, 1864.

He that never loved before,
  Let him love to-morrow!
He that hath loved o'er and o'er,
  Let him love tomorrow.

C. G. Prowett, 1882.

Let him learn to love tomorrow who hath never loved of yore;
Let him love again tomorrow who hath learnt to love before.

W. H. Porter, 1909.

Know'st thou love? Tomorrow mind him!
Know'st him not? Tomorrow find him!

Sir Thomas Warren, 1911.

Now learn ye to love who loved never—now ye who have loved, love anew.

Sir Arthur Quiller-Couch, 1912.

Tomorrow shall be love for the loveless, and for the lover tomorrow shall be love.

J. W. Mackail, 1912.

Tomorrow love comes to the loveless, tomorrow lovers
love again.

R. W. Postgate, 1924.

Tomorrow be lovers who never were lovers and they that were
lovers be lovers again.

Lewis Gielgud, 1951.

This last, I must confess, has for me more of the feel of the original than most efforts, but Parnell's version (1720) has been so long with me that I doubt if it can be displaced.

Let those love now, who never loved before;
Let those who always loved, now love the more.

Like the majority of its rivals it suffers from excess wordage. Only Mr. Postgate, among those I have quoted, gets near to the nine words of the original.

Pater, alas, made no effort. He merely described the setting, the night scene in Pisa, the young men pouring forth their chorus "as they bore their torches through the yielding crowd, or rowed their lanterned boats up and down the stream." Then, next morning, "the long procession started betimes."

At the head of the procession the master of ceremonies, quietly waving back the assistants, made way for a number of women, scattering perfumes. They were succeeded by a company of musicians, piping and twanging, on instruments the strangest Marius had ever beheld, the notes of a hymn, narrating the first origin of this votive rite to a choir of youths, who marched behind them singing it. The tire-women and other personal attendants of the goddess came next, bearing the instruments of their ministry, and various articles from the sacred wardrobe, wrought of the most precious material; some of them with long ivory combs, plying their hands in wild yet graceful concert of movements as they went, in devout mimicry of the toilet. Placed in their rear were the mirror bearers of the goddess, carrying . . .

But why should one ever stop? Who can resist a show, or Pater, or Marius? Above all, *Marius the Epicurean*. "Cras amet qui nunquam amavit, quique amavit cras amet."

PETER WILKINS

Every library is full of people we would like to know more about. When they are fictional, the curiosity is essentially idle. They are the author's creatures and, as Dickens showed with his alternative ways for Pip and Estella to behave on the last page of *Great Expectations*, they can be anything he or we may desire. But with real people it is different. Thus and thus were they, and we long to know just how it was. Borrow's old apple-woman on London Bridge, the man from Porlock, M. Magny of the famous literary dinners—on the printed page they are wraiths seen in glimpses, yet there was a time when they were living men and women. And none was ever once more alive than that "lady not only of high dignity of spirit, such as became her noble blood, but of excellent understanding and lively talents," Elizabeth, Duchess of Northumberland. You do not have to rely on Boswell's word alone. There is Horace Walpole's tribute to her as "a heap of jovial contradictions". She befriended poets and wrote poetry herself. She intrepidly went at night to see the Cock Lane ghost. She printed Goldsmith's *Edwin and Angelina* for him and had Percy's *Reliques* dedicated to her. For me, however, these things are as nothing to the fact that she was the original of one of the most engaging heroines in fiction—Youwarkee, the second Mrs. Peter Wilkins.

At least she was Youwarkee's original in mind. But, as her creator, Robert Paltock, was careful to point out, not in body. For Youwarkee was not only gracious and comely, she was also built in such a way that she could fly. Where Robert Paltock got his conception of "flying Indians" from is a mystery. He was born in 1697, and while any man who had heard of Icarus did not need to await the later fantasies of space travel to imagine an airborne people, his description of his creations is a detailed, convincing, beautiful piece of work. (It is more beautiful than M. Boitard's efforts to depict them in line; these are as lumpish as most eighteenth-century fashion plates.) We know Paltock lived in Clement's Inn, and Arthur Bullen, to whom we owe so many things and who resurrected *The Life and Adventures of Peter Wilkins* some 70 years ago, pictured him as a dreaming recluse turning from "the vulgar paths" of fame and money and determining instead to keep his fine feelings by writing a charming romance. (What things the old Inns could do to lawyers if they were not fully employed!) But whatever its origins, Robert Paltock's *Peter Wilkins* broke upon a fairly appreciative world in 1751. That was also the year of Gray's *Elegy*, Smollett's *Peregrine Pickle*, and Fielding's *Amelia*. And for a certain class of readers, of whom I am one, there is no sense of incongruity in mentioning it in the same breath as these three.

There have been few generations in which *Peter Wilkins* has not had a few strong supporters. So assorted a trio as Lamb, Southey, and Sir Walter Scott all lost their hearts to it. Coleridge declared it to be "a work of uncommon beauty" worthy to be put alongside *Robinson Crusoe*, and confessed that he had thought of writing a third such tale himself, to make a triptych. As for Leigh Hunt, he more than once went into dithyrambs, for "a sweeter creature than Youwarkee is not to be found." Bullen's own introduction to his 1884 edition is a nice essay in the art of appreciation.

Coleridge was only partly right in linking *Peter Wilkins* and *Robinson Crusoe*. The beginnings of both stories are rather similar, and for the first hundred pages or so the tale is merely picaresque, and Peter Wilkins's adventures thus far might well have been written by Defoe. But once we come—to quote the title-page—to

> His Shipwreck near the South Pole; his wonderful Passage thro' a subterraneous Cavern into a kind of new World; his there meeting with a Gawry or flying woman; whose Life he preserv'd, and afterwards married her; his extraordinary Conveyance to the Country of Glums and Gawrys,

or Men and Women that fly. Likewise a Description of this strange Country, with the Laws, Customs, and Manners of its Inhabitants, and the Author's remarkable Transactions among them

we are in a world Defoe, at any rate, did not encompass. For Paltock had a poet's imagination. And some of his descriptions of scenes and events have a sense of wonder and a delicacy allied to their matter-of-factness which weave an enchantment all his own. One can never read of Wilkins's first hearing the strange, seemingly disembodied, aerial voices without thinking of that other wonderful scene of Rima and her companions in the forest in *Green Mansions*. And the description of Wilkins's marriage night—all praise to Bullen for having overcome his self-voiced doubts and dared Victorian prudery by keeping it in—is worthy to be compared with Yeats's great poem *Leda and the Swan*.

The Life and Adventures of Peter Wilkins is not all idyllic. Nor are all the "flying Indians" angels. There is a revolution; such a civilized implement as a cannon; some executions take place. But all these things are not so much larger than life or smaller than life as in some curious way detached from life. Yet Peter's own domestic happiness with his Youwarkee never becomes mere fairy tale. Their dealings with each other are those of two rare human beings. Whether or not Rousseau read *Peter Wilkins* I do not know. It must have delighted him if he did. The tale goes its persuasive way until Youwarkee dies and Peter decides to return to England once more. Part of the persuasion lies in Paltock's having burked no difficulty, funked no description, invented names and titles, and even scraps of language, as he goes along. I shall not be at all surprised if Sir Edmund Hillary and his companions come back with a wonderful tale that they have discovered the land of Graundevolet somewhere in the region of the South Pole.

Peter Wilkins is, I think, not now in print. But it was once in Everyman and it is one of those books you will see from time to time in one garb or another in the sixpenny boxes. It is well worth that and much more. I hope it may be revived. Maybe the best means would be for history to repeat itself. In its first run of popularity it was a subject for spectacles and pantomimes. Cannot one of the more literate producers—best of all, Mr. Disney—be persuaded to take it up? It is pleasant to think of dear, dreamy, old Robert Paltock of Clement's Inn rising, after two hundred years, to the dizzy heights of "the book of the film".

CONRAD'S WOMEN

We were playing Ifs. "What do you think would have happened," the question was asked me, "if Rita had married Joseph Conrad?" Not wanting to think too hard, I idly retorted: "We should have had a better and happier book than *Joseph Conrad and his Circle.*" But the question has stayed in my mind since. Not so much regarding Mrs. Conrad. That would be an impertinence. She was, poor woman, yoked to a genius, and the fact that she was not one herself was hardly her fault. Whether in any circumstances Conrad's life would have been a gay and carefree one is doubtful. Even a Rita de Lastaola would not be likely to have transformed that grave and brooding, and sometimes agonized, nature. But she might well have robbed the world of three or four great works.

The works are there, thank goodness, and personally I have always put *The Arrow of Gold* among them. This is unfashionable. It is also said to be uncritical. Few writers on Conrad have been prepared to place the book in the first flight of his works, or indeed to say a good word for it. Miss Bradbrook, in her fascinating and original *Joseph Conrad: Poland's English Genius*, says straight out: "He does not succeed here." The subject was one "which cut so deep that he had never attempted it before . . . The very writing is for the most part turgid and clogged." Perhaps because it was the first book of Conrad's I ever read, and because there was the excitement that I was in my teens and that it had just come out, it has never lost for me its life and passion. Conrad himself used these two words in going to the heart of the matter. He attempted no literary appraisal of it, but devoted his subsequent preface to stressing that it was written in what had then seemed England's darkest hour and that its subject had been with him for many years, "not so much a possession of my memory as an inherent part of myself." And that subject "and no other" was "the quality of initiation . . . into the life of passion."

The Arrow of Gold, then, is autobiographical. How much so (adding to Conrad's categoric assurances) has become more and more apparent through the years. It has been known for long enough that there *was* a Mr. Blunt, "*Américain, Catholique, et gentilhomme*," and that Conrad did fight a duel with him over the girl he calls Rita de Lastaola. But any new bit of the jigsaw that can be fitted in (they are bound to be few, as these were the events of Conrad's earliest, darkest, and naturally unrecorded days) invariably confirms what Conrad himself said of those pages in *The Mirror of the Sea* dealing with Rita, and the whole of *The Arrow of Gold*:

> The pages and the book form together a complete record and the only assurance I can give my readers is, that as it stands here with all its imperfections it is given to them complete.

Conrad, although he qualified this to Sidney Colvin so far as the Rita of the Tremolino was concerned, was invariably a truthful man.

It was starting from this point that Mr. E. H. Visiak in *The Mirror of Conrad* last year took large chunks from *The Arrow of Gold*, substituted Conrad for "Monsieur George", and presented what Conrad had called "a story between two notes" as the matter of fact of his life. I remember seeing this rather severely dealt with in one review at the time; but I do not know that Mr. Visiak was not inherently right. Whether we are ready or not to accept the idea that Conrad the artist had no hand whatever in *The Arrow of Gold*, the fact is that there was a young woman of the antecedents and character Conrad gives Rita (our ignorance of her actual name is of little consequence) and that, amidst all the gun-running, Conrad fell passionately in love with her. Mr. Oliver Warner, who wrote the best and most comprehensive short study of Conrad, in Longmans' "Men and

Books" series some five years ago, doubted whether the relationship was likely to have been serious on Rita's side. This is possible. *The Arrow of Gold* hardly contradicts it. It does not in any way weaken the effect of the episode on Conrad himself.

That it coloured his subsequent life, Conrad affirms. I believe it also coloured his view of women. No one, so far as I know, has made a thorough study of the women in Conrad's novels and stories. Mr. R. L. Mégroz devoted a few pages to it in *Joseph Conrad's Mind and Method* but they were only enough to suggest how rich such a study might be. If one here and now declared that a common factor could be found in all of them, no doubt various Conrad enthusiasts would write in and ask me how Aissa, Nathalie Haldin, and Mrs. Gould, to name only three, could be fitted in to the same pattern. Well, I will be bold enough to make one or two generalizations. Conrad could embody certain virtues in a woman, but no woman character of his comes fully alive unless she is passionate. Conrad's finest woman characters are all foreigners. Even when he gave them English names their characters are essentially foreign. Conrad depicted any number of convincing English men. He never drew a rounded English woman. Conrad's best men characters are trying to get or to keep within the shape of things as they are; Conrad's best women are alien to it or trying to get outside it. Which brings me back to Rita and to what is perhaps Conrad's most explicit word on the experience. In another letter to Colvin, written a few days after *The Arrow of Gold* was published, he called it

> this emotional adventure fated to end as it ends in a world not meant for lovers and between these two beings both outside the organized scheme of society not because they are *déclassés* in any sense but because of the origin of one and the deliberate renunciation of the other.

Whether Rita ever got inside "the organized scheme of society" no one knows. Conrad did and in some ways felt an exile thereafter.

MOCK LAUREL

Gentle book-hunting is a pleasant occupation. To amble idly through the second-hand shops with a watchful, hopeful, but by no means anxious or purposeful eye; to be delighted if, by any chance, after 20 years of searching one does come across a copy of Trollope's *Marion Fay* or *Castle Richmond*, the second volume of Kirke White's *Remains*, or John Stuart Mill's *Three Essays on Religion*; to be almost equally happy to come out with nothing at all—these are delights for a questing but a quiet mind. Patience is everything. The years are long; we are in no hurry; there is plenty to read meanwhile. And if the day ever does come when, going up or down stairs in Cambridge, or Edinburgh, or Guildford, or Tunbridge Wells, we suddenly come face to spine with Godwin's *Mandeville* then the pleasure will be all the greater because the encounter has had to wait half a lifetime.

But there is one interesting consequence of being no mighty big-game hunter. (First folios, black letter, and all the rest of that esoteric paraphernalia are beyond me in more ways than one; I want books only to read.) It is the books in the highways and the byways, the sixpenny boxes, and the barrows that one does meet again and again. Unregarded, unwanted, their ubiquity heightens their distress. What success they must have had in another age to be still so plentiful. What care and enthusiasm was once lavished on them. The attractiveness of their get-up adds to their come-down.

Among such volumes the works of Stephen Phillips take a high place. In their ribbed, comely green and gold, with the laurel wreath still bright upon the cover, they are unmistakable. Which volume is it this time? *Herod*? *Ulysses*? *Paolo and Francesca*? The *Poems*? Sometimes they stand all together. Although we have done it so often before, a certain mixture of wantonness and wonder makes us turn to the pages of press notices Mr. John Lane invariably included before the back cover. "Mr. Phillips is a poet, one of the half-dozen men of the younger generation, whose writings contain the indefinable quality which makes for permanence" says *The Times*. "Mr. Phillips is a poet already of noble performance and exciting promise" according to Richard Le Gallienne. "He sees clearly, feels intensely, and writes beautifully; in a word he is a true poet" is a quotation from William Archer. "We possess in Mr. Stephen Phillips one who redeems our age from its comparative barrenness in the higher realms of poetry" runs W. L. Courtney's tribute. And so one could go on and on. Leigh Hunt, Tennyson, Racine, even Shakespeare, are all called into the account. The unfortunate Churton Collins linked Phillips's name with those of Sophocles and Dante.

What happened? How did it all come about? So far as Churton Collins was concerned he "discovered" Phillips as a youth, urged him to write poetry, and, perhaps, felt he had to back up what he was responsible for. But what of the others? And what of the public which bought five editions of the *Poems* in a year? Or the "awe-struck, spellbound" undergraduates at Oxford when "a grave and thoughtful young man . . . with the features of a Greek god" (the description is by Mr. Horace Bleackley) rose before them and for 20 minutes recited his own poems "fresh and pure from the heavenly spring"? Or Sir George Alexander, or Beerbohm Tree, who both believed in his dramas?

At this point the old doubt sneaks in again. Is it we who are wrong? Will Phillips yet come into his own again? One turns once more to "Marpessa", hailed at the time as one of his masterpieces.

So
When the long day that glideth without cloud,
The summer day, was at her deep blue brow
Of lilies musical with busy bliss,
When very light trembled as with excess,
And heat was frail, and every bush and flower
Was drooping in the glory overcome;
They three together met . . .

Surely it is still spurious stuff? "Christ in Hades" is no better. (I am deliberately choosing what were reckoned his triumphs.) As for the once famous verse dramas, they are not unreadable but they are dead. Not a spark of heat, or light, or force, or beauty, or any animation remains. Nor can we believe there was ever any there in the first place. This is not a case of a writer's reputation sinking into a trough after his death, to rise to its true worth in a later generation. Phillips was played out long before he died. He lived only 51 years, yet during the last decade he was more than once near starving, and penniless.

Poor Phillips. One does not resurrect his story in order to make fun of him. He was in youth an attractive creature. His weaknesses destroyed him. He was his own worst enemy. But in a way all these things are irrelevant. The fact is one cannot escape his derelict books to-day. And they are the ones written at what was the height of his powers. They are his best. When one thinks of the other poets who were also making their way then—Housman, Kipling, Alice Meynell, Francis Thompson, William Watson, Laurence Binyon, and Yeats—and asks how in the midst of such work Phillips's now lifeless efforts could command such extravagant critical and popular acclaim and create so great a furore the mind boggles. At this point I suppose I should propound some paradox to explain it all, be capable of some original solution. Unfortunately I am not. The thing has puzzled me for 30 years. I still do not know the answer.

A BENNETT QUARTET

It is good to know that the Arnold Bennett Society recently held its first annual dinner, even better that they ate at the George Hotel, Burslem. For the George Hotel, Burslem, is said to be "The Dragon" of *Clayhanger*, and of it Bennett wrote:

> The history of human manners is crunched and embedded in the very macadam of that part of the borough, and the burgesses unheedingly tread it down every day and talk gloomily about the ugly smoky prose of industrial manufacture. And yet the Dragon Hotel, safely surviving all revolutions by the mighty virtue and attraction of ale, stands before them to remind them of the interestingness of existence.

Bennett was 42 when he wrote those words. He already had a number of books, including *The Old Wives' Tale*, behind him. He was, indeed, both physically and artistically past "the middle of life's journey." Yet he held firmly to those last four words. He privately printed his first issue of *Things that Interested Me* in 1906; he gave his friends another collection in 1907; he published a completely different volume *Things that Have Interested Me* in 1921, another in 1923; another in 1926. Of all the novelists who have ever written none has believed more deeply in, or clung more fiercely to, the interestingness of life.

That, more than anything else, I think, is what will bring readers to Bennett for a long time to come. He had other attractions too, of course. He was an honest craftsman. One of the most widely read of novelists, he read with a purpose. When he read or wrote he knew precisely what he was doing. He was dogged and industrious. I profoundly admire the author of *The Old Wives' Tale*; it is the man who, over thirty-two years, wrote the three volumes of

Journals that I have an affection for, and almost reverence. His creative gift was probably small. His feelings could be powerfully moved but rarely soared. He was not a genius. It is wrong to say he had no style. He had so individual a style that one cannot pick up one of the true canon (Heaven knows how one explains away the pot-boilers) without at once knowing it is a work by Arnold Bennett that one has in one's hand. Yet because he was so deeply interested in everything, from his mother's funeral to the behaviour of a fat, crochety, repulsive, middle-aged woman in a Paris restaurant, his observation was sure, his characterization was true, and his invention never flagged. So, while his books vary in stature possibly more than those of any other author, they are almost unfailingly readable.

Geoffrey West, in *The Problem of Arnold Bennett*, a very small book now nearly twenty-five years old but still, to my mind, the most penetrating appreciation made of Bennett, reminded us that in his *Journal* 1929 Bennett had remarked:

> I have written between seventy and eighty books. But also I have only written four: *The Old Wives' Tale*, *The Card*, *Clayhanger*, and *Riceyman Steps*. All the others are made a reproach to me because they are neither *The Old Wives' Tale*, nor *The Card*, nor *Clayhanger*, nor *Riceyman Steps*. And *Riceyman Steps* would have been a reproach too, if the servant Elsie had not happened to be a very sympathetic character.

Of these four books I would, if we were going to establish precedence, myself discard two. I have never been able to understand the enthusiasm for *The Card*. It might just as well have been called "The Cad". Even if Edward Henry Machin was "identified with the great cause of cheering us all up" I would rather have had it done by a more attractive character. *Helen with the High Hand*, *A Great Man*, or *Mr. Prohack* are far more entertaining works.

The *Clayhanger* trilogy admittedly has not the unity or the timelessness of *The Old Wives' Tale*. Nothing else Bennett wrote could approach the poignancy and majesty of that famous scene in the room above the pawnbroker's shop in Deansgate, Manchester, where Sophia sees Gerald dead. But simply because it is not *The Old Wives' Tale*, *Clayhanger* has been misprized. Darius Clayhanger, Auntie Hamps, Mr. Shushions, Hilda Lessways, even Big James, are no ordinary creatures. There are some memorable episodes. There is nothing half-hearted or half-size in the conception. I, moreover, am not one of those who believe *Clayhanger* is less because the trilogy was completed. In *Hilda Lessways* Bennett attempted a *tour de force* and brought it off. Interest in Edwin and Hilda does not peter out in *These Twain*.

The Old Wives' Tale, *Clayhanger* . . . What should go next on the list? *Imperial Palace* is spiritually empty. *Anna of the Five Towns*, *Leonora*, *The Price of Love*, can none of them, good as they are, take that high place. *Whom God Hath Joined* can. Because it is an early work, written before Bennett was famous, it has never been fashionable. By all but a few critics it has been badly underrated. It has passion, and gives us one of those dramas of acceptance which Bennett saw as part of life's tragedy. Annunciata Fearns, her father and her mother are three of Bennett's completest character studies. The book has not lost any of its power after fifty years. To complete the quartet I would unhesitatingly choose *Lord Raingo*. If the three other books are pure Enoch, always the better and more fundamental of the two Bennetts—this is the best Arnold. Its political sketches are brilliant; and should any future generation be interested in some aspects of life in England in the 1914–18 War, then it could have no better guide than the knowing Bennett.

May the Arnold Bennett Society have many more annual dinners. I only wish it were possible for Sir Max Beerbohm to be the guest of honour at one of them, the menu of course including "Christmas pudden and scruts".

HE WENT, SINGING

"Death came leading Fame by the hand." Why those words of Helen Thomas's have been constantly going through my mind, I do not know—unless it be the striking contrast between her husband's story and that of Stephen Phillips. The first and most obvious difference, of course, is that Edward Thomas was a true poet. But further, Thomas knew little success and had no acclaim during his lifetime. All the work he will be remembered by was done during the last 30 months before he died. And in many ways his permanent reputation did not start growing until nearly 15 years later, after his widow had published her two haunting books.

It is as well to get this particular matter into perspective. *As It Was* and *World Without End* are to my mind imperishable. They tell in the simplest possible language, and direct from the heart of the woman who loved him, a poet's youth, love, life, struggle, and death. They have sent many people to Thomas's works who might have found their way there much more slowly otherwise. They led Mr. Robert Eckert to collect Thomas, to write his life and publish his most useful bibliography. They primed the pump. But the crucial point is that the well of pure, unaffected poetry was there all the time. Thomas's work lives in its own right, not because of his story. His wife's book would be a beautiful work even if he had been a bad poet. His stature as a good poet would be undiminished had no word about him ever been written.

What that stature is has been said once for all by Mr. Walter de la Mare. After reciting, in his foreword to the *Collected Poems,* some of Thomas's loveliest works and declaring "*their* word is England" he goes on

When, indeed, Edward Thomas was killed in Flanders, a mirror of England was shattered of so pure and true a crystal that a clearer and tenderer reflection can be found no other where than in these poems; neither in "Clare and Cobbett, Morland and Crome," nor among the living, to whom he was devoted in Hardy, Hudson, Doughty. England's roads and heaths and woods, its secret haunts and solitudes, its houses, its people—themselves resembling its thorns and juniper—its very flints and dust, were his freedom and his peace. He pierced to their being, not through dreams, or rhapsodies, not in the strange lights of fantasy, rarely with the vision that makes of them a transient veil of the unseen. They were to him "lovelier than any mysteries." "To say 'God bless it', was all that I could do."

Thomas was somewhere in his thirty-seventh year when Robert Frost persuaded him that his true bent was poetry. His life up to that time—the hack work, the drudgery, the misery of the articles and the volumes to be turned out at rates such as £37 10s. for 60,000 words, the even greater misery if no commissions were forthcoming—is now well known. The story has been so dramatized, however, that it has rather obscured one important fact. It was absurd that Thomas had to churn out volume after volume, from things he could put his heart into such as his *Richard Jefferies* and *The Happy-Go-Lucky Morgans* to studies of Swinburne, Pater, and Borrow, *The Feminine Influence on the Poets*, and even a life of Marlborough. But the point that must be made is his conscientiousness. He was never less than competent. None of the books is unreadable. Hard work, common sense, good, clear writing went into all of them. Whether he is saying of *Marius the Epicurean* that "As in *The Child in the House*, the central character is neither wholly Pater nor wholly someone else" or is pointing out that Marlborough "has suffered in memory because he was not loved except by his wife", he is always an honest craftsman using his skill and intelligence, no matter how tired or heavy-hearted he might be.

Skill and intelligence, however, are transient things, and I am not among those who believe Thomas was a great prose writer so far unrecognized. *Horae Solitariae* is his pleasantest volume, *Richard*

Jefferies his best. But all of them give way to the one volume of his poems. One hundred and ninety-five pages contain the 140 lyrics; which is good enough evidence there is nothing forced or pretentious. Many of them are deceptively short and simple, but they have the power to create beauty, to ease the heart, and to evoke a whole world of memories. "Lob", "The Mill-Water", "Lights Out", "The Brook"—one could go on quoting titles. Amidst all the singing, there is no monotony. From the charming opening of

> If I should ever by chance grow rich
> I'll buy Codham, Cockridden, and Childerditch,
> Roses, Pyrgo, and Lapwater,
> And let them all to my elder daughter

to the closing lines of "Adlestrop"

> And for that minute a blackbird sang
> Close by, and round him, mistier,
> Farther and farther, all the birds
> Of Oxfordshire and Gloucestershire

mood and metre are always subtly changing. The beauty, the integrity, the unforced singing remain constant.

> Now all roads lead to France
> And heavy is the tread
> Of the living; but the dead
> Returning lightly dance

wrote Thomas in "Roads". It was not quite true of himself, for he went voluntarily; his genius more and more fully bursting into song; serenity and confidence and peace of mind coming to him at last. It was not to be for long. He joined up in July, 1915, and was killed in April, 1917. Of his final leave at Christmas, his wife has written in a way that warns all others off the ground. There are few passages more moving in English literature. The homely scene, the children being bathed in front of the fire, the reading from Shelley, the last cup of tea in bed the next morning, the leaving of the poems, there is everything here for tears. And I am not ashamed to say that as I read the pages for possibly the twentieth time they still come.

THE FAIR S. S.

I do not know what Dr. Johnson would have said to Johnnie Ray, could they have met, unless it were to give the same advice that his own sage gave to that other youth who could scarce repress the starting tear. The Great Cham might, indeed, have said nothing at all. He might not have been impressed. Had he not seen this part of the performance done even more elegantly some considerable time before? From the London Palladium to the Thrale home at Streatham may seem a far cry. But ever since I read the notice of Mr. Ray's performance in *The Times* the other day there has been floating about in my mind the tantalizing, beguiling, half-formed vision of Sophy Streatfeild, "the weeping bluestocking", "the meek Minerva", "the fair S. S."

Readers of Boswell alone know her not. Dr. Johnson was too naturally reticent a man where his friends' private affairs were concerned to bandy names before outsiders. It is true he once wrote "If Streatfeild has a little kindness for me I am glad." But that was in a letter to Mrs. Thrale, and it is interesting that he mentions her in no letters other than those to Mrs. Thrale. Readers of Mr. James L. Clifford's fine life of *Hester Lynch Piozzi* (*Mrs. Thrale*) will know why. So will those who have delved in *Thraliana* or Abraham Hayward's edition of the *Autobiography, Letters and Literary Remains of Mrs. Piozzi.* There are glimpses of her in Fanny Burney's *Diary*, and although there the truth about Miss Streatfeild's place in the Thrale household is not revealed it is from Miss Burney that we get the best description of the accomplishment that made Sophy famous. For Sophy could weep at will. She would be sitting, and talking animatedly, and smiling in company. Mrs. Thrale, who loved to show off all her lions, would suddenly coax and urge "Do cry a little, Sophy, pray do!" Then the "crystal tears . . . rolled gently down her cheeks!"

> Such a sight I never saw before, nor could I have believed. She offered not to conceal or dissipate them: on the contrary she really contrived to have them seen by everybody. She looked, indeed, uncommonly handsome; for her pretty face was not, like Chloe's, blubbered; it was smooth and elegant, and neither her features nor complexion were at all ruffled; nay, indeed, she was smiling all the time.

And Sophy would repeat the performance time and time again.

A sense of drama tempts one to put in a parenthesis after the word performance and call it "her one little act". But this would not be true. Sophia Streatfeild may be immortal because she wept in such company but she had other accomplishments. Born in 1754, she followed Hester Lynch Salusbury as the favourite pupil of the ageing Dr. Collier. He had a capacity for arousing juvenile passion and both girls had a great attachment to him. He taught the teenage Sophia Greek and, as Mrs. Thrale wrote later, "obtained from her excess of tenderness for him, what I could not have bestowed." Dr. Collier died in Sophia's arms, was buried at her expense, and for years she wore black on the anniversary of his death. He taught her well. Mrs. Thrale, who, in between her bouts of jealousy, could sum up Sophia dispassionately, said "Wit she possessed of none" but "she has ten times my beauty and five times my scholarship." She had a Greek library. (But Johnson said that "taking away her Greek she was as ignorant as a butterfly.") She also had a fatal weakness for exercising her charms. When it was Mr. Thrale's turn to be the victim the matter became serious.

There were 13 years difference in age between Sophia Streatfeild and Mrs. Thrale, so they did not overlap at Dr. Collier's. They met by accident at Brighton in the autumn of 1777. Mrs. Thrale was 36, Sophia 23. She quickly won Mrs. Thrale's heart. "Her face is eminently pretty, her carriage elegant, her heart affectionate, and her mind cultivated." She had "an attractive sweetness". Soon she was a member of the Streatham circle, "part of the family", godmother to Mrs. Thrale's latest child. And soon Henry Thrale's roving eye had been caught by hers. By December, 1778, Mrs. Thrale was writing:

> Mr. Thrale is fallen in Love *really & seriously* with Sophy Streatfield—but there is no wonder in that: She is pretty, very gentle, soft and insinuating; hangs about him, dances round him, cries when She parts from him, squeezes his Hand slyly, & with her sweet Eyes full of tears looks so fondly in his Face.... A Man must not be a *Man* but an *It* to resist such Artillery.

There was a terrible scene at dinner when Thrale, in order to get Sophy, who had a cold, out of a draught, suggested she should change seats with Mrs. Thrale. The wife took it as an omen of what was to come. Burke and Johnson were present; the Doctor was challenged by Mrs. Thrale for not having objected. Both were abashed.

Even Thrale's paralytic stroke did not cool his ardour. The affliction had been worth it, he said, if only to see Sophy again. He thought Sophy semi-celestial. He used openly to press Sophy's hand to his heart. And yet, while being desperately jealous, Mrs. Thrale never doubted the affair was platonic. The one thing she was certain of was Sophy's chastity. For despite all the men in her life—and at different times she had affairs of the heart with Lord Loughborough, and Dr. Vyse, the Archbishop of Canterbury's chaplain—she succumbed to none of them, and none of them to her.

> How she contrives to keep bishops, and brewers, and directors of the East India Company, all in chains so, and almost at the same time, would amaze a wiser person than me [Mrs. Piozzi noted]. I can only say let us mark the end!

Earlier the same sharpened sensibility had observed "Few people, however, seem disposed to take her for life—everybody's admiration, as Mrs. Byron says, and nobody's choice."

So, astonishingly, it was throughout her days. Sophy outlived all her admirers. She married none of them. She might have become Mrs. Vyse—that affair lasted over eight years and seems to have been the most serious—unfortunately he had an invalid wife already and could not get a divorce. But even that supposition is doubtful. There was something in Sophy, despite her beauty, her brains, her smiles for most men, her capacity to command tears at will, that always stopped her short. Austin Dobson called her "a prude-coquette", which is as good a guess as another. After the death of Mr. Thrale, Hester and Sophy became distant. Mrs. Thrale publicly snubbed Miss Streatfeild at an Assembly in 1789. They met peaceably in 1802. In 1815 Mrs. Piozzi did not know if Sophia Streatfeild was still alive. In 1821, in the very last months of the eighty-year-old Mrs. Piozzi's life, there was an inquiry from Sophia as to her old friend's health. Sophy herself died in 1835, in her eighty-second year, to be remembered for ever by her tears rather than by her Greek.

GETTING TOUGH

The stream of "tough" American novels that, for the past twenty-five years, has flowed across the Atlantic has now dwindled. As if to replace it there is a renewed interest in Zola. A number of his works have been published in new English translations. It is a good moment to recall that American disciple of Zola who unites the two streams and the work of his which played so large a part in giving the "tough" American novel birth.

When Frank Norris's name is mentioned, the books it generally conjures up are *The Octopus* and *The Pit*. They were his most successful novels. But so far as literary history is concerned *McTeague* is more important. American critics have found in it some of the seeds of both Dreiser's and Steinbeck's work. It also has claims to be the parent of Mr. James M. Cain's *The Postman Always Rings Twice*. (Hemingway stands rather on one side; his most characteristic work is not urban.)

Literary ascription is a pleasant enough exercise (or game of make-believe?) for the specialists. What the ordinary reader wants to know is whether a book is entertaining, compelling, or otherwise worthwhile in itself. For me *McTeague* is a powerful and haunting work. First published in 1899, it now slightly dates. Also, novelists have become so much more professional since then that here and there it may seem contrived. But as a study of miserliness, of the way in which a windfall can ruin almost all who come in touch with it, and of primitive, unintelligent emotion running amok and destroying its human vessels it is masterly. Hurstwood, in Dreiser's *Sister Carrie*, is often cited as a wonderful study of the slow disintegration of a human being. Norris inexorably multiplies the process.

McTeague is a dentist in San Francisco; a shambling giant, slow-witted, good-natured, capable of savage fury when roused. His while life centres on his concertina, his canary, and his slick friend, Marcus Schouler. The two can hardly be called David and Jonathan. But they are devoted. So great is their friendship that, taken aback by the force of McTeague's passion, the bear leader gives up his girl, Trina, to the bear. Trina, frightened at first, finds happiness in submitting to her brutish admirer. She becomes McTeague's wife. Clearly, she must not only humour him but manage him and contrive for him. All goes well until she wins 5,000 dollars in a lottery.

The three characters are affected catastrophically but differently. Marcus feels that somehow or other McTeague has done him out of the money. Had Marcus married Trina would he not now be lord and master of her possessions? At first the impact on McTeague is small. It grows into a murderous obsession as Trina denies him any access to her hoard in spite of disaster, poverty, and hunger. For it is on Trina herself that the money wreaks its greatest havoc. She not only invests it to keep it intact, but devotes her whole life to adding to it. The bear cannot look after his affairs. In his own interests what small sums he earns must be wheedled or filched from him. Soon, she is worshipping the money for itself. The first climax comes when Trina triumphantly steals 60 cents from her husband at the same moment as he is running away with her accumulated savings of over 400 dollars. Later, he murders her for the original 5,000. Marcus, meanwhile, has had his revenge on McTeague by denouncing him as unqualified, thus robbing him of his livelihood. Finally, when McTeague is fleeing as a murderer, Marcus sets out to capture him and the money. The last scene takes place in Death Valley. McTeague kills Marcus, only to find himself handcuffed to the corpse and facing an inevitable end. By the two men lies the 5,000 dollars.

To tell the plot barely is to do the book much less than justice. It is tough, but there is nothing bare about it. From the opening page, where we meet a replete McTeague, fast asleep in his own operating chair after Sunday dinner, a whole small world begins to unfold. In the manner of Mr. Hitchcock's slowly swinging camera at the beginning of one of his thrillers, Norris shows us the "Dental Parlors", the street, the rooming house with its inmates. There is an absurd old couple, making delicate and genteel love without ever saying a word to each other year after year. There is Maria Macapa, the semi-mad Mexican woman who looks after the lodgers' rooms, who steals McTeague's gold fillings, and who tells a tale of a wonderful gold dinner service her parents once possessed. She, too, is murdered for her dream in the end. The junk dealer, Zerkow, marries her just to be able to hear of the great gold service whenever he wishes. After Maria bears him a child her delusion leaves her. She can no longer remember the service. This convinces Zerkow she really has it and is hiding it from him.

By now it will be clear why I started with Zola. But Norris was no mere copyist. The fascinating thing about *McTeague* is its 100 per cent. Americanism. *Maggie*, *McTeague*, and *Sister Carrie* are often cited as the three progenitors of the American realistic novel. But, more than Crane or Dreiser, Norris gave the genre its trans-atlantic character. Tough he certainly made it, but in some indefinable way, without making concessions, he shot through the sordidness and squalor a gust of fresh air.

OFF THE GOLD STANDARD?

Tell me the poetry a man can recite and I will make a fair guess at his age group. For the sponges we are in youth soak up two kinds of verse: that of the established canon which appeals to us, and whatever in contemporary writing fires our imagination. To be precise, it is most likely to be poetry just passing out of being contemporary. The young do not get on to the newest thing, but to the newest that seems on the way to becoming established. So it is that many men (and women) in what I still like to think of as vigorous middle age have an abashed predilection for quoting Flecker.

This first came home to me in a romantic fashion. Being held up in Honolulu during the War, waiting for some corner of a bomb-bay into which we could be stowed, a fellow victim and myself arranged to meet at midnight on the terrace of the Moana Hotel. There, under the great banyan tree, at our feet the surf gently rolling up Waikiki Beach (a triumph of advertisement over Nature, if ever there was one), we took it turn and turn about to recite poems to each other till our repertory was exhausted. And when we finally went to bed about 3 a.m. I suddenly realized what a stand-by Flecker had been to me. In fact I seemed to know more of his work by heart than that of any other poet.

How many bells, I wonder, do "Saadabad", "Rioupéroux", "The Old Ships", "Yasmin", "The War Song of the Saracens", and "The Golden Journey to Samarkand" ring with the young to-day? Flecker has not been well served by the anthologists. The Oxford Book of Modern Verse has only three of his poems; the Albatross Book of Living Verse one; the Faber Book of Modern Verse none. Robert Lynd put two of Flecker's best pieces into his collection, but then one could always be sure of Lynd. Richard Church's *Poems of*

Our Time 1900–42, one of the most representative and most intelligently arranged of all modern anthologies, has "The Old Ships". And yet Martin Secker's noble edition of the collected poems runs to well over a hundred items with very little juvenilia. We are a long way away from the days when it could be confidently proclaimed that Flecker's work "like some masterpiece of Greek sculpture . . . will be found to epitomise its period"; that he would "be read and admired centuries after those who were his contemporaries have passed away"; and that "in the years to come generations of poetry-lovers will be eager to know what kind of man he was."

Was this all far-fetched? Might I just as well throw away my long-hoarded first edition of *The Old Ships* (complete with mermaid removed from the later covers)? Or is Flecker merely in the usual trough? (Forty years after death is a long time to stay in it.) Clearly if he is going to journey through the generations and the centuries, some of his cargo will have to go overboard. Looking at them again lately I found *The King of Alsander*, Flecker's only novel, better than I had remembered it; the *Collected Prose* not so good. Neither, I think, has any chance of survival. And as a letter-writer Flecker was ordinary. We are left then with *Hassan*, *Don Juan*, and whatever we choose to keep from the poems.

The two plays have rather been Box and Cox to each other. For many years Flecker was known almost solely as the author of *Hassan*. *Don Juan* was just another play he had written. But slowly it has, in estimation, crept up to its more famous fellow and, in some people's view, even passed it. The fact is that *Hassan* needs to be superbly well done (which also means extravagantly mounted) not to seem tinsel. *Don Juan*, as George Bernard Shaw was the first to see—and as a television performance some time ago reminded us—exists in its own right. Don Juan; Framlingham, the Conservative Prime Minister; his two daughters; and the soothsaying Owen Jones are all flesh and blood in a way Haroun, Rafi, Pervaneh, and even Hassan himself are not. *Don Juan*, moreover, has for the past 20 years had an almost topical relevance. Flecker knew nothing of modern dictatorships or of the hydrogen bomb, but the poet in him seized the deep anguish of the moral dilemma in choosing between peace and war.

For, no matter in what form Flecker was writing, he was always purely and simply a poet. For that reason I myself think *Hassan* will prove the more enduring play of the two. The golden road to Samarkand may have got a little oily of late, and in poetry as in so many other things we have temporarily gone off the gold standard. But both plays will come back to the stage from time to time as new producers with imagination and courage and the love of the running line arise. And on many shelves and in many hearts they will long find a place. So will such poems as "Tenebris Interlucentem", "To a Poet a Thousand Years Hence", "The Old Ships", "Rioupéroux", "Stillness", "Pavlova in London", "In Phaeacia", "Santorin", "Brumana", "The Old Warship Ablaze", and "Saadabad". Their harmonies and melodies may seem uncomfortably pleasant to the ear in this cacophonic age. But Flecker spoke truly when he said in the preface to *The Golden Journey to Samarkand* that he had written "with the single intention of creating beauty". He fulfilled his intention. Surely that is something which will last?

SHAKESPEARE WAS NOT A FRENCHMAN

Messrs. Nordhoff and Hall, I seem to remember, once went on a Pacific cruise in their small boat accompanied only by the *Encyclopædia Britannica* volume *Med to Mum*. In something of the same spirit I took away with me for a weekend in the country the second series of Rémy de Gourmont's *Promenades Littéraires*.

To call Rémy de Gourmont a man of all work in letters (as Saintsbury once did Gautier) would be to give a false impression. There was nothing solid or humdrum about him. A maid of all work would be a better description. His intelligence often seemed feminine; he could be subtle, sensual, and graceful. Again, it is necessary to restrict the description to John Bull's traditional idea of a French maid. At the same time, although I have never seen a complete bibliography of his works, the fly-leaf of a posthumously published collection of his essays listed nearly 50 volumes. They include novels, stories, plays, poetry, and criticism. It is true that in almost all these fields he was overshadowed by his near contemporaries. That is no reason for not reading him. Heaven help our mental digestion (and our touch with common humanity) if we ever get to the point of reading nothing but the greatest works. But by any standards his novels are thin (his short stories are much better), his plays unremarkable. His poems, particularly the *Litanies*, are his best creative work.

There is one field, however, in which Gourmont fully comes into his own. That is criticism. I have spoken of his intelligence. Here it had full scope. He did not confine his studies to literature. He ranged widely; he wrote vigorously. Indeed, when thinking of this

—by far the greater bulk of his output—one hesitates to draw a line between creative and critical work. In the seven volumes of the *Promenades Littéraires* he discusses such diverse subjects as Nietzsche, Renan, Bret Harte, Heliogabalus, Homer, George Meredith, and "the natural woman". He also wrote reflections and character studies. In other series of works he sought to be a philosopher but cheerlessness would keep breaking in. He was never dull. For some 20 years—say from 1894 to 1914—he was, as Thibaudet has acknowledged, France's most considerable essayist. Thibaudet saw him as a spiritual child of the eighteenth century, the descendant of Bayle rather than of Beyle, and said of him that he had a lively awareness of folly, a nose for stupidity (which nevertheless attracted him), and that he threw on the conventional, the successful, and the official a cruel light. He carried what learning he had lightly and he wrote a pleasant, untortuous French.

But to come back to my volume two. It yielded good value: notes on Villiers de L'Isle-Adam, the *Dernière Mode* of Stéphane Mallarmé, Hérédia, Mme. de Noailles, Baudelaire and Racine, Chopin and George Sand, Balzac's teachers. (In this essay Gourmont develops the idea that for 60 years before Balzac French literature had been strongly influenced by English writers. Certain strains in Balzac, Hugo, and Vigny all had English origins. "Our poets and our story-tellers escaped from Young only to succumb to Thomas Moore and Walter Scott: they were liberated from Ossian to be enslaved by Byron." In Balzac's particular case, he argues, there was also the influence of such eighteenth-century writers as Richardson, Godwin, Goldsmith, and Sterne.)

It was the essay *Stendhal, Racine et Shakespeare*, however, which held me longest. Gourmont is severe on Stendhal's early work comparing the two dramatists. Shakespeare excited Stendhal, Racine bored him, is Gourmont's summing up of the business. But he goes on to make other points. One is that Shakespeare and Racine marked the apex, and the end, of dramatic tragedy in both England and France. Tragedy required a certain kind of audience and the seventeenth century provided it on both sides of the Channel. Another is that in 1824, when Stendhal wrote his comparison, the French theatre had, except for "some misleading imitations by Voltaire and Ducis", never presented Shakespeare at all. And even since then, Gourmont adds, every single effort to translate Shakespeare into French has failed. He goes further. If some of Shakespeare's plays have succeeded in French versions it is precisely because they are not faithful translations. "Literal Shakespeare" in French would be not only incomprehensible but insupportable. French taste has no place for such riotous riches as are to be found in Shakespeare's style. Shakespeare's work is packed with detailed fancies; French taste urges the suppression of every useless detail. Such is Gourmont's argument.

Is not the same true in reverse? Where is the perfect translation of Racine? And if we had it, and were frank and honest, would it be at all to our taste? The more one thinks about it the more one begins to wonder whether untranslatableness is not a sign of ultimate greatness. Why it should be so is open to speculation; the fact will bear assertion. Not even Scott's genius could make anything but a hash of *Goetz von Berlichingen*. However much we may admire Carlyle's magnificence, never would we dare to claim that he either has given us any true work of Goethe's. Even lesser lights such as Schiller and Heine have defied translation. Generations of French writers have wrestled with Milton. What Englishman can claim to have given us the authentic Dante? And beyond them all, there is Homer, baffling every century, every nation, every language.

I came back from my weekend wondering whether the great "world writers" are not the only ones who are truly national; also whether Rémy de Gourmont is not due for a revival. He died in 1915, overshadowed by what then seemed a world cataclysm. The new generation in the 1920s were attracted to him, but their hopes came up against his scepticism. Would he have more appeal for their children?

EMINENTLY VICTORIAN

I was fortunate in my first encounter with Lily Spender. The Victorian three-decker novel has always had a great attraction for me. Found, as they usually are, in country houses (and, occasionally, vicarages), being invariably the worse for wear, showing that sometime or other they have been read by the family as a whole—and there is nothing so friendly-looking as a well-worn book—easy to read with their comparatively small page area and large type, the volumes can offer the most beguiling of encounters. Admittedly one has disappointments. Some are so sententious that even their last-century atmosphere has no charm. Others are thoroughly bad. But every now and again one comes alongside a three-decker to find it still cleared for action, ready to board your attention, and to make an assault upon your feelings at once. Such a one was *Godwyn's Ordeal.*

"The hot weather was not yet over at Dullerabad." A good, workmanlike, opening sentence. The first page introduces the reader to "an unusual scandal", immediately overleaf stands the officer on trial for firing at a brother officer; on page 4 is his dying wife awaiting the verdict—and away we go, with a motherless child, to a Devonshire village, a love story, a wicked countess, an anonymous letter, a rift, happiness on the final page, and in between a little Kingsleyish Christian socialism centring around the affairs of the local mill. At any rate, the story—and some rain—made me go on to *Both in the Wrong* and *Mark Eylmer's Revenge,* both of which I found still better. In subsequent years I must have read six or seven more of Lily Spender's novels or volumes of short stories as I have happened to come across them; none as good as these, but all pleasant and competent.

In truth, the books would hardly be worth writing about were it not for the woman herself. Lily Spender, or Mrs. John Kent Spender, as she proudly signed herself, was far more remarkable than her works. The wife of a highly skilled and successful doctor in general practice—at one time he was physician to the Mineral Water Hospital at Bath—she was faced with the fact that her husband was something of a saint. One of his sons has told us that "he would not take a fee from any clergyman, priest, or Nonconformist minister." Even in those early days, the 1860s and 1870s, he had a free room in his surgery as well as the paying one and was always busy transferring patients into it. He "ought to have been a Dean", kept up his Latin and Greek, spent at least an hour every day with some good author, and had a reputation as an authority on rheumatism. He also had eight children. It was these who caused his "radiant and beautiful" wife to find her vocation. "Early in her married life she decided that though my father's income might be enough for necessities, it would not be enough for the good things we ought to enjoy. So she set to work to write—a formidable undertaking for a young woman at that time—beginning with essays on the German poets" (and other things) "and then plunging boldly into the three volume novel . . . She found a public almost immediately and it remained faithful to the end."

That end was happily a long way off. Her first novel appeared in 1869, when she was thirty-four, her last was published posthumously in 1895, the year of her death. Through those twenty-six years she wrote continuously and, according to the same son's fond record, effortlessly. "I have never seen a quicker writer; she never seemed at a loss for a plot or an idea; her pen flew over the paper." She would write anywhere, in any room of the house even though it were filled with noisy romping children, if necessary on the landing. One of the books is dedicated "To my five elder girls and boys, to whom this first volume was read as it was written on the seashore during a happy summer holiday." And as the list of her books grew, so did her various "funds". For Lily Spender wrote strictly with a purpose. First there was the fund to send the four boys through the university. At £400 each that demanded £1,600. This accomplished, there was the fund for family holidays as far afield as Switzerland and Italy. Finally, when the children were launched and holidays had become individual affairs, there was the fund to add to her husband's savings to enable him to retire and to provide for their daughters thereafter. And, wrote her son in 1927, "I am to this day administering a Trust which is distributing the income of the residue to various members of the family." He was J. A. Spender, the editor of the *Westminster Gazette*. He tells the story in his autobiography *Life, Journalism, and Politics*. The memory of it has always moved me. I never cease being surprised how few people now know it.

We are beginning to see the men and women of the nineteenth century in a truer light. Nothing is nobler than the way in which the greatness of the women's characters so often matches that of the finest of the men's. But too often, alas, their purpose brought a streak of hardness. It is to be seen in James Mill's remarkable mother, in Florence Nightingale, in Jane Welsh Carlyle, even in Christina Rossetti. But Lily Spender—and so far as character goes I dare to put her name alongside these—seems serene and unspoilt. Her achievement was prodigious; the sums she raised were real money in those days. Her children's fame—Harold Spender was another of her sons—testifies to her excellence as a mother; as a writer she has her column in the *Dictionary of National Biography*. If any of her other books come my way I shall piously read each one of them.

MAN TO MAN

Fortuitously, the last four books I have read have in one way or another concerned themselves with politics. They were too curiously assorted a quartet to have much in common—*The Masters*, by C. P. Snow, *Eisenhower, The Inside Story*, by Robert J. Donovan, *Felix Holt*, by George Eliot, and *The Last Hurrah*, by Edwin O'Connor—but they left me with one dominant thought. Mr. O'Connor's novel is the ironical-realistic story of an up-to-date mayoral election in an American city. It showed that television and other modern devices there were only a veneer covering something strangely similar to English politics in George Eliot's post-Reform Bill Midlands borough. Mr. Donovan's ability to draw on Cabinet minutes to compile a record of the Eisenhower administration stressed the differences between American and British political habits at a higher level. But it was Mr. Snow, who keeps his story closely confined within an imaginary college of the University of Cambridge and who deals solely with the election of a Master, who made me feel I was at the inner core of politics.

Where is this? "Politics," said F. S. Oliver, "is the endless adventure of governing men." Beyond and above that, however, among the politicians themselves, it is the inexhaustible art of managing men. Because of that, so many books, particularly novels, which are said to be political are hardly about real politics at all. For all their weaknesses in other directions—outrageous stories, the impossible Phineas Finn, melodramatic irrelevancies—Trollope's so-called "six political novels" are. (It is a pity that because the series must embrace the life story of Plantagenet Palliser and Lady Glencora *Can You Forgive Her?* has to be read as a kind of prelude. It is one of the few tedious novels Trollope wrote, the hearty comic business of the Widow Greenow's two suitors is tiresome, and the book must have put more people off the rest of the sextet than anything else could.) Leave the parliamentary scenes in all these books on one side, let the main political actors get together in their caucuses and clubs, watch the ineffable Duke of St. Bungay exercising his influence, and you are at the heart not only of British politics but of those of Roosevelt, Machiavelli, and Thucydides as well.

Disraeli, too, knew what he was about. It is certainly good for Conservatives every now and again to be reminded of his warning about "the two nations" but *Sybil* has never seemed to me a major political novel. It is elsewhere, particularly in touches in *Endymion*, that we find the true stuff of politics. No man knew better than Disraeli that it is not what is done in the limelight that matters but what happens when man meets man in private. This is the day of mass forces and mass media. They have to be taken into account. The management of public opinion is an exercise and can, indeed, be an art. These things take up much of almost every politician's energies and time. But, as F. S. Oliver himself showed, it is the rarer, subtler, occasions—often sudden flurries—when even among colleagues and comrades the battle of wills is joined that ultimately decide events. Augustus beat Antony, Walpole beat Bolingbroke. Metternich beat Napoleon, Lloyd George beat Asquith. For me at any rate that is the essence of political history.

Of all the occasions and mighty events described in the six volumes of Sir Winston Churchill's *The Second World War* I know none which has the same tenseness and the same drama as the closing scene of the first volume. It is 11.0 a.m. on May 10, 1940. Thirty-six hours have passed since Neville Chamberlain's disastrous "victory" in the House of Commons. Being an honest man, he has come to face the facts. Halifax and Churchill have been summoned to meet him. The three men sit round a table. One of them is about to cease to be Prime Minister; one of the two others is about to succeed him. The question is which. They are all alone. The tumult, the shouting, the House of Commons, the newspapers, the masses, the politicians, the Party machines, the secretaries, the wirepullers on the fringe—all have died away. Now there is nothing to guide them but their judgment and their will. On the outcome of their talk hangs perhaps the fate of the world.

In centuries to come much of the history of the last war will die away. But I do not believe the story of this single meeting will ever fade. Rather, as the stars brighten when the night falls, it will gleam more and more. Historians will put their telescopes to it. Every scrap of reminiscence or evidence that can throw any light on the influences that played on these three men in those preliminary 36 hours will be scrutinized and discussed. The "very long pause" after Neville Chamberlain had finished speaking which Sir Winston Churchill describes, his emphasis on his own silence, will be X-rayed to reveal their exact significance. Maybe some Shakespeare centuries hence will make of the scene another Misenum. It would not be unworthy.

It was for reasons such as these that I found Mr. Snow's novel so exciting. He deliberately works on the smallest possible scale. His electors for the Mastership number no more than 13. They slowly line up six-six. It is the odd vote that will settle the matter, deciding not only the identity of the next Master but also the future character of the College. Because he is dealing with what is in essence a closed world Mr. Snow is able to make his characters more introverted and liable to more emotional display than men usually accustom themselves to in larger communities. Being dons they are also more outspoken with each other. But no one who has ever been a member of a board at a time of struggle for power, no one who has watched a crisis resolve itself at the top of a great organization; above all, no one who has seen the inner play of politics will be able to deny that the same characteristics and the same considerations come into play. *The Masters* is a microcosm of politics, none the less true because the issue at stake is relatively so small in the scale of world events. But to these men it was everything; and no man can put into any battle of wills more than the whole of himself.

ARNOLD ALIVE

I see that Everyman's have republished Matthew Arnold's poems and it puts in my mind the question whether any other Victorian poet is more assiduously kept in print. I am not arguing from this that he was among the greatest; there are doubtless accidental causes why through the years the handy volumes made up from the poems come out in one form or another and always find a welcome. For one thing Arnold was in bulk a middle poet and in quality an unusually equal one. As a result of both these things it is easier to make, with slight variations, an acceptable single volume out of his total output than it is to do so, say, for the far more voluble Tennyson or the far more dynamic Browning, in both of whom, perhaps because of their bulk, inequality is a dominant feature.

Arnold is also a far more elusive Victorian. I am not referring to the Marguerite episode, or to the long silences—from 1855 to 1867 and from 1867 to 1882 so far as the publication of significant poems went, yet as the middle date included "Dover Beach" and the last one produced "Westminster Abbey" there was, as Quiller-Couch has pointed out, no falling away in mastery—or to the impossibility (although Nature somehow did it) of fusing the poet, the professor, the critic, and the schools inspector into a whole man. But if the man as a whole has never been seen clearly, neither has the poet as a whole, or the critic as a whole. When the B.B.C. were engaged in the long months of planning and inquiry which made Sir George Barnes's project on *The Ideas and Beliefs of the Victorians* the most memorable series of talks that the Third Programme, or indeed broadcasting anywhere, has given us, nothing was more fascinating as the weeks went by than the fluctuating estimates of Arnold's importance. In the end, I thought, he received less attention than he deserved. (I remember Humphry House speaking of Matthew Arnold's "melodious whine", a phrase I never forgave him.) But Arnold survived this, as he did Froude's enthusiasm and Saintsbury's faint praise, Hugh Kingsmill's denigration, and Sir Max Beerbohm's theory that all that was wrong with him was his whiskers. Neither a popular issue of *Cromwell* and *Alaric at Rome* some 50 years ago nor the fact that the single collected edition of his works has for a long time been inordinately expensive set him back. Serenely, unspectacularly, but determinedly, Arnold trudges on.

His progress, even in his lifetime, puzzled many. As "Q" has said,

> The steps by which a reputation grows, the precise moment at which it becomes established, are often difficult to fix. The poems, negligently though they had been received at first, must have helped: and since men who improve an office are themselves usually improved by it, assuredly the professorship helped too. The lectures on Homer which adorned Arnold's first tenure of the Chair strike a new note of criticism, speak with a growing undertone of authority beneath their modest professions, and would suffice to explain—if mere custom did not even more easily explain—why in 1862 he was re-elected for another five years. But before 1865, no doubt, the judicious who knew him had tested him by more than his lectures, and were prepared for *Essays in Criticism.*

I believe the explanation for Arnold's enduring, and perhaps increasing, hold through the 67 years since his death is equally practical. During those seven decades the world has alternately suffered and enjoyed—with much more suffering than enjoyment—the most astonishing vicissitudes. Through them all, contemplative minds in each generation have found something in Matthew Arnold they had come across nowhere else. He is one with his beloved Senancour and Amiel. Moreover, though Arnold's voice is fixed forever and nothing can alter it now, we hear slightly different tones in it as the tumults of our times supplant each other. Readings of "Dover Beach" in 1875, 1915, and 1955 would all have had a different impact. So it is with many of Arnold's other poems. So it is with his prose. Even the *Discourses in America*—and although it is said to be the prose work by which Arnold himself wished to be remembered no one would claim it is popular or even well known —has a remarkable appropriateness to our present dilemmas. The lecture on "Literature and Science" could well be read by any educationist arguing over the merits of an Arts degree to-day. The lecture on "Numbers" is even more strikingly topical. And some months ago I was asked to lend my copy of *Literature and Dogma*, which has not yet come back to me.

If Matthew Arnold the man remains elusive there has been one attempt to capture him which came nearer to doing it than all the others. Some six years ago Isobel Macdonald gave us *The Buried Self*. It is the kind of book I usually dislike, a biography in the form of a semi-novel. But the writer's touch was so sure, her researches had been so thorough, and her dialogue and episodes were so well documented—never did I believe I could read that kind of book, with the notes chapter by chapter, and so enjoy it—that not only Arnold himself but the Victorian setting of those years from 1848 to 1851 suddenly glowed with life. It is a book I recommend to all those who are interested in Matthew Arnold.

Their number will increase. Arnold is so unobtrusive a companion, so calm a guide. I have gone back to him time and again during these past 30 years; in each decade finding a deeper meaning He is the friend of quiet, pitying us that we should

> . . . see all sights from pole to pole,
> And glance, and nod, and bustle by;
> And never once possess our soul
> Before we die.

The irony has more than once been noted that Arnold, the enemy of Philistinism and the mechanical age, died running for a tram. It is not often enough added that his haste was to meet his daughter.

A NOT-SO-LOST LADY

It may not have been so very wise to produce this season, nine years after her death, a new volume containing three of Willa Cather's short stories, and those not of her very best. American literature is still so vigorous, young, and forward-looking that, as yet, a writer needs the stature of a Hawthorne or a Melville to be revived. All the same, there was no need for the critics to treat her quite as if she had been one of the Pilgrim Mothers; quaint, remote, archaic, belonging to a world that is gone. Reading some of the notices of *The Old Beauty* I could not help feeling that the bright young reviewers looked upon Willa Cather as about contemporary with her own beloved Sarah Orne Jewett. No one would have thought she had been modern enough to pass judgment on D. H. Lawrence and the later Thomas Mann, and to be shrewd about Katherine Mansfield.

Admittedly Willa Cather was neither a Hemingway nor a James M. Cain. (In passing it is worth observing that the "tough" American novel is not so very new, not even twentieth-century. One of the "toughest" of them all, Frank Norris's *McTeague*, about which I have written earlier, was published way back in the 1890s.) She wrote in a traditional style. She was to some extent a regional novelist. Her generation still looked to Europe for its literary standards and to the heart rather than to the solar plexus for its emotions. In *Death Comes for the Archbishop* and *Shadows on the Rock* she gazed back to an American continent in which the church was more important than the drug-store or the cinema. Artists, musicians, men and women of sensibility were to her more vital and more interesting beings than boxers or gangsters. Yet she was no reserved maiden aunt, timidly withdrawn into a world of her own inside her own parlour. At one time she edited a highly competitive magazine in New York. At all times she was concerned with the impact of society, whether it were in city, or country, or desert, upon strong or weak men and women.

Almost everybody who has written about Willa Cather has spoken of her delicacy. The first meaning of this word is fineness of texture, and in that sense the epithet is just. But it can also mislead by implying frailty. The most abiding impression Willa Cather's work leaves is of her strength. Take, for instance, *My Mortal Enemy*. It is one of the shortest and seemingly simplest of all her books. Young Myra Driscoll runs away with Oswald Henshawe, from riches to eventual poverty, and although they remain lovers to the end she regrets her "error" with increasing rancour. No concessions are made to romance in the relations between the two; even the devoted, patient Oswald's middle-aged strayings of heart and other weaknesses are firmly given. The tale is touching and true; it is also enduringly bitter.

For that reason, in spite of all its power and much as I respect it, *My Mortal Enemy* is not a favourite of mine. For while Willa Cather looked at human beings clear-eyed and did not flinch from recording what she saw, she was essentially a Stoic at heart. She accepted because she understood. This comes out most clearly in three of her novels—*My Antonia*, *A Lost Lady* and *Lucy Gayheart*—and on them I will stake her claim to last. Each, moreover, is distinct—in approach, in texture, in technique. Some readers have seen a deliberate contrast between Marian Forrester, the "lost lady" who could not withstand the deprivations of a wrecked husband and a country life, and Antonia Shimerda who lost *her* fineness when she deserted the land for the city. It is a false comparison; as false as the impression such a synopsis gives of both women and of both tales. Only a modern critic could strip them down to that, leaving out the fact that in each case the story is seen through the eyes of a boy who was in love with the heroine and remained so all his life although he turned away from her. In spite of all their vicissitudes neither Marian nor Antonia can lose her attractiveness. The settings, also, the pioneer hardships of *My Antonia* and the feeling of youth and sunrise in *A Lost Lady*, make them books one does not forget. One speaks of them as others did of Lucy Gayheart.

In Haverford on the Platte the townspeople still talk of Lucy Gayheart. They do not talk of her a great deal, to be sure; life goes on and we live in the present. But when they do mention her name, it is with a gentle glow in the face or the voice, a confidential glance which says: "Yes, you, too, remember?" They still see her as a slight figure always in motion; dancing or skating, or walking swiftly with intense direction, like a bird flying home.

Few books can have had a more enchanting opening than that. Even fewer have managed, without making a concession to truth or reality, to maintain the enchantment to the end. Lucy, her watch-maker father, Harry Gordon, who loved her, Clement Sebastian, whom she loved, her sister, the Haverford folk, take possession of heart and mind as quietly, as calmly, as certainly as do the characters in a novel by Turgenev. The story can be seen as a tragedy. It is also a triumph. Here all bitterness has been purged. Only love, and grace, and pity, and beauty, and thankfulness remain. If anyone still wants to charge Willa Cather's writing with having had its day I will put in *Lucy Gayheart* as rebuttal and let the verdict rest.

BORROW'S LETTERS

It is good these autumn days, when a walk through the woods can mean more to the naturally reflective than the joys of high summer, to sit in one's study in the early evening and to conjure up the links between walks and books. Immediately one's eye goes to the shelf holding *Lyrical Ballads*. Has anything better ever come out of a walk than *The Ancient Mariner*, conceived and, in part at least, composed by Coleridge and Wordsworth as they roamed the Quantock Hills? That was a walk to give birth to a masterpiece; there is to my mind only one candidate comparably to close one. It was done 10 years earlier. Who can ever forget those "several turns in a *berceau* or covered walk of acacias" which Gibbon took between 11 and 12 on the night of June 27, 1787, on completing *The Decline and Fall of the Roman Empire*?

Both these walks have one thing in common. They were in essence a form of leisure. A far different walk was that of George Borrow from Norwich to London in December, 1832. He did the journey of 112 miles in 27 hours, spending only 5½d. on the way, laid out (as he himself proudly recalled in middle age) on "a pint of ale, a roll of bread, half a pint of milk, and two apples". Then 29, with already a fantastic life of wandering and picaresque adventures behind him, completely unknown, except by a Lowestoft parson who had been impressed by his gift for languages, Borrow was on his way to keep a rendezvous with the officials of the British and Foreign Bible Society and—without anyone knowing it—with Posterity.

The mass of books are like the mass of people; at a distance it is hard to tell them apart. But now and again there is a book which, by the peculiarity of its size, maybe its colour, the individuality of the lettering on its spine, even the way its binding has faded, can be identified at a distance, no matter in what surroundings you come across it. For me such a book is *Letters of George Borrow to the British and Foreign Bible Society*. If ever you see it, as I sometimes do, in the second-hand shops I commend it to your attention.

One of the great strengths of the British and Foreign Bible Society has always been that while they are men with a mission they are also shrewd and hard-headed people. Even though he made a good impression on the sub-committee, Borrow was not taken on trust. He was sent back to Norwich with a number of appropriate books, but without a teacher or even a grammar, and asked to show if he could acquire the Manchu language in five or six months. Little can his new employers have realized the rare bird they had captured. Within a month he is criticizing the existing Manchu version of St. Matthew; before the end of the time, he announces he has mastered the language. By that time also the Bible Society found they had a vigorous, attractive, and ebullient correspondent.

Learned philologists have long since convinced everybody that Borrow was not in their class. He would never have delighted succeeding generations if he had been. He was a man of action. By September, 1833, he was in St. Petersburg, not only translating but also proselytizing and soon suggesting that he should be sent 5,000 miles farther on to Kiachta on "the frontiers of Chinese Tartary", where not only Chinese caravans but also Chinese children could be encountered and where "there would not be much difficulty in disposing at a low price of any quantity of Testaments." Both Borrow's life and at least a smallholding of English literature might have been greatly different if Borrow had been allowed to go to China. But, his work in Russia done, he was, at his own suggestion, sent to the Peninsula instead.

As Mr. Darlow, the admirable editor of the letters, pointed out, Borrow's proposals to the Society made it clear he set out "with some idea of a book like *The Bible in Spain* already in his mind". And when Borrow, his adventures over and safely home again, sat down to begin his masterpiece the Bible Society "cheerfully forwarded" to him all the letters he had written them. (How they came back again, and were "lost" for a time in the crypt of Bible House and therefore unavailable to Dr. Knapp when he was writing his Life of Borrow is told by Mr. Darlow in his preface.) Borrow made sometimes verbatim use of them. It may be asked, therefore, why anyone should read the letters instead of *The Bible in Spain*. Perish the thought! The one is a work of art; the others were glimpses of life. But even though we are not, as Augustine Birrell once said, "all Borrovians now"—for a new generation has grown up since then—Borrow will always have his circle. The Lives of him have, by and large, not been good; most of the efforts to "interpret" him have been ludicrous. The doubts about him remain. Was he a romancer, an impossible man, a semi-humbug? After the last and most learned pundit has finished, I will still be ready to put in the evidence of these letters. (And he made use of less than a third of them in *The Bible of Spain*.) No man could have kept up a pose over so many years in such extraordinarily different sets of circumstances. The committee of the Bible Society were, as I have said, shrewd and hard-headed men, and though they came to know that their rare bird was also a stormy petrel they kept their respect for him to the end of his life. Above all—what will concern the ordinary reader most—the *Letters of George Borrow to the British and Foreign Bible Society* are like no other letters between covers. Their story, the telling of it, and the teller are all unique.

FOUR MODERN POETS

If words were regulated by law, modern would long ago have been contraband, because incapable of definition. A sharp-edged, sharp-sounding word in itself, the more you consider it the vaguer it becomes. "Of or pertaining to the present and recent times, as distinguished from the remote past" says the Oxford English Dictionary. But when one turns up "recent" one gets little further on: "Lately done or made; that has lately happened or taken place." Proceeding to "lately" we are given the definition "recent".

This may seem mere fun and games; and H. L. Mencken—a lament for the Sage of Baltimore—once declared there was no more enchanting companion to outlast the longest lifetime than the large O.E.D. But when one is put to it, as anthologists are, to justify their limits, then the exercise can become very real. "Modern Poetry", "Selections from the Modern Poets", "A Book of Modern Verse"; no two compilers mean quite the same thing. In one's youth the beginning of the century provided a convenient—though artificial—dividing line. Then it was the First World War; but, as we slowly perceived it was really a thirty years war we had been engaged in, that lost its force. Sometimes it is done by the age of poets. "I have included no writer who was over 25 in 1956" declares some eager enemy of senescence, overlooking the fact that very often it is the young poets who hanker after traditional style and thoughts, and the old ones who experiment.

"Pertaining to, or originating in, the current age or period": this secondary definition seems more hopeful. What kind of poetry most truly pertains to the current period or age? Where is its starting point? For myself, to-day, if I had to stand and deliver I should firmly choose Sir George Rostrevor Hamilton's *Hospital Ward (of this generation)*.

The World is sick, and we sick men
Listen for feet upon the stair:
And far off when we hear them, when,
Nigh to despair,
We think we hear them, we cry out
With hope and mockery and doubt
And blasphemy and prayer.

How beautiful the feet of them,
Thy messengers of peace!
But are they Thine? Shall they condemn,
Or bring release?
When all the thousand steps are climbed . . .

I know it is maddening to leave off there. But just as, when a child has wilfully played only seven notes of the scale, we cannot rest till —sometimes long after—we have gone to the piano and struck the eighth; so, too, I am hoping that some readers will find something gnawing inside them until they know the whole of this fine poem. You will find it in Sir George's *Unknown Lovers*.

Hospital Ward was written in 1930. I find it necessary to jump some twenty years to mention another poem which moved me with the same force, and the feeling that it was both destined for the years and intensely modern. If Rostrevor Hamilton's *Hospital Ward* enshrines in a grave beauty some of the deeper feelings of those who can still feel in this war-ridden, science-beset century, Mr. James Kirkup's *A Correct Compassion* surely fixes for readers generations hence another equally true and equally revealing aspect of our time. From its first, swift, aseptic line

Cleanly, sir, you went to the core of the matter

it cuts into the mind as coldly and as precisely as the surgical operation it celebrates.

Hilaire Belloc has told how he first came across one of Miss Ruth

Pitter's poems "spelt in the old seventeenth century fashion", and some who know and admire her work may be surprised to see her described as a modern. Yet "Reverse the flight of Lucifer" and "1938," with its closing lines

> Let us go down together,
> Having despaired of wisdom:
> The earth is as fruitful as ever,
> The sea still teeming with fishes,
> The sun still lusty; but we
> Have failed to love, and must perish

is surely as authentically of our day and plight as anything could be?

> I had a silver penny
> And an apricot tree
> And I said to the sailor
> On the white quay

When these words, beginning Mr. Charles Causley's *Nursery Rhyme of Innocence and Experience*, were first broadcast in the middle of a Third Programme selection of contemporary poetry some three or four years ago, thousands must have sat up and taken notice. At any rate, I was told that the B.B.C. had numerous inquiries about Mr. Causley the next day, and many homes must now be the richer by housing his small booklet *Farewell Aggie Weston*. For Mr. Causley, with all his derivativeness and disarming simplicity, represents a fourth strand in our modern poetry. Thanks to the B.B.C., poetry has once again become spoken. The ballad, the singing line, the straightforward metres have reasserted themselves. Alongside the newer poetry that is a challenge to the mind has come a new-old strain that is pleasant to the ear. And I often even wonder, heretically, whether, where Mr. T. S. Eliot is concerned, Old Possum will not outlive Alfred Prufrock.

This may seem perverse, or at least highly idiosyncratic. And it can be pointed out that not one of the four poems I have singled out has a line devoted to a full-stop, a monosyllable spread over two lines, a word spelt backwards, or anything that remotely looks as if it had been written by archy or mehitabel. But then I am Philistine enough to believe that even in this hydrogen bomb age the poetry that will endure will be that which continues the line of tradition, however much it may strip, fashion, or embellish it; true modernity resting in the way it uses new thoughts, accents, or cadences to crystallize the temper of the age.

CHRISTINA LIGHT

Every novel reader must have his favourite moment of truth—that instant when, because of some character's speech, or an incident, or a description, a book will suddenly come alive and stay in the memory always. My own, I think, is in *Roderick Hudson.* Henry James has been describing how, while Hudson, in the presence of his friend and patron, Rowland Mallet, was sculpting the beautiful girl, Christina Light, her hair had become disarranged and loosened.

"My dear young man, hands off!" cried Mrs. Light as she came forward and seized her daughter's hair. "Christina love, I'm more surprised than I can say."

"Is it indelicate?" Christina asked. "I beg Mr. Mallet's pardon."

Mrs. Light gathered up the dusky locks and let them fall through her fingers, glancing at her visitor with a significant smile. Rowland had never been in the East, but if he had attempted to make a sketch of an old slave merchant calling attention to the "points" of a Circassian beauty he would have depicted such a smile as Mrs. Light's. "Mamma's not really shocked," added Christina in a moment, as if she had guessed her mother's by-play. "She's only afraid that Mr. Hudson may have injured my hair and that, *per conseguenza*, I shall fetch a lower price."

Poor Christina; one is never likely to forget her beauty, her enigma, or her tragedy after that.

Henry James could not do so either. In the preface to *The Princess Casamassima* he has told us how for 10 years after he had finished *Roderick Hudson* Christina Light refused "to be laid away with folded hands in the pasteboard tomb, the doll's box to which we usually relegate the spent puppet." He put it down to her restless vanity. Also to his conviction that he had not completely recorded her. But he makes it clear that the driving force came far more from her than from him. She had known herself to be striking once, "and couldn't resign herself not to strike again." And so she did. From her first sudden irruption (in *Roderick Hudson*) upon Rowland and Roderick in the gardens of the Villa Ludovici, accompanied by her mother, the Cavaliere, and the poodle—one sees only later what a wonderful piece of dramatic arrangement the whole scene is—to our last sight of her beside the dead body of the little *anarchiste manqué*, Hyacinth Robinson, on the closing page of *The Princess Casamassima* she is challengingly alive all the time. Of her beauty I can say only that I am less prepared to take Helen's on trust.

I have spoken of her tragedy. Some may deny it. After all, except on the one occasion, she followed her own star. Was it not Roderick Hudson and Hyacinth Robinson who died? Who can tell whether, as Paul Muniment, the man who had a gift for being right, prophesied, the Princess Casamassima did not go back to her husband's riches in the end? But would that not have been for Christina the most cruel blow of all?

Consider her story. Brought up in the belief that she is the daughter of two Americans, she has, ever since the age of five, been told "twenty times a day" by her horrible mother "that she's a beauty of beauties, that her face is her fortune, and that if she plays her cards she may marry God knows whom." As a child she was hawked round the money-lenders so that they could see on what good physical security they were making their loans. But she has more than beauty. She has will; she has wilfulness; she is, as Madame Grandoni says, "a mixture of good passions and bad—always of passions"; and with all these things goes a desperate, pathetic desire to achieve integrity. Her mother is determined to marry her to the colourless but wealthy Prince Casamassima. She momentarily thinks she may find an escape in Roderick Hudson. Then she decides to repudiate both the Prince and Hudson. Her mother, like some Clytemnestra, kills her hope with the threatening revelation that she is the illegitimate daughter of the Cavaliere.

In *The Princess Casamassima* she has broken free once more, in the strange Herzen-like phantasmagoria of Bakunin's London. Henry James never did anything more consummate than the way in which he made the coming together of these two worlds credible. Christina uses her wealth to help foster the dreamed-of revolution; taking up the little bookbinder, Hyacinth Robinson. But I am not concerned with the tale—although it is for me by far the best James ever told—but only with Christina. There is still her third attribute, that of being an enigma.

Not the least part of Christina Light's quality was that no two people saw it alike. Rowland Mallet could think her "corrupt, perverse, as proud as a potentate, a coquette of the first magnitude, but . . . intelligent, bold, and free." To Roderick she was a will-o'-the-wisp; to Hyacinth a radiance. For Prince Casamassima she was an ineluctable despair. Madame Grandoni, who stuck to her longest, thought her heart was "maybe a gold mine . . . at the bottom of a very long shaft." But none of these impressions was of any consequence. All that mattered was what Christina was to herself. A would-be great actress on the stage of life, she fled part after part for fear it was make-believe. Herself sprung from corruption, she fought to ensure that everything except the fatal marriage she was forced into should be incorrupt. Inherently selfish, even little Hyacinth in his last hours comes to see that in her selfless passion to relieve others she is only relieving herself. Yet in a world of pretence, and chicane, and mistrust, time and again she makes the child's eager plea to be trusted. Sincerity is all to her, if only she can divine it. Surrounded by insincerity, the last words she was ever to speak to Rowland Mallet were "I *was* sincere."

What ultimately became of her I do not know. She must be long since dead. But that last remark should form only one part of the triptych of her epitaph. On the other panels I would put Madame Grandoni's ringing tribute, "She'll speak the truth always", and her creator's conviction that she could do nothing *banal.*

BLIND MAN'S BUFF

It is perhaps natural that I, more than most people, should be interested in chance encounters with the famous, although, contrary to what is generally believed, I remember what they said to me far more vividly than anything I may have said to them. The only six words that Arnold Bennett ever addressed to me, for instance, are inescapably held in my memory. They were so surprising. Seeing him lost in the crush at a provincial first night in a theatre I knew well and he did not, I showed him where his seat was, to which he replied, "Thank you for this charming solicitude." Similarly, my sole contact with George Bernard Shaw, on the telephone this time, was when I rang him up in the middle of the day to tell him that Dr. Axham, whom he had championed as Herbert Barker's one-time anaesthetist, was dead. "Well," said Shaw—rather crossly, I thought—"I am not, and I am having my lunch." But it is of a third encounter I want to write to-day. For one thing, although we never met or even spoke together, its memory is pleasant. For another, it led to the filling in of a small, admittedly unimportant but to me not uninteresting, page in literary history.

I must have been fortunate in my youth; many of the book acquaintances I made then—without anyone to advise or guide me—have not worn out their companionship in later life. Among them was Kai Lung. So when in 1936 his *Golden Hours*, his *Wallet*, and his *Mat* were all rolled up into one volume I could not resist suggesting in print that it should have been called "A Celestial Omnibus." This came to Ernest Bramah's notice and—strange man that he was—he was greatly pleased and wrote to tell me so. We corresponded. Now Bramah had always fascinated me as a writer, and particularly as the begetter of Kai Lung. How had it come about? He was such an oddly diverse author; had so many original ideas. As if Kai Lung was not enough in himself, there was Max Carrados, the blind detective—another hero of my youth, and that remarkably prescient novel (the 1947 coal crisis in reverse) *The Secret of the League*. There was also the *magnum opus* I had never read but had heard respectfully talked about, his *Guide to the Varieties and Rarity of English Regal Copper Coins*. How on earth had he come to think up Kai Lung? I asked him.

The genesis of Kai Lung, he told me, went back 45 years. At that time, having left the post of sub-editor on Jerome K. Jerome's *To-day*, he joined "two or three similarly minded young men" whose scope was "to do anything in literary, artistic, or journalistic spheres: to write books, stories, articles; to illustrate magazine matter, to supply cartoons and full pages . . . in short to do almost anything for anybody." So much a band of brothers were they that they held all things in common. This extended to ideas. "If one struck a plot which he thought suited another's style more than his own . . . he passed it on." Among the band was one whom Bramah called X. One day X said to him, "I've got an idea for a short story that I think might suit you." X then "outlined the bare essentials of *The Story of Yung Chang*—before the days when mathematics were understood in China a young man worked out the system of calculation which he took to an idol manufacturer. Unfortunately the system, perfectly reliable up to 100, broke down with cumulative effect at that point so that all transactions above 100 resulted in an increasing loss."

"I think [Bramah added] that that was as far as my obligation went, though our financial difficulties, coming on about then, supplied a few touches of personal, topical, colours. The detail of having a story-teller [Kai Lung] to narrate did not arise till I was committed to the format—which, I think, obviously suggested such a feature. With regard to our respective shares in the story X was generous but I think just. When we had written anything actually in collaboration we were accustomed to sign it with a name combining parts of both those concerned. When I came to typing

Yung Chang and said 'What name shall I put to it?' his immediate answer was 'Oh, your own, of course—there's no question about who wrote it.' As I have since drawn on the Kai Lung formula for about forty short stories and one full length book it is naturally satisfactory to have had this made plain from the beginning."

At first, Bramah said, the idea had not excited him. For months it lay idle in his mind. X asked him more than once why he was not getting on with it. Bramah even thought of passing it on to someone else. Then eventually "the story was written in snatches during my homeward journey from King's Cross to Muswell Hill—generally by the last train (11.45 I think it was, for we were working very long hours and were all dog-tired). Some Chinese families lived in that neighbourhood at that time and I often found myself sitting in a railway carriage opposite members of them. Possibly their placid inscrutable faces and courteous way unconsciously helped somewhat." The story went the rounds, was rejected everywhere, till it was taken for *Chapman's Magazine* "provided an assurance could be given that it was entirely original." This, as Bramah said, could be taken as either an insult or a compliment. He decided it was the latter; screwed them up from three guineas to four guineas; the rest is known.

One thing is not. Who was X? After all, he had the seed and the wisdom to know where to plant it. The other day, reading Kai Lung again, it suddenly occurred to me that Bramah had given me a clue. In return, so he had told me, he had given X the idea for a story called *The Rival Rain Makers*, which X had got published in the *London Handbook*, 1897. Eagerly I went in search of a copy. *The Rival Rain Makers* was there all right. But the author, alas, was our old friend Anon.

ANNALS OF THE POOR

Whenever political novels are discussed—and they are one of the few literary subjects that regularly shine within the penumbra of a general election—pride of place is generally given to Disraeli and Trollope. I would not say a word against either of them, except to point out that if it is an election you want to read about, *Ralph the Heir* is a much better book than any of the more famous Palliser series. But during these recent days the question has been going through my mind: What is a political novel? Is it only a novel about politics? Or can it also be a work of fiction from which political consequences may flow?

If it can be the latter, then alongside the two high and mighty names there should be placed two much less well-known. For the dominant theme of politics during the past 40 years, certainly from 1911 to 1951, has been the emergence, establishment, and acceptance of the idea of the welfare state. And for some 20 years before the First World War, from 1894 to 1914, there was a series of books that, I think, helped to awaken the conscience of the nation. Admittedly social consciousness was in the air; one has only to read Lowes Dickinson to recapture its nobility of spirit. Many writers tried their hands at this new kind of prose and fiction. Innumerable names can be mentioned. But the two I want to recall particularly are Arthur Morrison and Richard Whiteing.

Indignant Dickensians—why are Dickensians so often indignant? —will want me to go back to a much earlier date. Peace, peace! All praise to Dickens. But he was too much before his time to be effective politically in this context. There was no more typical Victorian than Bagehot and, as Asa Briggs has recently reminded us in *Victorian People*, "Bagehot believed that 'the character of the poor is an unfit topic for continuous art,' and attacked Dickens's poor people because they were 'poor talkers and poor livers, and in all ways poor people to read about.'" Something, however, happened between the 1850s and the 1900s. I believe it was the two jubilees, particularly the Diamond Jubilee of 1897. *Recessional* is perhaps the most famous literary reaction to that event, and Kipling has told how he wrote it and sent it to *The Times* because of "a certain optimism that scared me". That optimism scared, and shocked, many people. Was it surprising that two other journalists —and when so many just limitations are put upon the pretensions of our craft let us all the more glory in the fact that all three were journalists—should have sensed amidst all the self-congratulation the growing of doubt and stirring of conscience?

Arthur Morrison's *Tales of Mean Streets* appeared in 1894 and *A Child of the Jago* in 1896. In neither, it is true, is there any explicit pointing of a moral. But the moral was there, and some social workers were quick to seize upon it. Never before had the life of the poor been so frighteningly depicted, without palliation or caricature. To this day a reading of *Lizerunt* in *Tales of Mean Streets* makes one feel desperately unhappy. Richard Whiteing's *No. 5 John Street*, which came out three years later, in 1899, was frankly a piece of crusading. It was also a better novel. Whiteing made the whole point of his tale turn on the fact that it was a report to some faraway, South Sea islanders on the England of the Diamond Jubilee. He rubbed things in by choosing as his observer to live in the "four-storied hovel in the very heart of a slum which lies between two of the finest thoroughfares of the West End" a young aristocrat who is constantly getting reminders that he is missing "the season" only a hundred yards away, and hunting, and country house parties, and all the other indulgences of the comfortable part of England of that day. In the preface to a new edition in 1902—the year Morrison's most powerful work, *The Hole in the Wall*, appeared—Whiteing became even more explicit. He avowed his purpose. He discussed "What should we do?" And he came to the conclusion—

striking in view of all that has happened since—that "as a regenerative scheme, the pursuit of wealth for its own sake is a dismal failure. It makes far more ills than it cures."

Thereafter, throughout the Edwardian era, there was a growing preoccupation with the plight of the working class. Whiteing returned to the theme in *Ring in the New*, a poor book but interesting because it tries to see things from the woman's standpoint, in 1906; and in *Little People*, which runs to sentiment, in 1908. Sentiment was, indeed, creeping in. Stephen Reynolds's *A Poor Man's House* (1908) is one of the better examples, and good old William De Morgan cast a golden glow over Sapps Court and other places as he re-lived his mother's charitable excursions of 50 years before. Then, like an angry, dispersing discord, scattering all complacency, came 1914, Robert Tressall's *The Ragged Trousered Philanthropists*, and the War. Tressall's is a savage, bitter, powerful, and in parts unfair book, but it had influence in its day. 1914–18, homes for heroes, the years of unemployment, the second ordeal, final assault, to-day's welfare state—these 40 tumultuous years are too recent yet to be history. But when the literary and social parts of that period come to be written I hope that at least a footnote will be spared for Morrison and Whiteing. As for Gissing, I will explain why I have left him out another week.

QUIET BUT TRUE

The death of the *Brooklyn Eagle* a few weeks ago aroused many thoughts in me, but none has remained so tenaciously as that of John Bailey. The English mind rolls, I suppose, as much as the English road, but from Brooklyn to the Athenaeum, or better still to Wramplingham, is a diversion that did not enter even Chesterton's head. But substitute Paumanok for Brooklyn and all is clear, for few can think of the *Brooklyn Eagle* without recalling that Walt Whitman was once its editor, and I, at any rate, can never think of Walt Whitman without there coming vividly to my mind whole paragraphs and images from John Bailey's book on him in the English Men of Letters series.

Even when repaying debts of gratitude it is as well to keep things in perspective. Bailey was not a great enough writer for it to be said of him that he is now in the inevitable trough that follows the death of all geniuses. His fame never soared so high that this generation had perforce to bring it low. At the same time the particular setting of his lifetime (1864–1931) did tend to do him less than justice. A fine Shakespearian critic, he was obviously not in the same class as Bradley; a lover of the English grand masters, his relish was faded out by the gusto of Saintsbury; a Johnsonian of distinction, he wrote in the shadow of Birkbeck Hill and the rising sun of S. C. Roberts; his work on Milton was soon overtaken by that of Dr. Tillyard; nominated for the chair of Poetry at Oxford by Mackail, H. A. L. Fisher, Dean Inge, and Bradley among others, he saw it given to Garrod. Yet it would be wrong to deduce therefrom that Bailey was merely a second-best in all these fields. The truth is that working over the same ground he reaped a different harvest.

The first thing one notices about Bailey's best books is that they are all about writers and their writings, not about critical abstractions. The second is that they are all short and most thoroughly readable. Finally, although their learning is sure and their values and feeling unerring, they are all addressed to a popular audience. Both *Dr. Johnson and his Circle* and *Milton* were written for the Home University Library, *Shakespeare* for the English Heritage series, and *Walt Whitman* for English Men of Letters. It is true there were other books—*Poets and Poetry* is still worth reading, while the essay on "Shakespeare's Histories" in *The Continuity of Letters* is the best short piece I know on that subject—but it is on these four that what readership Bailey is likely to have in future will rest. And the work they will do is neither unimportant nor less than noble. We have few enough writers who can stir the young and take the newcomer by the hand, making him feel he has a safe, sane guide in the land of wonder; the easiness of the talk coming from the profundity of the knowledge, and the quietness of the judgment from a true and yet anything but hidebound instinct. "He was," said *The Times* after his death, when reviewing the pleasant volume of his letters and diaries edited by his wife, "beyond doubt one of the best critics of his time, a conservative with a liberal outlook." Twenty years have gone by since that was written, but the judgment still stands.

Mention of his letters and diaries may make some wonder about his life. Essentially it was a quiet life. He had political hankerings, once fought Sidney Webb for a seat on the London County Council, and stood in two parliamentary elections. Happily he lost all three contests. For though, thanks to his happy marriage, he moved easily and with a certain pleasure in political circles, loving to note down *mots* of Balfour and others, and attempting some political character sketches, that was not his world. Nor was the study either. He was far too great a lover, in Rupert Brooke's sense, of the truer pleasures of life to be so confined. Oxford, his "beloved Lakes", Norfolk, good talk, correspondence with his friends, his presidency of the Literary Society, his clubs, his work for "Scapa" and the National Trust, charitable interests—all these things took up as much time as his writing for *The Times*, *The Times Literary Supplement*, and his books. To-day they have little importance in showing the kind of man he was unless they found some reflection in his books. He himself said that what he had in him was short essays rather than a *magnum opus*, and that his line was "not the historical but the interpretative study of poetry", and at first glance it might seem that few of his activities can have much bearing on that. Yet closer scrutiny convinces one that they informed much of his work, and above all one book.

For in running through those fields in which some might say John Bailey had perhaps been superseded I deliberately left out Walt Whitman. Many of his friends trembled when they heard he had undertaken the work; he himself called it, half-way through, "an uncomfortable task". Yet to my mind it is a *tour de force*, still the best single volume on Whitman that I have read. All that is best from the beginning to end of Bailey's life can be caught in undertones in it. It is not even a bird's cry from the Norfolk boy to the lad on Paumanok shore; the man who had known personal agony in 1914–18 understood the tenderness and love of the Civil War poems. But what nonsense it is to talk of any good work, full of honesty, insight, truth, and sincere yet simple writing, ever being superseded. Literature has many mansions and the name of John Bailey on any door is a guarantee of entering at least a modest one of them.

PLUS ÇA CHANGE

A hundred years ago to-day* one of the most famous cases concerning European literature was decided in Magistrate's Court No. 6 in Paris. As late as the middle of January, 1857, Flaubert had thought that the prosecution against him on account of *Madame Bovary* would be dropped. The *Revue de Paris*, in which *Madame Bovary* had been appearing, was hostile to the Government, so he was convinced the action was political and could be fixed. His moods alternated. One day he thought he had a fair chance of being acquitted; the next he was affirming "I expect no justice whatever. I will serve my prison term." At last on the eve of the full hearing he wrote to his friend Dr. Cloquet that "at 10 a.m. to-morrow I shall honour the swindler's bench by my presence", adding, presumably in the hope of getting some feminine support, "Ladies are admitted but a decent and modest dress is essential." He did one other thing, and for this we should be eternally grateful. He engaged a shorthand writer to take a note of the proceedings.

Centenaries are usually mere acts of piety. And in such a case as this, where the right verdict was given and Flaubert gained instead of suffering from the action, it might be thought there was nothing more to be said. Nevertheless there are two points to be made. The first is that posterity has in general been unfair to the prosecution. The second is the relevance the arguments then used have to the identical problems of literature and the law with which we are still wrestling.

Because the idea of trying to suppress masterpieces is hateful, succeeding generations have echoed Flaubert in denigrating the way in which the case against him was conducted. Even so fair-minded a

*Feb 7, 1957

literary historian as Albert Thibaudet spoke of the prosecutor's "ridiculous address". But when one studies a photograph of Mons. Pierre-Ernest Pinard he seems anything but a ridiculous man. And a careful reading of his speech shows him to have been not only sincere, serious-minded, and fair, but also something of a literary critic.

He began by giving the court a detailed account of the story of *Madame Bovary*. It is true he did this in order to suggest that Flaubert's sub-title should not have been "Moeurs de Province" but "The story of the adulteries of a provincial woman." At no point, however, does he misrepresent. He does not overstate his case. When he passes from the general to the particular he bases the charge that the work is offensive on four episodes. The first is Emma's seduction by Rodolphe. The second is the scene when Emma has religious stirrings after her serious illness. The third is her affair with Leon. The last is the setting of Emma's death.

In quoting long extracts from these particular chapters M. Pinard allowed himself the kind of comments which a living Q.C. might indulge in. It was not so much Emma's fall as her glorification of it which was dangerous. Flaubert's scenes were "admirable painting if one considers only the skill; execrable painting if one has any regard for morals". Flaubert wrote "platitudes about marriage, poetry about adultery". The test for the court was surely the kind of person likely to read such a novel. Would it be most likely to be picked up by political economists and sociologists or by young girls and married women? After a hundred years of justifiable satisfaction that Mons. Pinard lost his case—and let us not forget that far from being only his case or the Government's case it was also the case of the scores of indignant readers who had protested to the *Revue de Paris* (and somewhat scared them) as the instalments came out—I think it is time that a little justice was done to him.

Maître Sénard's speech for the defence, as it was made on the right side and was successful, has always been admired. Have we not, however, taken the judgment too much for granted? France in

1857 was far from being a free society. Judges everywhere had to be careful, most of all in Paris. Therefore when the magistrate said *Madame Bovary* merited severe censure, and that Flaubert had not paid sufficient attention to the bounds which even the lightest literature should not pass, he was doing the least that could be expected of him. Many a magistrate would do the same to-day. But, in that historic judgment of February 7, 1857, he found the charge not proven and acquitted all the defendants. Even by those who can recite the case in some detail his name is not known. As another act of justice it should be printed to-day. It was M. Dubarle. Indeed, the whole verbatim report of the proceedings might well be republished. For it shows how little ground we have gained. Were a new *Madame Bovary* to appear, the same evidence might well be given and the same speeches made. The one thing we could not be equally sure of is that there would inevitably be a magistrate as enlightened as M. Dubarle to try the case.

I cannot close this voluntary on the theme of "Plus ça change" without one final adornment to the tale. Among the strongest letters of protest the *Revue de Paris* received while the instalments were being published were those from pharmacists who said that the character of Homais was an unjustified slur on their profession.

JOINT EFFORTS

"There, but for the grace of God, go I" is a reflection that comes naturally only in later years. I was young and ardent when I first strayed into what was for me the enchanting world of Southey's letters. Here was a man in all truth. Even his faults were likeable. Who that surrendered to Southey's spell in his letters could fail to echo Thackeray's tribute to his life: "It is sublime in its simplicity, its energy, its honour, its affection." What trials he had to bear, and how his family life solaced him. Then suddenly, when Southey is 60, his beloved daughter, Edith, gets married; and within 24 hours he is writing to his friend Henry Taylor the quite serious observation: "As my household diminishes there will be room for more books." How shocked I was! This God had feet of paper after all. It was many years later that walking in a long and solemn funeral procession that wound its way through a provincial city I caught sight of a handsome row of red, black, and gold volumes in a bookseller's window. And immediately the service was over I hurried back to buy the set of Besant and Rice that I have treasured ever since. I remember that even as I paid the bill I was thinking that Southey was avenged.

Besant and Rice. The collocation came as trippingly off the tongues of their generation as "blackberry and apple" did in a later one and as Laurel and Hardy has done in our own day. Of all collaborations it was one of the most remarkable. Little is known about James Rice to-day beyond the fact that he was editor of *Once a Week*. Besant is still a name remembered and revered—is not his bust with a most superb pair of *pince-nez* upon the Thames Embankment? He became a devoted and noble social worker, the begetter of the People's Palace, a founder of the Society of Authors, the historian of London. Rice had nothing to do with any of these things. Yet if ever one man's fame was made by another, Besant's was made by Rice.

For when all Besant's "good works" are forgotten, *Ready Money Mortiboy* will remain. And *Ready Money Mortiboy* was Rice's idea. Rice was the best type of editor, being satisfied to create through others. He suggested to Besant that he should write a novel. He gave him the plot. He gave him more plots. *The Golden Butterfly*, *'Twas in Trafalgar's Bay*, *The Monks of Thelema*, *My Little Girl*, and many other tales were the result. The collaboration lasted for 10 successful and highly profitable years; then Rice ailed and died. Besant wrote 20 or more novels on his own after that; hardly one of them is remembered to-day. Yet Rice had no claim to fame in his own right. He wrote nothing of consequence alone. He would hardly have been a name even while he lived if it had not been for Besant.

This was perhaps the perfect, inevitable, essential collaboration. So many others seemed forced, the lesser light invariably doing the forcing. How Kipling ever came to collaborate with Wolcott Balestier to produce *The Naulahka* has always been a puzzle, though Mr. Carrington in his excellent life of Kipling went some way towards solving it. Balestier was obviously a most persuasive young man. There is an essay about him by Edmund Gosse which shows how others also fell under his spell. Stevenson's collaboration with Lloyd Osbourne was a different matter. For years it was decried and even deplored. The adulators of Stevenson could not bear to feel that even the most feeble star could twinkle near their sun. Clearly affection had a good deal to do with Stevenson's willingness to collaborate. But although it would be absurd to pretend that Lloyd Osbourne was in any way on a footing with R.L.S., the collaboration was not a sham. *The Wrong Box* is like nothing else Stevenson wrote and there are individual notes both in *The Wrecker* and *The Ebb Tide*. However small it was, Lloyd Osbourne had something to contribute.

Exactly what it was is hard to determine. Lloyd Osbourne in his prefaces to the Tusitala edition of Stevenson's works was modestly explicit about the machinery of the joint efforts; nevertheless one would have to study all the manuscripts to see exactly what his contribution amounted to and even then one might not be certain. There was all the talk before the writing. That we can never recapture. Perhaps the most revealing remark was the one R.L.S. made to Osbourne when they were working together on *The Wrecker*: "It's glorious to have the ground ploughed, and to sit back in luxury for the real fun of writing—which is re-writing."

A collaboration which was much less happy was that of Conrad and Hueffer. Despite all his brashness and dogmatism I have always suspected that there was a fundamental uncertainty in Hueffer (or Ford as he later called himself). His patronizing air towards Conrad, particularly after Conrad's death, has done him a disservice with many people. For Ford was a good writer himself. The Tietjens series, and even more *The Good Soldier*, deserve great respect. And, generally unattractive as Ford's writings about Conrad are, there are passages in his *Joseph Conrad: A Personal Remembrance* which are of great interest. Conrad and Ford collaborated in three works: *Romance*, *The Inheritors*, and *The Nature of a Crime*. None of them deserves to rank in the true Conrad canon. It is interesting that when Conrad came to write a special preface for each volume of the collected edition he wrote none for the first two of these works. And the preface he did write for the subsequently issued *The Nature of a Crime* rather gives the game away—as far as so punctilious a gentleman as Conrad could bring himself to do such a thing.

All collaborations are something of a mystery. One could go on to examine many more names in double harness; the mystery would still remain. And lest collaborations be thought of as almost inevitably second-class works, let it be remembered that one of the greatest of all pieces of English literature was, in essence, a collaboration. As Sir Arthur Quiller-Couch was never tired of pointing out, the authorized version of the Bible was the work of 47 men, all of whom in some miraculous way found their pens taking wings. The work seized them individually till collectively they were uplifted and inspired.

LILY BART

I have been re-reading *The House of Mirth.* It is a book which is rarely completely out of my mind for long. There was a time when this puzzled me. It is not a great work (though I think it the best thing Edith Wharton wrote, far better than the more highly praised *Ethan Frome*). It is neither true tragedy nor comedy. Though the world it deals with is not, in these post-war times, as dead and gone as Mrs. Wharton thought it was in the 1930s, it is insignificant in the scheme of things to-day. *The House of Mirth* is a story about essentially trivial, aimless, worthless, people. I should, therefore, be hard put to it to answer the question why I have taken the book up time and again. I should be—but I am not. Let Mrs. Wharton herself give the reason. (She does so in her autobiography *A Backward Glance.*)

> A frivolous society can acquire dramatic significance only through what its frivolity destroys. Its tragic implication lies in its power of debasing people and ideals. The answer, in short, was my heroine, Lily Bart.

Lily Bart is a fascinating creature. And in at least one thing she is highly original. The essential secret of all the great women characters in literature is said to be their mystery. Where would Cleopatra, Beatrice, and Anna Karenina be if there ever came an end to the arguments about them? To drop down to a much lower, and more appropriate, plane, half Christina Light's attraction is her enduring enigma. Neither in *Roderick Hudson* nor in *The Princess Casamassima* did Henry James allow us fully to understand her. But Lily Bart is presented to us whole. Nothing is reserved, neither of her strength nor her weakness. If at any moment she appears to become unpredictable the reason can only be that we have not been watching her carefully enough. Sometimes it is difficult to do so, because she can be such an attractive and sympathetic companion. But her defects are never sprung on us. They are there from the opening pages. She acts in character at every point of the story. The fascination is not to guess, but to observe, exactly what that character is.

She had an upbringing strangely like Christina Light's. A hard-up childhood and youth, a mother who was "a wonderful manager" and who studied Lily's beauty "with a kind of passion", an adolescence in which that beauty slowly budded to her mother's lament for their lost comforts and the constant reassurance to Lily, "But you'll get it all back, with your face." Mrs. Bart's last adjuration before she escaped from dinginess by dying was, "Don't let it creep up on you and drag you down. Fight your way out of it somehow —you're young and can do it."

Fight Lily did. Ostensibly under the protection of a highly respectable, dull, and only moderately well-off aunt, she won for herself one of the places at the top of the greasy pole of New York society. She found that with her beauty, her charm, her gifts of perception and natural grace "there was room for her, after all, in this crowded selfish world of pleasure." Misfortunes she had had. They had made her supple instead of hard. Only one thing further was needed to consolidate her success and to transform the greasy pole into a comfortable throne, whence she could queen it without fear or struggle. She should get married. So far, through a mixture of bad luck and fastidiousness, this consummation had eluded her. "She had several times been in love with fortunes or careers, but only once with a man." At the story's opening she is 29, "eleven years of late hours and indefatigable dancing" are beginning to show, and she is on her way to a country house partly determined to capture and wed the dim young millionaire, Percy Gryce.

Only at the book's close does one appreciate the skill of its beginning. Lily has missed her train to Bellomont. In Grand Central

Station she meets Lawrence Selden, vaguely in her circle but really a detached observer of it. For one thing, he has not the money to afford it, for another, he is both Stoic and Epicurean. Lily cannot afford it either. She, too, had fastidious tastes—once. But whereas Selden's detachment has preserved him, Lily's standards have become corrupted. Their meeting, so casual, so trivial, is the beginning of her slide to disaster. Ironically it was a momentary re-establishing of her values that led to her ultimate undoing. She felt no deep affection for Selden at first; it took her some time even to perceive how his presence "always had the effect of cheapening her aspirations, of throwing her whole world out of focus." But when Selden unexpectedly turns up at Bellomont she lets Gryce slip from her grasp (half-believing she can easily recapture him later).

In turn, through a misunderstanding, she loses Selden. Then, by becoming the pawn in another woman's fight to avoid divorce, she loses her place in the exclusive world. Level by level, she sinks down through the different layers of society, always indomitable, always brilliant, always—despite the worthlessness of all she is fighting for and the tawdriness of her weapons—maintaining a final integrity. For throughout she has it in her power to re-establish herself by using some letters to Selden written by the woman who has ruined her. This she never does, although she trembles on the verge of it. And she uses her last money to repay a debt in which there had never been dishonour. Poverty and an overdose of chloral remain. Selden, having finally made up his own mind, arrives too late.

I have said *The House of Mirth* is no true tragedy. It causes neither awe nor compassion. Nonetheless it is a beautifully constructed, extremely well written, and finely controlled work. It might be argued that the two events which finally precipitated Lily Bart to disaster were both injustices to her. The fact remains that if she had been other than she was they could not have harmed her at all. She has all the instincts for poetry and nobility; she had not the fibre to sustain them. Even towards the end of her long plunge downwards

She had rejected Rosedale's suggestion with a promptness of scorn almost surprising to herself; she had not lost her capacity for high flashes of indignation. But she could not breathe long on the heights; there had been nothing in her training to develop any continuity of moral strength: what she craved, and really felt herself entitled to, was a situation in which the noblest attitude should also be the easiest.

That was one cause of her failure. Balancing it was another. As one of her friends said of her:

That's Lily all over, you know: she works like a slave preparing the ground and sowing her seed; but the day she ought to be reaping the harvest she oversleeps herself or goes off on a picnic . . . Sometimes I think it's because, at heart, she despises the things she's trying for.

The day will come, I am sure, when I will again want to meet Lily Bart.

WHERE THE SEA SUCKS

The poems a man recites to himself are probably among his most private possessions. But, for the purposes of this article, I must confess that there cannot have been many weeks in these past 30 years when I have not at least once gone through the lines of "Dover Beach" in my mind. I have a profound respect for Matthew Arnold. And among all his works "Dover Beach" says more to me than anything else.

That means I have not read it since I was young. At least, not attentively. Does one ever examine the detailed lineaments of a constant companion? If one does, it is almost invariably to get a shock. Can he or she really be like that? The familiar features seem to dissolve. A stranger is in front of us. It says much for the comforts of familiarity that what one then sees is not so attractive as what one knows. So it was when some time ago I heard a speaker on the B.B.C. quoting Arnold to illustrate a point and saying:

> Listen! you hear the grating roar
> Of pebbles which the waves suck back, and fling,
> At their return, up the high strand . . .

"Suck back"! The man, I thought, has slipped up badly. He can have no ear at all.

Last weekend, however, I was looking through Mr. John Hayward's excellent *Penguin Book of English Verse*, and "Dover Beach" caught my eye. Remembering the B.B.C. misquoter I stopped to make sure Mr. Hayward had got it right. I received not one shock but three.

Come to the window, sweet is the night air!
Only, from the long line of spray
Where the ebb meets the moon-blanch'd sand,
Listen! you hear the grating roar
Of pebbles which the waves suck back and fling,
At their return, up the high strand,
Begin, and cease, and then again begin,
With tremulous cadence slow, and bring
The eternal note of sadness in.

(I have quoted a longer extract than is strictly relevant in the hope it may send new readers to the whole poem.)

Now I really was disturbed. The *ebb* meeting the moon-blanch'd *sand*, as well as the waves *sucking* the pebbles back. Had I been misquoting Arnold all these years? I went to the *Oxford Book of Victorian Verse*. It backed Mr. Hayward up. So did five other anthologies or collections of Arnold I had by me. This was a bad business. It would be hard to alter the mind's gramophone record after half a lifetime. Moreover, I felt strongly my version was the better.

The first ray of hope came from Mr. Louis Untermeyer's *Albatross Book of Living Verse*. He had "sand" and "suck" but not "ebb". Then I began to come across all kinds of variations on the three disputed words. At last I got back to the 1885 collected edition of Arnold's poems; and there was firm land and safe water once again:

Where the *sea* meets the moon-blanch'd *land*,
Listen! you hear the grating roar
Of pebbles which the waves *draw* back . . .

"Dover Beach" was as I had always known it.

The divergences may seem too trivial to worry about. I do not think they are. Fortunately I am not learned or subtle enough to belong to Hazlitt's "occult school" of critics: "They discern no beauties but what are concealed from superficial eyes, and overlook all that are obvious to the vulgar part of mankind." But I was born and brought up by the sea's edge, and of all the sounds that have penetrated to my sub-sub-conscious those of the sea meeting the moon-blanch'd land, and of the grating roar of pebbles drawn outwards by the retreating wave, must be among the clearest. "Sea" and "draw" are for the two operations beautifully onomatopoeic. The incoming wave spreading and dissipating itself over the land, particularly at night when all other sounds are stilled, does so with a hiss. The word "sea" conjures up the sound as immediately its following words present the image. When the waves go out, the sea does not suck the pebbles. The sea, as Cowper once remarked, may have to house the sprat, but it does not suck anything less than islands in a tidal wave or great ships in a storm. Rivers may be heard to suck small things, but not the sea. What the sea does is to move the pebbles slightly outwards in the "long, withdrawing roar" Arnold speaks of later, and the word "draw" is exact both for the action and the sound. About "land" and "sand" I do not feel so strongly. You get assonance either way. Personally "blanch'd land, Listen" is pleasanter than "sea . . . sand"; and "land" sounds more majestic and in keeping with the poem's general argument.

But let us go to Arnold himself. "Dover Beach" appeared in *New Poems* in 1867. Arnold wrote "ebb . . . sand . . . suck". A second edition appeared in 1868 and already Arnold, with true instinct, had begun to amend it to "ebb . . . sand . . . draw". So it remained in the *Collected Poems* of 1869 and 1877. In 1878 it became "sea . . . land . . . draw". In 1881 "sea . . . sand . . . draw". In 1883 "sea . . . land . . . draw". In 1885 the final edition that Arnold (who died in 1888) saw through the press had "sea . . . land . . . draw". So it stayed in the posthumous 1890 edition. Arnold hovered between "sand" and "land" almost to the end, but he stood firmly by "sea" and "draw" for the last 10 years of his life. I know Mr. Hayward has committed himself in general to using the earliest texts, but Arnold must, unless all the different variations are printers' aberrations, have pondered the matter many times. And *The Penguin Book of English Verse* is so obviously destined to have a great educative influence with the new generation that I hope in subsequent editions Mr. Hayward will make an exception to his rule and restore "Dover Beach" to its full, final glory.

PLAIN OR FANCIED

A number of critics seem to have been rather baffled by Mr. Richard Church's new novel, *The Dangerous Years*. It has obviously left one after another of them with a certain sense of unease amidst their admiration for its integrity and its craftsmanship, but there does not seem to be any general agreement about the reason why. I wonder if it is not one of the very strokes in the book which are meant to make for verisimilitude. Mr. Church, both in his autobiography and in his novels, has shown that he is not only a great lover of music but that all his life he has been seeking to pierce to the heart of its mystery. He is one of the few novelists who have been able to depict musical genius convincingly; the master of that small band being, for me at least, Henry Handel Richardson. The *deus ex machina* in *The Dangerous Years* (if one can call so human a small boy by so august a title) is the child prodigy, Adrian. Child prodigies rarely convince us. But Adrian does—until in the Alpine hotel where he is staying he meets an elderly man with "a massive and grim mouth under the grey moustache". The man is Schnabel.

I must confess that real people in novels affect me as actors do when I see them inserted into an animated cartoon. Instead of adding to the sense of reality they destroy it. Rather than being larger than art they are invariably smaller than the author's own world. One must draw a distinction, of course, between those characters who are so shadowy in history that the novelist can do with them what he will without any violation of our conception or knowledge and those who are fixed, famous figures. Stevenson had a completely free hand with James Stewart in *Kidnapped* and *Catriona*, for instance, because we have no clear idea what the Appin murderer (or martyr?) was like. Actually Stevenson, quite deliberately I think, did little with him. (For all the ordinary man knows of Alan Breck he is a completely fictional character.) But let Dr. Johnson, or Gladstone, or Byron enter a novel, however perfunctorily, and at once conviction vanishes. Again one must differentiate between novels which are wholly historical, where only two or three characters are fictional, and those where it is the other way about. The historical novelist is not seeking to create a world of his own but to recapture one that once existed. No reader of Scott can deny that the Young Pretender is one of the most vivid figures in *Waverley*. On the other hand, his forerunner in *Henry Esmond* is but a stage figure. One can, of course, be challenged with Lord Beaconsfield. What—to take only one example—about *Endymion*? Does the fact that it is a *roman à clef*, that almost all the characters are but faintly disguised, and some, such as Wellington, Lord John Russell, and Peel, not at all, ruin it? Of course not. *Endymion* is an enchantment. Each time one picks it up it has a new charm. But it is a masque, a ballet, a contrivance, a whatever you like to call it, but not a novel.

There is another kind of "real people" in novels which is in no way a drawback. Mr. Harry T. Moore, in *The Intelligent Heart*, has once again told how everything, and almost everybody, was grist to D. H. Lawrence's literary mill. We had long known that Jessie Chambers (E.T.) was the Miriam of *Sons and Lovers*—and among Mr. Moore's many achievements is to have disentangled the whole relationship and interaction between the young Lawrence and the young Jessie more persuasively than it has been done before—but Mr. Moore has managed to identify a whole host of Lawrence's relatives, neighbours, and acquaintances, whom he used in his stories and novels. Conrad did the same thing. In his case, trouble was sometimes not even taken to change the name.

There are two reasons, I think, why this practice, and the knowledge of it, lessens neither one's pleasure in reading the resultant fictions nor one's admiration for their authors. The first is that we know nothing about the originals. There is no mental shadow to get between us and what the writer would have us see. The second is that no matter how well a writer may know another human being he cannot comprehend him fully, as his Creator made him. In this age of the psychologists we appreciate better than we once did how right Oliver Wendell Holmes was when he insisted that six people were involved if John talked to Thomas. Therefore it is never a real person an author can put on to the written page. Certain characteristics, idiosyncrasies, lineaments he may take merely photographically. But something will come from himself, however faithful to truth he may try to be. As Holmes pointed out, neither John's ideal John nor Thomas's ideal John can ever be the real one. The art of creation is going on in all our relationships all the time, whether we set pen to paper or not.

It is this question of creation, it seems to me, which is at the root of the matter. We do not feel that Mallock's *The New Republic* or any of Peacock's tales are spoiled because the greater part of the cast had living originals. Rather do we want to have the fun of identifying them. For what are they but diverting and most obvious puppets? The author is not seeking to introduce reality into the world of the imagination, or fancy into what we know to have been real. Everything is larger than life dared to make it, and therefore deliberately unreal. We can accept such a convention and be satisfied. But in a book which is meant to be, above all, a work of the imagination, real people are best kept out of the way.

LA NUIT DE MAI

A hundred years ago to-day* Alfred de Musset died, and the fact makes a full third of them fall away in the memory. We are once again in those good, gay, creative years of hope, the early 'twenties, when a better world seemed to be being made. A French company is visiting England to forge new ties of shared experience after those of a war. The high spot of the season is the appearance of Le Bargy in *Le Marquis de Priola.* But the main work falls on two ardent and hard-working young people, Pierre Fresnay and Rachel Berendt. They present us with plenty of Molière, of Rostand, of Théodore de Banville, of Musset. Above all, of Musset. There comes back that enchanted moment when one first heard

Poète, prends ton luth et me donne un baiser

and was given seizin of *La Nuit de Mai.*

The two strands of Alfred de Musset's genius have woven in and out curiously to make his fame. In the article which Sainte-Beuve devoted to him on the first available Monday after his death (*Madame Bovary* took that of May 4), Musset is appreciated almost exclusively as a poet; Sainte-Beuve, who had hitherto had reservations, coming out forthrightly with

Tant qu'il y aura une France et une poésie française, les flammes de Musset vivront comme vivent les flammes de Sapho.

That has hardly been the judgment of recent years. While the

*May 2, 1957

reputation of Musset the dramatist has never stood higher in France, I am assured by those who should know that his poetry has for a long time lacked a wide public to appreciate it. The eclipse has been all the more marked because the regard for his plays has actually grown. Nearly all of them have been, and many still are to be, seen on the Paris stage. Some continue in the repertory of the Théatre Français. Vilar at the Théatre Nationale Populaire and Jean-Louis Barrault at the Marigny have since the war both helped forward Musset's fame with a new generation; Vilar with a particularly fine performance of *Lorenzaccio*. In this connexion a guiding idea has persisted through a hundred years and more. Even while he was alive it was possible to allude to Shakespeare when writing of Alfred de Musset. Sainte-Beuve did so at least twice. And to-day the attraction in Musset's plays for a French audience is said to be his "fantaisie Shakespearienne". Shakespeare is too well known in France—and in spite of some insuperable difficulties has been too well translated—for French critical opinion ever to put anything but a stiff gap between the two men. But what French dramatist achieves a smaller gap? As one of the most discerning of Frenchmen was heard to say the other day, "*Lorenzaccio* is the nearest thing to Shakespeare in the whole of the French theatre."

I doubt, however, if it is for such rare fare that Musset is loved by the multitude, or by the ordinary English reader. *Lorenzaccio* is a noble effort that falls short of perfection. It is impossible to imagine how one could add one iota of improvement to *Les Caprices de Marianne*. We return to it time and time again; some because they see Musset himself in both Octave and Célio; others because there is the inevitability of life itself in the way comedy turns to tragedy not with a lightning stroke, but with a gathering relentlessness. It is part of Musset's genius that his greatest "comedies"—*On ne badine pas avec l'amour* is another fine work—should end with a hammer blow of Fate, but the gayer "proverbes", such as *Il faut qu'une porte soit ouverte ou fermée* and *Il ne faut jurer de rien*, all have their charm. They are to be seen if that is at all possible; if not, they can make their effect when they are read. But for me, if I had to lose in one way or another the greater part of the nine volumes of Musset's collected works, including even the stories and *La Confession d'un Enfant du Siècle*, the catastrophe would not be complete so long as *Les Caprices de Marianne* and the *Nuits* were saved.

For whatever may be the taste in Paris it is Musset's poems that hold me even more firmly than his single stage masterpiece. The four "Nights"—with *La Nuit de Mai* surpassing the others in beauty as *La Nuit d'Octobre* does in depth, the *Stances à La Malibran*, *Namouna*, some of the sonnets, all the songs, many of the lyrics have an inexhaustible magic. It may be possible for the editor of a French literary monthly to hold that Musset is not a "number one poet", although he graciously added that any anthology of French poetry which did not include something of his "would be unjust"; literary appreciation undergoes the strangest mutations. But we need not worry about fashion. Indeed I console myself that often the fashions that shock the most are the shortest-lived. There are signs that the "surrealist school" of poetry criticism has been rediscovering Musset with some approval. Aragon speaks well of him. Philippe Soupault is about to publish a new study of him. This, combined with the centenary exhibition to be held later this year by the Bibliothéque Nationale, may set yet a newer cult. Who knows? Alfred de Musset is to-day a hundred years young. He will not die.

For it is the marvellous youth we should remember. Mme. Berendt explained to us from the stage at the last curtain call that the secret of Musset is that he is the poet of youth. For that reason I have said nothing of George Sand, or his weaknesses, or his excesses, all of which helped to make him old. Nor will I look up a particularly painful memory of him at a party in his closing years. It is here on my shelves, but it shall stay closed, as does the page, in another volume, containing that terrible portrait by Pompeo Batoni of Prince Charles Edward in later life. I prefer to remember the eager, proud, and handsome boy who, still in his teens, burst into the circle of Vigny and Hugo, facing the world with wonder in his eyes and reciting his verses with joy in his heart. It is by such the Muse wishes to be kissed. It is to such that, no matter what may come after, ordinary men and women give their affection also.

GEORGE GISSING

It is time I paid my debt to George Gissing, or at least explained why in discussing those authors whose writings on the poor had stirred the social conscience fifty years ago I left him out of account. Gissing wrote as grimly and as vividly about the submerged parts of society as anyone. Often, as in *New Grub Street*, he did so from personal experience. His very titles proclaim his purpose—*Demos, The Unclassed, The Nether World, Workers in the Dawn, The Emancipated.* He was a better artist and a more considerable literary figure than such men as Morrison or Whiteing, Tressall or Reynolds. Yet whatever the place of his books to-day—and I want to suggest later that for some of them it is reasonably high—so far as social or political effects go he had no influence at all.

The commonest complaint against Gissing is that he is too gloomy. (Indeed Dr. Johnson's "inspissated gloom" is much more appropriate to *The Nether World* than to any amount of darkness in *Macbeth.*) Another is that he whined; still another that he railed too much. I do not believe the cause lies in any of these things. We get a better clue from the fact that by the time the leaven of Gissing's earlier novels should have been working he had escaped from the worst of his own miseries, and that the book of his which is most read, and by which he is now principally remembered, *The Private Papers of Henry Ryecroft*, is the record of his escape.

The truth is that Gissing disliked the poor. He himself describes Ryecroft as "a man of independent and rather scornful outlook". Mr. Frank Swinnerton, whose book on Gissing remains after 43 years the truest, most sympathetic, and most penetrating study there is, points out that not only was he temperamentally an egoist, but that Gissing had never lived in the spirit of the London poor. "In the books about the lower classes," says Mr. Swinnerton, "there is a lack of exact knowledge, due to his temperamental lack of sympathy with the life he is describing." H. G. Wells went even further. After calling Gissing's upbringing in the chemist's shop at Wakefield one of "repressive gentility", he shows how "he was entirely enclosed in a defensive phraseology and a conscious 'scorn' of the 'baser' orders and 'ignoble' types." Gissing was an aristocrat *manqué*, his pity was self-pity, and, in that strange subconscious way that the English have, the public came to know it.

Would such a barrier have been impassable if Gissing had had even that as a firm standpoint? Gissing had no firm standpoint. Wells said of *The Crown of Life* that it was illuminating because it revealed that to Gissing the "crown of life" was love in a frock-coat. One has only to remember what he himself attained where love was concerned to know he had no standards. And lest I be misunderstood I would say his first marriage was far more to his credit than his second. Morley Roberts's *The Private Life of Henry Maitland* (which under the guise of fiction is an intimate biography of Gissing) has been attacked for its inaccuracies, for the indelicacy of such a strange act of friendship, and for revealing things that are best left hidden. Enough years have now gone by for us to enjoy its fascination, and what a lifetime of reading Gissing has convinced me is its psychological truth. Maitland-Gissing is a creature of exquisite aspirations and gross tastes, sensuous and sensual, artistic and vulgar, indignant at misery and with a terror of reform. And yet——

And yet, like so many other Englishmen not one iota better—some far worse—he had one inestimable gift. He could write. Too often he wrote for bread and his adored dripping. He had neither the sureness of ear nor the brilliance of fancy unfailingly to triumph over such circumstances. But when he did, the result was enduring. Personally I have a particular liking for *Demos*, but most critics would not put it among the best three or four of his books, and when one is possibly coaxing new readers to an author it is best not to be idiosyncratic. With *Thyrza* one is on sure ground. The two so dissimilar working sisters, Thyrza and Lydia Trent, are real people. Thyrza's beauty and goodness are not things we have to take on trust; her sad, frustrated love for Egremount is moving and tender. Although the story is far from gay, the writing is the warmest and most poetic in any of Gissing's novels. *Thyrza* can stand equably alongside most Victorian novels. *The Nether World* is a fiercer, gloomier, more powerful tale; you cannot know one of the essential Gissings without it.

Indeed, the moment one begins to compile a list of Gissing's best books one sees what an assembly of contradictions he was. *Thyrza, The Nether World, New Grub Street, Born in Exile, The Private Papers of Henry Ryecroft, By the Ionian Sea, Charles Dickens*—where is their common denominator? How reconcile the first four with the last three? In fact, I have placed them in this order deliberately, to make the point of what I have been saying. For, of course, the only common denominator was the quirked character of that ill-starred, *déclassé*, self-destroying but essentially likeable writer of thwarted talents, George Gissing.

ANOTHER WORLD

I am no Proustian. I have read *A la Recherche du Temps Perdu* three times in these past 25 years and I hope to do so at least once again before I die. To my mind it is probably the only enduring long work written in our time. Its 12 volumes are as majestic and truthful—even down to the nasty mudbanks—a flow through Time as the river Thames is through space. But, whenever I am borne upon it, my relation to the real Proustians is that of a pleasure steamer passenger compared with a Thames waterman. For one thing, I like Combray better than Paris or Balbec and the childhood scenes more than the grown-up ones. The Guermantes, Cambremers, and Verdurins bore me. I think Proust got the Baron de Charlus badly out of perspective in the proportions of his picture. (In contrast there is his unerring handling of Mlle. Vinteuil's vice.) I have no desire ever to know what was the famous "little phrase" from the sonata, though I accept fully all it could accomplish. Elstir and Bergotte both leave me cold and Berma fails to convince. I would never have gone to the Proust exhibition at Wildenstein's because of them.

Why did I go? And why did I find myself staying on and on? Because Proust captured out of his memories, mounted, and set out in his show case, specimens from a stagnant world, much as a lepidopterist might mount his captures from around a pool on a summer's afternoon. It was high summer for Proust's particular world; the blast of 1914 was to wither it all. There was much grace and beauty, and even simple, unaffected pleasures, but some pretty nasty things crept about the undergrowth. And here in a London gallery were not only relics of Proust and manuscripts of Proust, but also evocations of Proust's raw material. Photographs, portraits, paintings, drawings, some of the actual belongings, of the Proustian circle and what one may loosely call his originals. Here and there, it is true, are some who do not look too comfortable. Both Carlyle (gloomily) and César Franck (quizzically) seem to be asking what they are doing *dans cette galère*. It will infuriate the Proustians, and underline the fact that I am not one of them, when I say that all the cathedral photographs seem equally ill at ease.

But when one comes to the pictures of Illiers, to the society paintings by Beraud and the photographs by Nadar (what a debt posterity owes to the egregious, intrepid, and surely immortal Nadar), to Proust's waistcoat or his handwritten report about his duel, to Anna de Noailles's parasol, to Laure Haymann, and Louise de Mornand, to Reynaldo Hahn, and Tissot's wonderful study of human still-life *Le Cercle de la Rue Royale* (a grand collection of Mr. Pooters they are) one is completely captured. At one moment I even felt Arnold Bennett looking over my shoulder. Gazing at the massy, heavy Bronte-ish hair of Cléo de Merode one could sympathize, as apparently Bennett could not, with the New York impresario who announced on large posters: "Tonight Cléo de Merode will show her ears."

But something beyond the mere fact that it was largely a trivial world is slowly registered. It is the appreciation of what an alchemist Proust was. Comparing these people, who actually lived (and in some cases are still alive), with the characters in *A la Recherche du Temps Perdu*, there are only three who strike one as being in themselves larger than art. The first is Madame Weil, Proust's grandmother. If ever there was a face of character this is it. The second was Marie Bernadacki, who, the catalogue tells us, was the model for Gilberte. She looks an enchanting person. The third, I regret to say, is Robert de Montesquiou. I have sometimes wondered whether it was my distaste for his character that made me always feel the Baron de Charlus was one of Proust's few failures. Now I am convinced it was not.

I have said that I think Proust's masterpiece will endure. Possibly it will do so longer in the English language than in French. This is no mere paradoxical praise of C. K. Scott-Moncrieff's superb translation (which really does make it otiose for an Englishman to labour through the original), but because in a curious way this river of a novel has more to tell us, more unaccustomed nerves to set responding, more strange harmonies to vibrate, than it has for the French. Nor is it likely to be overtaken by anything of its own kind in our language. But it would be wrong to believe it will ever be read by the hundred thousands, as Stendhal, or Dostoevsky and the other great Russians, or even Balzac are read. Frankly, it is not easy to read. The proportion of those starting out with *Swann's Way* who manage to persist through to *Time Regained* will remain small, though larger than that of those who encompass *La Comédie Humaine*. As with Sibelius's second symphony, *A la Recherche du Temps Perdu* is a tantalisingly long time in mounting the platform of its final triumphant theme. (Not the least astonishing thing about his great work is that immediately after he had finished the opening of it Proust wrote the end, and then filled in all in-between.) But when that final theme is fully displayed what a memorable and moving thing it is. Proust himself once summed up his purpose as "psychology in space and time". But just as no great painting can be described by measurements, so is no written masterpiece capable of being reduced to a formula. All that one can say is that Proust magically brought into the novel certain apprehensions about time and life and memory which had never been there before.

One last thing should be added. In starting out on *Swann's Way* you give hardly any hostage to fortune. If you get through all the remaining ten volumes so much the better. If you do not—if you refuse at the vicious parts—you will still have something worthwhile to retain. Proust's opening movement is, for me, his greatest work. One can come to it on its own, if necessary, again and again.

PANACHE

The enthusiasm and energy of American scholars when they confront English literature are well known. The discoveries, the treasures, the manuscripts flow in a depressing stream westwards across the Atlantic; in due course the great new editions of Boswell, of Walpole, of Coleridge flow back. What is not so well known is the good sense of American universities and colleges, particularly the newer of them. Having come perforce late into the field, they find that even their wealth cannot accumulate great collections of incunabula and other rare masterpieces. So, looking to the future, they more modestly invest in the masters of our own times. You come across a Hardy collection here, the beginnings of a Conrad one there; Rupert Brooke and the Georgian poets' manuscripts somewhere else. And one college, I believe, has decided to go nap on Cunninghame Graham.

Close on 25 years ago now, some time between his eightieth birthday and his death, I suggested in an article that there should be a collected edition of Cunninghame Graham's works. Various people were interested, even enthusiastic. I had correspondence with some of them, including Tschiffely. It is necessary to say something about Tschiffely, if only to keep the record straight. On the face of it, the literary combination of Cunninghame Graham and Tschiffely was such an odd affair. Tschiffely does his great ride and Cunninghame Graham hears of it. Cunninghame Graham writes a glowing account in *Writ in Sand* and helps to make Tschiffely. Then Tschiffely publishes his book, becomes famous, and devotes much of his writing years to proclaiming the books and deeds of Cunninghame Graham. Tschiffely produces *Rodeo*, a collection of Cunninghame Graham's stories and sketches. It includes the piece "Tschiffely's Ride," and Cunninghame Graham writes a preface.

The thing that must be stressed is the disinterestedness there was behind it all. No one would ever have dared to have accused Cunninghame Graham of literary log-rolling. But Tschiffely's ardour was equally selfless. He won Cunninghame Graham's heart because he had accomplished a ride on horseback such as no man had ever done before. Cunninghame Graham won his heart because he was a natural enthusiast suddenly confronted by a phenomenon with a *panache*. The rest followed, whatever the consequences to either of them. And now they are both dead; there is no collected edition; I doubt if there ever will be. Also I have long since come to the conclusion it is as well.

Cunninghame Graham is greatest as a legend. Exactly how and where we first encounter it hardly seems to matter. Believing that Shaw will last, I am convinced that future generations will, as those of the past, first meet him in the epilogue or footnote to *Captain Brassbound's Conversion*. So encountered, he is irresistible. How magnificent to burst upon that scene in the House of Commons with its superb "I never withdraw." Then there are the Epstein bust and the Rothenstein and Lavery portraits. No one can fail to be held by such a man. Or you come across him in the company of Conrad or Hudson; or in some memory of the famous Trafalgar Square riots. Always something of his daemon leaps out. He was not a fencing master for nothing. You are held; you do not forget; you decide to explore.

It is to be hoped you will explore the life as well as the works. (Of course, Tschiffely has written it.) Strange as it may seem to say of so good a writer—and when he ranked among his literary peers it was no time of pygmies—he was even more outstanding as a man than as an author. It has been loosely said that everything he wrote was autobiographical. Certainly he had known all his characters; had lived most of his stories and episodes. Perhaps because of this there is a curious dead level about them, so that, if they are read in bulk, they become monotonous. Imagination can wax and wane with its creations. But the writer who has been there, seen everything, finds even his most fantastic narrations adopting the uniform of verisimilitude.

Is it perhaps because of this that so many people place "Beattock for Moffat" as his masterpiece? Euston Station is a far cry from the pampas, and Andra is, on the face of him, brother neither to sheikh nor gaucho. But the tale has a drive, a touch, an imaginative force withheld from far more stirring recitals. Similarly I place as high as anything in *Mogreb-El-Acksa* his few pages "A Memory of Parnell" and "Lift up Your Hearts", based on his six weeks in gaol. Here, too—even though these were actual experiences—his imagination was powerfully aroused, for in both cases he had been confronted with something he did not really understand.

But when all his wanderings and adventures have been taken into account, when all his stories and sketches—there must be close on 150 of them; he was for some years a prolific writer—have been read, it is with Latin America that Cunninghame Graham will always ultimately be identified. Here his only equal is Hudson; and while he could not approach the finest effects of that great prose artist, he had a closer feeling for South American life and history than Hudson had. Some of Cunninghame Graham's best writing is to be found in his historical works. And it is in his life of Francisco Solano Lopez, *Portrait of a Dictator*, there comes that superb piece of scorn that has long been my favourite Cunninghame Graham quotation:

> His bust has been stuck up on the place where he was killed; not fighting, but endeavouring to escape into the woods. He died as he had lived, to the last an egoist, leaving his mistress and his children alone and undefended, whilst he endeavoured to skulk off.
>
> His bust defiles the dark recesses of the Tarumensian woods. So far no bust of Judas mocks Gethsemane.

Could anyone but a Scottish *hidalgo* think and write a blast like that?

SANS PEAK

Wars, social upheavals, minor cataclysms, and subtler influences all tend to compartment the history of the novel into more or less clearly marked periods. When, for instance, Mr. Gerald Bullett wrote his excellent little book, *Modern English Fiction*, in 1926 he remarked on the "curious and convenient chance" that the beginning of this century marked a hiatus. Meredith and Hardy (as a novelist) lay firmly on the further side of the line; only Henry James and George Moore straddled it at all untidily, and they were hardly of the same generation as Mr. Bullett's. For him, in 1926, the outstanding living novelists were Wells, Bennett, Galsworthy, Conrad, and E. M. Forster. (D. H. Lawrence was put to jostle with James Joyce, Virginia Woolf, T. F. Powys, and May Sinclair in a chapter called "Eccentricities," from which he has long since angrily broken out.) But now, thirty years on, the great men of the 'twenties are dead or have ceased writing fiction. One cannot help wondering whether we have not arrived at another dividing line in the history of the English novel.

It is as well, in considering this, to get one or two things clear first. We are told that the English novel is not what it was. This has been said for well over a century. And if one looks at the great peaks, from Defoe to Fielding, to Scott, to Thackeray, to George Eliot, to Meredith, to Hardy, to Conrad, then it does admittedly seem as if there were a gap to-day. But there is, lower down the range, a certain critical snobbery where novels are concerned. Few things are more satisfying than to recall former pleasures, and it is great fun to realize there is an almost inexhaustible treasure trove of Victorian and Edwardian fiction in the London Library and in the older public libraries throughout the country. Long may the prospecting continue. To make out, however, that it is anything more than semi-precious stones we are digging up is either to be smitten with blindness or to suffer from a complete lack of judgment. Bulwer Lytton, William Black, Samuel Warren, Besant and Rice, Wilkie Collins, even—dare I say it in view of what I am going to say next?—Robert Louis Stevenson have good stories to tell us and a power still to entertain. I believe that as practitioners in narrative, in the delineation of character, and in the weaving of a plot they all have their equals among us to-day.

I am sure that never were so many good, competent novels being written as are now being published. The question is whether there are not too many. It is impossible for any one reader to keep track of all of them (and I am confining myself in this article to English novels only, ignoring all those from America). Thanks to Freud, to the social revolution, to the unease of our age, to the rise of the story of detection, violence, or thrills into a vast category of its own, it is often impossible to see the wood for the trees. But a generation which includes such writers as L. P. Hartley, Joyce Cary, Graham Greene, Richard Church, Elizabeth Bowen, Charles Morgan, Storm Jameson, Anthony Powell, cannot be said to be a poor period for the novel.

The best way to come to some conclusion is, perhaps, to split the field into four: the titans, the novelists, the story-tellers, and the rest. Taking them in reverse order: owing to the rise in competence and the drop in morals, the rest is both better and worse than it has ever been. Among what I will call the story-tellers the level, I should think, can rarely have been higher. It would be interesting to put up Edwardian or Victorian teams to match Nevil Shute, C. S. Forester, Georgette Heyer, and any other three the reader cares to think of. (At the apex, this section of the field is very good indeed and exclusive. I doubt if there are more than six writers of near the same calibre.)

When we come to the novelists, however, their number is legion. Looking at the good ones only, they attract, and they gleam, like the thickest poppies among a field of corn. One does not know where to begin to pick them. They form the staple fare of the better circulating libraries. They are reviewed intelligently and faithfully in the weekly periodicals and Sunday newspapers. They have their deserved hour, or week, or month of fame. And then, seemingly inexplicably, they die. Nothing can be more cruelly salutary to the sensitive reviewer than to see, a year or two later, the remaindered, second-hand, or discarded copies of novels that he was so appreciative of, and hopeful about, when they first came out. Maybe they die from their very profusion; maybe it is something to do with the economics of publishing; maybe in some future generation they may be resurrected, though I doubt it. But, whatever the reason, they wither far more quickly than they deserve, for many of them are cleverer and more conscientious than those which have survived from a previous age.

There remain the titans. How many have there been in the past 237 years of the novel? How foolish we are to expect there should always be one with us. The last, in the sense that he dominated young and old in his generation and every new work of his was a national event, was Meredith. But 50 years is a little time in which to find his successor. It is foolhardy, but all the more stimulating, to try to see what those 50 years have given us, below the topmost peaks, in memorable or significant novels. The British have a natural hankering after dozens, so 12 is chosen as a quite arbitrary number. Here is one list:

Lord Jim, Conrad 1900
Kim, Kipling 1901
Green Mansions, Hudson 1904
The Old Wives' Tale, Bennett 1908
The History of Mr. Polly, Wells 1910
Howard's End, E. M. Forster 1910
The Good Soldier, Ford 1915
Of Human Bondage, Maugham 1915

Women in Love, Lawrence 1920
To the Lighthouse, Woolf 1927
The Fortunes of Richard Mahony, Richardson 1930
Brighton Rock, Greene 1938

MR. ANTI-CANT

The time was late April, 1872. The place, the Indian Ocean. Mr. James Fitzjames Stephen, Q.C., was on his way home from Calcutta. He had had a gruelling two and a half years as member of Council, being as busy and as energetic as one of his greatest predecessors, Macaulay. He had not been well. Faithfully and successfully as he had laboured, enhanced as his reputation was among the elect, his future was not altogether certain. Surely now was the time to relax and recuperate for the fray ahead.

Fitzjames Stephen, however, was a Victorian. Relaxing was not one of their strong points. The first day out he gets through a volume of Sainte-Beuve. He reads German and brushes up his Italian. He writes long letters. He converses with other passengers. With time still on his hands he decides to revert to his old love, journalism, and to write an article a day till the boat gets to Suez. There is at first some distraction because from the comfortable spot he has chosen his iron chair disturbs the ship's compass. But on April 27—according to his brother Leslie Stephen, who tells the tale in his life of Fitzjames—he can report that he has been "firing broadsides into John Mill for about three hours." The book which all too little of the world now knows as *Liberty, Equality, Fraternity* was being born.

And what broadsides they were. Has any other volume on political philosophy so forthright an opening? Already, in the first paragraph:

> It is one of the commonest beliefs of the day that the human race collectively has before it splendid destinies of various kinds, and that the road to them is to be found in the removal of all restraints on human conduct, in

the recognition of a substantial equality between all human creatures, and in fraternity or general love. These doctrines are in very many cases held as a religious faith. They are regarded not merely as truths, but as truths for which those who believe in them are ready to do battle, and for the establishment of which they are prepared to sacrifice all merely personal ends.

Such, stated of course in the most general terms, is the religion of which I take "Liberty, Equality, Fraternity" to be the creed. I do not believe it.

Stephen was, in fact, a friend and admirer of Mill, and went a long way with him. But there came a point in Mill's great work *On Liberty* where Stephen's rugged realism, and perhaps his pessimism based on experience, pulled him up short. So one of the great arguments of the nineteenth century reached its climax. Mill himself was never to reply. He died almost as the articles—they appeared first in the *Pall Mall Gazette*—were published in book form. But John Morley and Frederic Harrison took up the cudgels and Stephen dealt with them in a long preface to his second edition a year later. He became debated, admired, hated, and eventually a Judge. This was his last polemical writing, and his best.

I do not propose to summarize the argument here. "Epitomes," said Shelley, improving on Bacon, "are the moths of just history. They eat the poetry out of it." Also I want to leave space to say something about the man. Interest in the Stephens has grown greatly in recent years. As Mr. Noël Annan pointed out in his admirable *Leslie Stephen*, "the Stephen alliance" is one of the most fascinating of our intellectual aristocracies. To my mind Leslie is by no means either a lone eagle or the king of his line.

The Memories of James Stephen, Leslie's grandfather, lately published, introduced us to a far more dynamic and rugged character. I still believe *Liberty, Equality, Fraternity*, when some publisher has had the vision to put it into one of the cheap libraries of classics, will outlast anything for which Leslie is now famous. Other books of Fitzjames are also worth reading if one comes by them. The three volumes of his *Saturday Review* essays, *Horae Sabbaticae*, contain 50 first-rate pages on Hobbes, and some sound sense on Gibbon.

Fitzjames Stephen has been called a swashbuckler. The best answer is that among the other Saturday Reviewers of that time were Maine, Morley, Mark Pattison, Freeman; and Stephen was regarded as being among his peers. Humbug he certainly hated. He could not abide cant. For some reason or other he disliked Dickens. But, whether he was appreciating or criticizing, he never left his reader in any doubt precisely where he stood. He is the least equivocal of writers. The result was that he wrote a clear, direct and forthright prose. I have never come across his first work, *Essays of a Barrister*, but I am sure that he began as he went on.

Although I believe it would be well if *Liberty, Equality, Fraternity* were more widely read to-day, I still think Mill has the better of the argument. *On Liberty* remains a true and noble book. Civilized man will have signed his death warrant if ever he abandons Mill's ideal. But Fitzjames Stephen insisted that even when reaching for the stars it was necessary to have our feet on the ground. Much subsequent history has justified many of his most pessimistic contentions. Indeed, I doubt if he is a pessimist by modern standards. Certainly he is a manly soul by any.

> We stand on a mountain pass in the midst of whirling snow and blinding mist, through which we get glimpses now and then of paths which may be deceptive. If we stand still, we shall be frozen to death. If we take the wrong road, we shall be dashed to pieces. We do not certainly know whether there is any right one. What must we do? "Be strong and of a good courage." Act for the best, hope for the best, and take what comes. Above all, let us dream no dreams, and tell no lies, but go our way, wherever it may lead, with our eyes open and our heads erect. If death ends all, we cannot meet it better. If not, let us enter whatever may be the next scene like honest men, with no sophistry in our mouths and no masks on our faces.

It is with these words *Liberty, Equality, Fraternity* closes. If anyone does wish to read it he should get the second edition.

OUT OF THE POST

I was asked the other day what was the most exciting thing I had read this year. I promptly answered that it was the first two volumes of the great Clarendon edition of Coleridge's letters; adding, possibly from some idea of a sense of justice, or because the one thing immediately made the other flow into my mind, that the most satisfying thing had been the new complete edition of Gibbon's letters.

The difference is more than a distinction, but I do not want to go into that now. More interesting was the fact that both these works were collections of letters. This is often said to be an age when letter writing is dead. I doubt it. However that may be, it is, possibly above all others, an age when letter publishing is alive. The awareness that has generally spread in this generation of the treasures that may still be awaiting discovery in old country house libraries and attics, the new standards of editing that are the result of both the manners and scholarship of the age, the resources in men and money (mostly dollars, it must be admitted) that can now be applied to such tasks have meant that this generation is being enriched by a remarkable collection of definitive editions of the great English letter writers—among them Dr. Chapman's superb edition of Johnson's letters; Mr. Ray's of Thackeray's; the Toynbee-Whibley Gray; Mr. Lewis's Walpole; with, possibly the crown of them all, the great Chicago-Cambridge edition of Burke's letters still to come. Here are riches; but there are lesser treasures also. Figures as dissimilar as George Eliot and John Stuart Mill have taken on some semblance of flesh and blood again for us through the work which has been done on their letters.

Maybe it is because the English are outwardly so reserved and phlegmatic a race that they have this great diversity and quality in published correspondence. As a kind of compensation, we let ourselves go on paper. France can, of course, point to Mme. de Sevigné, to Flaubert, and to Sainte-Beuve, but they cannot match our riches. Nor, for all the fascination of the Nietzsche-Wagner correspondence and the slowly unfolding Rilke letters, can the German language. When we summon up Gray, Cowper, Byron, Fitzgerald, Coleridge, Johnson, Keats, Southey, Walpole, Lady Mary Wortley Montagu, and Burke we have a team to beat the world.

What is more important, we have the material for almost endless hours of pleasure. If I had to advise a young man who wanted to specialize in a small library I do not know that I could put him on to greater enjoyment and profit than to advise him to collect volumes of letters. With whom should he start? That would depend on his character. Years ago I used to find the quietness and passivity of Fitzgerald charming. Undoubtedly nothing can take away from him the claim to be one of the greatest of our letter writers. But when I came back to him some time ago I found myself getting rather impatient with "old Fitz." He renounced the world just a little too much; by the end, his very unpretentiousness seemed rather pretentious. On the other hand, I have come to like Byron's letters more and more. Mr. Peter Quennell's two volumes, *Byron: A Self-Portrait*, in which he lets Byron speak entirely through his letters and journals, was a tremendous experience. While I was reading them I lived in another world. Byron pours forth radioactive fall-out all the time. Some of Keats's letters are among the most moving literature we have, and what shines through the whole is the remarkable strength of the man. But in a way it always seems to me that we have either too many or too few of Keats's letters. What there are do not quite allow us to see the man whole. They present a picture rather like that on our television screen. It is exciting, it is admirable. But we never cease to feel that there is surely some further knob we might turn to get the details just a little more into focus. For all our satisfaction, there remains a subtle discontent.

While we would not have one of Dr. Chapman's discoveries away, we know we have enough of Johnson's letters. Nothing to come could really add to or alter our affectionate image of the Great Cham. Neither Gray nor Cowper had the same force of character and, enchanting as their *kleine Nachtmusik* is, there is quite enough of it. Southey's six volumes we would willingly see stretched a little farther. He was a correspondent who always had something to say; his life was so busy and full; and yet the press of affairs or books or worries could never cloud his essential nobility. Of Scott we can never have enough. Everything that great man wrote instantly springs to life, no matter in what circumstances we take it up. Remove his own letters and journals from Lockhart's Life and the work falls dead to the ground.

But it is to the seventeenth century I would go for the most enchanting letter writer of them all. It is a century richer in correspondence than is sometimes thought. The letters of Sir Thomas Browne are not easily available, but are well worth hunting for. It is true that James Howell's *Epistolae Ho-elianae* were subsequently written essays rather than the unconsidered missives they appear to be, but they are none the less of outstanding interest. And—for me queen of all letter writers—there is Dorothy Osborne. Macaulay's essay on Sir William Temple put Judge Parry on to them and to Judge Parry and Mrs. Longe future generations will be eternally indebted. Since then there has been a fully annotated edition. Temple's courtship of Dorothy lasted seven years, from 1647 to 1654, and the letters we have cover only the last two years of this time. But they give us a woman so loving, so frank, so gay, and so vital that when we close the book we feel we have known her all her life. If, which Heaven forbid, all the sets of letters I have were ordered to go, and it was spared to me that only one volume should remain, without hesitation I should choose Dorothy Osborne.

RICHARD MIDDLETON

Fortunately there is no particular significance in choosing this week, or this year, to recall Richard Middleton. Only great men can survive the interest artificially aroused by their anniversaries. The appointed day arrives; the hungry critics dutifully blow away the dust and find enough to fill their columns; the reader takes their piety for what it is worth; the next day the subject, be he writer or politician or man-of-action, is really dead at last. Richard Middleton was not a great man; he had enough bad luck in his life to be spared this final misfortune.

Middleton's first mischance was his timing. Born in 1882, he came to manhood at the wrong end of the 'nineties; flourishing—as far as he ever did flourish—from 1905 to his death in Brussels in 1911, he struck a period which fed his physical and literary weaknesses. Little regarded in his lifetime—he committed suicide probably because he had not the means to live any longer—he was loyally overpraised after his death, invariably for the wrong reasons. Frank Harris, who should have known better, said some of his poetry was "finer than Herrick" and that "at twenty-five he stood as an equal among the foremost men of his time in knowledge of thought and of life." All of which is nonsense. But he is—thanks to George Saintsbury—at least in *The Cambridge History of English Literature*, closing a chapter that starts with Macaulay and proceeds by way of Keble, Coventry Patmore, and Andrew Lang to Dowson. Saintsbury is severe, rightly classes him below Dowson, and leaves one wondering, indeed, why he included Middleton as a poet at all.

I have never been able to understand the steadfast refusal of Middleton's friends to see that he was first and foremost a prose writer. They always grew indignant at the idea. Yet to-day, while there is not one poem in all his two volumes that I can remember, his essays still charm, and some of his stories so deeply etched themselves on my mind at first reading—over thirty years ago now—that I can still say passages from them by heart. As an essayist Middleton is at his best when, drawing on experience, his pieces shade off into almost a short story. Some of his short stories, too, are near-essays. But whether remembering childhood in fancy or in fact, he brings to the process a truly childlike eye, not only romantic but also seeing what was cold and cruel. In the one manner he suffered from being a contemporary of Kenneth Grahame, for he was never quite in *The Golden Age* class. But he could do things Grahame could not do. There are many essays in *The Day Before Yesterday* still worth reading; and in *The Ghost Ship* volume "A Drama of Youth" and "The New Boy" strike a note all his own.

With "The Ghost Ship" we come to the mansion Richard Middleton most surely inhabits. It is a small mansion; for those who value not only imagination but cadenced prose it is an abiding one. The well-known passage in which the customers of The Fox and Grapes see the pirate ship that has passed the summer in landlord's field "sailing very comfortably through the windy stars . . . Her portholes and her bay-window were blazing with lights, and there was a noise of singing and fiddling on her decks" is only one of many that are memorable. "The Ghost Ship" has not been over-praised—it is one of our best short stories—but, another misfortune of Middleton's, it has eclipsed almost everything else. "On the Brighton Road" and "The Conjuror" are tales one does not forget, and few men could have put more into the eight pages of "Fate and the Artist".

But for me the story of Middleton's which surpasses all others, even "The Ghost Ship" is "The Great Man". Knowing all that happened one can never cease wondering whether Middleton, when he wrote it, knew all that was to happen. The tale is simple, and clearly autobiographical. A defeated and disillusioned young writer meets an English resident in Brussels. They find they have common enthusiasms. The Englishman takes the writer home for tea. Under the influence of more grace and sympathy than he has known, stimulated by the interest of the Englishman's wife and sixteen-years'-old daughter, the young man expands, luxuriates, talks about himself and his dreams of the future. The visit ends; he is pressed to come again. "Like a man recovering from a terrible debauch" he knows he will not.

> "No, I will return to that house on the hill above Woluwe no more, not even to see Monica standing on tiptoe to pick her roses. For I have left a giant's robe hanging on a peg in the hall, and I would not have those amiable people see how utterly incapable I am of filling it under normal conditions. I feel, besides, a kind of sentimental tenderness for this illusion fated to have so short a life. I am no Herod to slaughter babies, and it pleases me to think that it lingers yet in that delightful house with the books and the old furniture and Monica, even though I myself shall probably never see it again, even though the Englishman watches the publishers' announcements for the masterpieces that will never appear."

Poor Middleton; there he wrote his own epitaph.

WHERE LIFE IS EARNEST

I know no Russian, but I find the development of the Soviet novel, so far as I can follow it in English translations, fascinating. The limitation, moreover, is perhaps not so severe as it sounds. For one thing, ever since the heroic efforts of Constance Garnett with Tolstoy, Dostoevsky, Turgenev, and Chekhov, Russian literature has been turned into English more copiously than that of almost any other language. For another, the Soviet authorities—no doubt for ends of their own—have produced a number of modern Russian novels, competently translated and printed, and sold at a price which, even if it makes one suspect their disinterestedness, also makes purchase practicable. But as all art in Russia is controlled, and as the Stalin Prize novels are presumably part of the authentic canon, some judgment is possible.

In the years immediately following the October revolution, Russian writing, as the Western world came to know it, divided into three strands. There were the works of what one may loosely call the authors of the old régime. They became *émigrés*. They wrote wherever they could find a resting place: Berlin, or Shanghai, or New York, or Paris. They sometimes did their best to make an equation with the new dispensation but their roots were in the old. Bunin, Aldanov, Remizov, and Krymov were of this band. Then there were the writers inside Russia: Alexei Tolstoy (who went back), Fadeyev, Veresaev, Leonov, Fedin. They were ostensibly writers of the new régime, for they were producing under it and often extolling its example. All the same they were no more than men of the transition. In spite of whatever apparent novelty or fury they exhibited they were rooted in the old tradition. Even Fedin's comparatively late *Early Joys: No Ordinary Summer* is no exception.

About the first warning of the shape of things to come—I am all the time concerned only with English readers—was Gladkov's *Cement.* In the twenty-six years that have passed since this third strand arrived on the scene it has become more and more dominant. Death has thinned the *émigrés.* The men of the transition have become old-fashioned. But the industrial novel, the story of men and women on the job, the expression of Russian idealism through a wholesale abnegation to the task in hand, has gone from strength to strength. I remember how in the middle-thirties I was struck by a vivid article by Ilya Ehrenburg about a Soviet library. Having described all the variety it had to offer, he added that far and away the most thumbed book in it was one on the theory of the two-stroke engine. The Russians have moved an astonishingly long way since then. But the didactic urge remains. Vitali Zakrutkin's *Floating Stanitsa*, which a friend brought back for me from Moscow last year, deals almost passionately with the rehabilitation of a fishery on the Don, one of the most dramatic chapters in it being concerned with an experiment in pituitary injections into bream. Antonina Koptayeva's *Ivan Ivanovich* does much the same thing for the Soviet medical service.

To me by far the most interesting of these novels has been Azhayev's *Far from Moscow.* It won a Stalin Prize in 1949; it has gone, so I gather, through many editions since then; and it has the incidental attraction of being an old-fashioned three-decker. Essentially the plot is simple. As part of the Russian war effort a pipeline has to be built urgently in the Far East. The local engineers, good men all, say the job will take three years. The Council of People's Commissars declare it can be done in one. So a construction chief (Party worker and Order of Lenin with bar) and two engineers are sent from Moscow to ensure that the "impossible" is achieved. Leaving on one side the engineering part of the tale—and it is well done—it is the human implications which are remarkable.

Once Moscow has pronounced, impossibility no longer exists.

You can challenge everything else if you are on the job. You can bully your men and be bully-ragged in turn by them in a way that would create strikes, riots, civil commotion, and apoplexy among both managers and shop-stewards in any capitalist country, so long as you leave this ark of the covenant unquestioned. The relations between the political and engineering bosses are a study in themselves. As for the men and women workers, one English critic, when the book came out, described them as models for boy scouts.

So indeed they are, and therein lies the 64,000-rouble question. Can a novel which is completely travestying spirit and conditions become a best-seller, and dare even the infallible Moscow bureaucrats give it the accolade? If not, then is this how the ordinary Russians see themselves; or have been persuaded to see themselves? And if they have, has not such uninhibited self-conscious rectitude implications which are far more formidable than Messrs. Bulganin, Khrushchev, and Molotov, all rolled into one? It may be said that such books are propaganda, as indeed they are. But they have been published as realistic novels—almost as documentaries—in Russia itself. Not even the much heralded breaking of Ilya Ehrenburg's recent book *The Thaw* into some semblance of non-Soviet personal feelings has been able to draw my mind away from this problem. Ehrenburg's flutter was, by Western standards, a very mild affair. There are already signs the break-out is destined to be short-lived. But the enigma of the modern Soviet novel remains.

THE ORATORS

There is a short period in adolescence when mental energy on an heroic scale seems particularly inspiring. It was this which first attracted me to Voltaire. I can still remember the thrill with which I read Rosebery's dictum on Napoleon that "he carried human faculty to the farthest point of which we have accurate knowledge." And, such is the healthy indiscriminateness of youth, I was even led, by some tale of his fantastic activities, to wade through the 1,500 pages of the *Memoirs of the Life and Times of Lord Brougham.*

Later on I was to find out how misguided I was. Historians have pronounced that Brougham's defects outweighed his virtues. His memoirs have been proved to be misleading and inaccurate. With all his great gifts he was denied the indispensable one of balance. His vanity ran away with his judgment. In the best Greek tradition his pride destroyed him—politically, at any rate. But he was not as unimportant as posterity has generally rated him. And he was never uninteresting. The man who can claim to be the creator of the Judicial Committee of the Privy Council, of the Central Criminal Court, of the modern prosperity of Cannes; whom Peacock put into *Crotchet Castle*, and of whom Thackeray could write in 1831 "I am glad the last King of England is a good one; really and truly I believe he will be the last. Brougham will be Lord Guardian or Lord Protector or something" has plenty to repay study.

Even the memoirs are not as black as they have been painted. First of all there is the date of their composition. Brougham, who talked at eight months, and had his first scientific paper read before the Royal Society at 18, started writing his memoirs in his eighty-fourth year, and finished them in his ninetieth. Parts of them are undoubtedly dull. The affairs of Queen Caroline are no longer absorbing, and here probably—having been a principal actor—Brougham is more partial than elsewhere. But it was an observant and enterprising young man who visited Denmark and Scandinavia in 1799 and Holland and Italy five years later. It was from Brougham I first learned of Sydney Smith's motto for the *Edinburgh Review* (of which Brougham was one of the founders) "Tenui musam meditamur avena"—We cultivate literature on a little oatmeal. Alas, it was discarded as being too flippant. And there are pictures of Lord Durham's craving for an earldom, of Mr. Pitt coming home to dinner "a good deal exhausted after his cabinet work" and restoring his strength by drinking quickly a bottle of port, of Lord Liverpool sending Lady Hester Stanhope four thousand yards of different ribbons from which to pick the colours for military decorations; and of Brougham himself discussing almost everything from Robespierre to differential calculus with Carnot. At the very end there are brief character sketches by this astonishing old man of Lord Holland, Lord John Russell, Louis Philippe, and Palmerston, about whom he can write in the past tense.

It is indeed as a writer of character sketches that Brougham will live as an author, if at all. I would not persuade anyone to go to the memoirs, but the five volumes of his *Historical Sketches of Statesmen who flourished in the time of George III* and *Lives of Men of Letters and Science who flourished in the time of George III* are well worth reading. I have seen two sets offered cheaply in recent second-hand catalogues and that put it in my mind to write about them.

All his life Brougham lacked the golden mean. This is as true of these volumes as of everything else he did. Few will want to wade through his pages of algebraical formulas (in the essay on D'Alembert) to-day. And he has little to tell us about Watt, Priestley, Cavendish, Davy, and Lavoisier that we cannot learn more easily elsewhere. But his essay on Dr. Johnson is noble, that on Rousseau full of vigour even though he thought Jean-Jacques's political works beneath contempt, and while admiring Gibbon's judgment, sagacity, and learning he lays into him heartily over his style. Brougham yields his richest harvest, however, in the three volumes on the statesmen. Here he comes fully into his own. He has, of course, a wonderful mine to quarry. What other reign can show us the equal of the two Pitts, Burke, Fox, Sheridan, Canning, Wilberforce, Grattan, Castlereagh, Wilkes, as well as the great lawyers? Nor does Brougham confine himself to England. He throws in Napoleon, Robespierre, Danton, Lafayette, Neckar, Carnot, Talleyrand, Mme. de Staël from France; Washington, Jefferson, Franklin from the United States; and Frederick II, Gustavus III, the Emperor Joseph, and the Empress Catherine for full measure. There are some 60 studies of "statesmen" in all.

Not many of them match up to the opening essay on George III himself, or to that on George IV. Some of Brougham's judgments, moreover, now seem arbitrary. He described Fox as "certainly the most accomplished debater, that ever appeared upon the theatre of public affairs in any age of the world", which can hardly be determined. He censured Nelson and denied genius to Ricardo. Sometimes he is superficial, and in his legal portraits too technical. But always he is clear, forthright, readable, and vigorous. And the fascinating way in which, in study after study, he makes oratory the first quality necessary for a statesman—the need to move, persuade, and convert his hearers in the House of Commons—reminds us of a day that is gone.

NADAR

Interest in the Second Empire is about due for a revival. Philip Guedalla called it "one of the finest stories in the world", but he did not manage to make it so. Yet it should be an attractive age for literary-minded historians of to-day. Were not Flaubert and Daudet its novelists, Dumas the younger its dramatist, and Baudelaire its poet? F. A. Simpson's two magnificent books, *The Rise of Louis Napoleon* and *Louis Napoleon and the Recovery of France*, make us lament that they should continue to remain an uncompleted masterpiece. Novels about the period have never given its full flavour. Daudet's *The Nabob* is too depressing and too cruel. Sainte-Beuve's letters to the Princess Mathilde are a great disappointment when one thinks what the volume might have been. (I await the forthcoming book on Princess Mathilde with muted hope.) The unexpurgated Goncourt journals, at last to be given to the world, will fill in one part of the picture. But such was the range of the Second Empire, its grandeurs and miseries, its aspirations and machinations, its astonishing rise and resounding fall, that it can probably not be seen whole through the eyes or in the light of any one of its great figures. As has been the case before, it might be better to use as a peg some lesser, but more diversely involved, figure of the age.

There is a special reason why, for many years now, my favourite candidate for this role has been Nadar. He was christened Felix Tournachon, but he once fought and won a lawsuit to establish that he was "the one and only Nadar", and it is by this assumed name he will always be known. Always is perhaps a long time, but Nadar was an exceptional man. It is not often given to one individual to figure in the encyclopaedias under three different headings. Nadar has his place in even the most summary histories of aviation, of photography, and of caricature. He was a writer for the theatre, a journalist, and a memorialist as well. He was curiously embedded in the pseudo-Napoleonic comedy-tragedy of social manners. Whether you read Baudelaire or Flaubert, Sainte-Beuve or the Goncourts, it is not long before you come across some reference to Nadar.

He was born in Paris in 1820 and was destined to be a doctor. He did become a medical student. But after some studies which Larousse describes as "fort irrégulières" he drifted to the borders of art and journalism. By the age of 22 he had already adopted the pen name of Nadar. It is ironical that the man who was to be so much a Second Empire period-piece should have withdrawn to Prussia as a consequence of the events of 1848. He must himself have felt it was a false move, for within a year he was back in Paris again, still trying to make a living by his pen. Whether these efforts did not sufficiently fill his pockets or exhaust his energies I have never been able to establish. But soon he took the decisive step for his fortunes—and indirectly for at least two strands of his fame. He opened a photographic studio. A natural artist, a caricaturist and illustrator of at least some genius, he was from the outset more than a mere "Quite still please; one . . . two . . ." operator. He had a wonderful eye for character. To this day Nadar photographs, faded and yellow as they may be, are worth studying. In the recent Proust exhibition at Wildenstein's the Nadar photographs of Proust himself, of Saint-Saens, of Alphonse Daudet, and of the Duchesse de Clermont-Tonnerre did not seem out of place amid the portraits or drawings by Jacques Emile Blanche, by Tissot, and by Sargent. Aided also by his caricaturing and writing activities, above all by his *Pantheon-Nadar*, in which, as *The Times* said, "he fixed picturesquely the traits of his most notorious contemporaries", he quickly became famous. He also made a fortune.

Success, however, only made him anxious to conquer other worlds—or at least the air. He became absorbed in the problem of flight. He built one balloon, and then another—the Géant—the largest that had ever been attempted. Being a natural showman, he suspended from it a wicker-work two-storied cottage. It flew with nine people on board—including Nadar and his faithful, intrepid wife. It nearly killed them all. It came to the Crystal Palace on show. But Nadar had already got beyond balloons. He proposed airships with propellers. He declared his faith in heavier-than-air flight. He wrote a book *The Right to Fly*, which was published in English and is in the British Museum. But these had to stay ideas only, for he suffered the fate of so many pioneers. He was ruined. Back to the darkroom he went to make some more money. Before he could do anything with it, there came 1870 and the Franco-Prussian War. Still, when Paris was besieged, he took charge of a balloon observer corps.

Forty more years of life were left to him—and before he died in 1910 he had the happiness to know his dreams had been justified by Blériot flying the Channel—but with the fall of the Second Empire his real life was over. His setting was gone. He wrote many books. The only one with any interest to-day is perhaps *Mémoires du Géant*. In it he made a reference to Flaubert, who wrote in approval of it to George Sand. Flaubert also sent him a copy of *Madame Bovary*, "à Nadar, avec une forte poignée de main." That copy has long been one of my few treasures.

ASKING FOR MORE

Although I shall not look forward with any particular interest to the forthcoming Oxford lectures on poetry, I have no feeling of having been robbed by the votes of the seven pound holders and others. For me, *Oxford Lectures on Poetry* will always mean A. C. Bradley, and *Shakespearian Tragedy*. Mr. Wilson Knight—the only scholar among the three candidates—will go on writing his admirable and remarkable books whether Oxford undergraduates elegantly chalk "Knight for Prof" on the university walls or not. And Sir Harold Nicolson has surer things to do than to add another volume to that section of the shelf of his works which contains his reflections on his reading.

Few critics have made a study of Sir Harold's output as a whole. The first thing that strikes one on doing so is how long that shelf of his works is. I have by no means a complete bibliography, but I can list at least some 36 titles over 35 years. The second thing is that while Sir Harold has been an industrious writer and a highly professional one—if, for instance, one wants to know what good pamphleteering can be, there is *Why Britain is at War*, with its superb opening about George Joseph Smith and the brides in the bath case—his work falls roughly into three parts, criticism, commentary, and history. The criticism should not be neglected. Tennyson has so far baffled every writer who has tried to make a synthesis out of him, but Sir Harold has succeeded better than most. His Swinburne and Verlaine are not major works, but they are interesting. If he is better on Byron's life than on his works, that is not to show a false sense of values.

The Nicolson commentaries are too well known to need any description. For years they gave a grace and distinction to the *Spectator* which no amount of general cleverness or smartness can replace. Conversational, they brought the very tones of his voice. Urbane, liberal, civilized, with now and again a rare touch of indignation or scorn, they were the epitome of his character. How far they ranged can be seen by just a few of the titles from *Friday Mornings*: The German Soul, Tsarist Russia, Shakespeare's Flowers, Fire Watching, Homer as a Poet of Nature, Foreign Names, The Dismissal of Weygand, Lutyens, Horace and the Italian Campaign. For more than 25 years also he has been one of the most attractive and accomplished of broadcasters. Future historians may well study *People and Things*, a selection of his B.B.C. talks during 1930 and 1931, and *Marginal Comment*, his weekly essays during 1939, to discover the true temper of the English people during two decisive periods of the inter-war years. For while he has a relish for the better things of life, he has never counted protection from the contemporary scene—however distressing or bodeful—among them. Many of his comments, read now 17 years later, glow with courage and prescience. Solaced by the centuries, he has lived in the hour.

And yet . . . ? Why was it that through 1950 and 1951 his friends and admirers waited so anxiously for the appearance of *King George V: His Life and Reign*, with a curious feeling that despite the sum total of all that had gone before Nicolson needed success in this particular task to justify himself? In a way it was a tribute to his powers. Had there not been *Lord Carnock* (his biography of his father), *Peace-making*, *Curzon: The Last Phase*, and *The Congress of Vienna* to portend them? For, so far, we have not looked at Nicolson the historian. These books had shown what, given the will and the concentration, a good historian Nicolson might be. Given one other thing also, that he should have been concerned with or lived near to the events he analyses or relates. Whether he is lightly disguising reality in such fictions as *Some People* and *Sweet Waters* or openly recording how M. Clemenceau behaved at Versailles, he has an artist's eye for a character and a situation. Things seen are his strength.

If that is so, and if he had this amount of achievement behind him, why then was there the passionate desire of his friends that he should pull off *King George V*? For the answer one must go to his weakness. Sir Harold has not only been a life-long reader but an unwearying annotator. More than once he has described—the latest occasion is in *Good Behaviour*—how for years he has marked his books, and made his own index on the fly-leaves. To me it seems that subsequent recourse to those fly-leaves has got in the way of the artist. Nicolson synthesizing things seen is of an altogether different order of writers from Nicolson collecting things read. He is best when quoting from experience, weakest when quoting from books. (This does not include his formal criticism.) And when one surveyed the 30 odd volumes up to 1950, isolated the tiny phalanx of true history, and thought of what might have taken the place of the rest, one realized that, appreciable as his achievement was, Nicolson still lacked a *magnum opus* to justify himself.

How triumphantly he provided it is now common knowledge. In this work all his gifts came to full flower. Is there a better life of an English monarch? But success brings its demands. The writing of good contemporary history is so rare that we feel impelled to ask for more. And although Sir Harold Nicolson recently broadcast in the General Overseas Service of the B.B.C. "On Being Seventy" (apparently, like what we were told about the ancient Chinese, counting his natal day as one) he is young enough and active enough to give us at least one more major work. If he has kept a journal, could we not have the first volume? Or a series of contemporary studies akin to Clarendon's character sketches? Or—what we still lack badly—a true portrait of the Edwardian age? These desires have one thing in common—the recognition that Sir Harold Nicolson has it in him to be the Saint-Simon of his day.

ON READING PLAYS

There was a time, not so long ago, when the only way for the great majority of people to know anything about plays was to read them. Much has been written about the palmy days of the theatre, but even in its heyday it served only a fraction of the people. And it gave them, especially if they lived outside three or four big cities, an even smaller fraction of the drama. The cinema, curiously enough, did not fill in either of the gaps. A film is not a play. Broadcasting did more. The remarkable achievements of Mr. Val Gielgud and his colleagues, their adventurousness, range, and catholicity, have not yet received proper credit. Shakespeare, Marlowe, Ibsen, Euripides have been given to over four million people at a time. Television, if its artists do not allow its technicians to run away with it, may do even more. Does this mean that the reading of plays will increase or decline?

The answer is subject to so many incalculable factors that I doubt if it is worth attempting. Far more interesting to me is whether the question matters. If the time comes when almost everybody can see plays need we care if many fewer read them?

There are those who say that the drama is three-dimensional; that seeing is all and that the stage is the thing. Against them are those, headed by Charles Lamb, who argue that some works at least, Shakespeare's greatest tragedies among them, cannot be adequately staged, that, as Bradley put it for him, "theatrical representation gives only a part of what we imagine when we read them." For myself, I sympathize with this view. But not where Shakespeare is concerned. I know no passage of Shakespeare, not even the loveliest music of *The Tempest* and *The Merchant of Venice* or the grand climaxes of *Othello* and *Macbeth*, that is not better in the playing. With Marlowe it is the other way about.

> And ride in triumph through Persepolis?
> Is it not brave to be a king, Techelles?
> Usumcasane and Theridamas,
> Is it not passing brave to be a king,
> And ride in triumph through Persepolis?

Not even Mr. Donald Wolfit, who is a magnificent Tamburlaine, can put as much exultation into that, can make it sound as "sweet and full of pomp", as I silently can to myself. As for the famous scene:

> Holla, ye pampered jades of Asia

with Tamburlaine entering "drawn in his chariot by the Kings of Trebizon and Soria, with bits in their mouths, reins in his left hand, and in his right hand a whip with which he scourgeth them", it can move powerfully when read; on the stage it looks just plain silly.

Some people might object that *Tamburlaine* is a special case; so barbaric and rodomontade as to be *hors concours*. But it is the same with *Doctor Faustus*. Never have I yet tensed myself, eager and expectant, in the theatre, for the great moment of

> Was this the face that launch'd a thousand ships?

without feeling let down when it came. For one thing, so few producers have the sense to keep their Helens out of sight. Or again, take *Dido, Queen of Carthage*. It has what has been to me one of the loveliest, most picture-creating, and most haunting lines in all literature. Cupid sings his song to Dido. She asks him, "where learn'dst thou this pretty song?" and he replies:

> My cousin Helen taught it me in Troy.

The actor (or actress) is not yet born who can get what I can out of that.

Ben Jonson, on the other hand, I find unreadable. For years I could not believe there was anything in his plays which the centuries had left undestroyed. Then, a year or two after the end of the War, I saw Mr. John Burrell's production of *The Alchemist* at the Old Vic and it burgeoned into life.

Eugene O'Neill's work reads better than it acts. One should perhaps make an exception in the case of *The Emperor Jones* because, if it is well done, the insistent beating of the tom-tom can have its effect. But even in this case, I think, the scenes in the forest are more potent if seen in the mind's eye than if they are physically represented. When we turn to *The Great God Brown* (with its business of the masks) or *Strange Interlude*, then the printed page has it every time. Barrie, for me, acts incomparably better than he reads. Coward's plays can be read if a vintage one of them was originally heard. Shaw is fun to read in short scenes, but any play read as a whole I find tedious. Yet, although the plays seem most undramatic, the fact is that some vital spark energizes them as soon as their lines are spoken. Shaw's genius has been acclaimed on more than one front. In some cases it has been mistaken for what was really superb talent. But this gift to write plays that can make not only the lines better than they are but the actors and actresses better than themselves was the quintessence of Shavianism, and was genius if anything is. Ibsen shows himself the greatest of modern dramatists in that whether read, or broadcast, or televised, or seen on the stage, he is unfailingly and inextinguishably alive.

There are, of course, many plays that do not lend themselves to print. They are all action and little reflection. There are others, such as Tennyson's and Swinburne's, Shelley's, and Addison's, which are freaks upon the boards. What Dr. Johnson's *Irene* would be like I cannot imagine. Such is my faith in the Great Cham that I have a sneaking suspicion we might be surprised. Meanwhile, it is there to be read, as are so many other plays. They are often better than other forms of reading, because if we are going to tackle them at all we cannot be passive. Every character, every change of speaker, every scene, is a challenge to our imagination. Play-reading at its best can be one of the seven lively arts. I am glad I do not have to specify what are now the other six.

"MONSIEUR DE CAMORS"

Years ago, when Europe was still young and gay, or at least innocent enough to believe that even if it was a world war which had tumbled Humpty Dumpty off the wall he could still be put together again, Heinemann's published a series called "Masterpieces of French Romance". I bought them as they came out and have them still. Tall and handsome they are, though both the blue and the gold have rather faded. But translations, paper, and type were all good; there were introductions by such writers as Henry James, Maurice Hewlett, and Andrew Lang; and a biographical study in each volume by Edmund Gosse.

Gosse was the editor of the venture as a whole. What has interested me many times since is his choice of works. With something like three centuries to range through he took his 12 "masterpieces" from a bare 60 years. They were: *Notre Dame of Paris* (1831), *Mauprat* (1836), *The Charterhouse of Parma* (1839), *Colomba* (1840), *The Two Young Brides* (1842), *The Lady of the Camellias* (1848), *The Black Tulip* (1850), *Madame Bovary* (1856), *The Romance of a Poor Young Man* (1858), *Renée Mauperin* (1864), *The Nabob* (1879), *Pierre and Jean* (1888). It was admittedly an astonishing six decades.

One book on the shelf has often nagged at me a little. The story goes that Sir Thomas Beecham was once asked at a rehearsal how a conductor with a huge symphony orchestra going full blast could detect a wrong note. He replied: "If someone showed you a handful of coins, said there was exactly ten shillings worth, and you noticed there was only one halfpenny you would not have to count the rest to know he was wrong." It has always seemed to me that in this case the halfpenny was *The Romance of a Poor Young Man*. It is true that it is still Octave Feuillet's most famous work: that it sold

40,000 copies in its first five years and has possibly topped the million since: that it is a delightful concoction, a sugar-plum of a book (highly appropriate this, for it is in reality a fairy-tale). It is true also that Sainte-Beuve, who devoted two *Lundis* to Feuillet in 1863, proclaimed it the most triumphant of his works. But alongside *Notre Dame*? And *Madame Bovary*?? And *La Chartreuse de Parme*??? No. No matter how bright and attractive and tinkling it is, a halfpenny it is seen comparatively to be.

It is not, moreover, as if Octave Feuillet had nothing to justify his keeping company with Stendhal, Balzac, Flaubert, and the rest. Sainte-Beuve ended his 1863 study with an appeal to Feuillet to leave his prettiness behind and to strike out into "the vast ocean of human nature". Four years later Feuillet did so. *Monsieur de Camors* is not only his masterpiece; it is, I think, one of Europe's also.

Unlike most nineteenth-century fictions it opens with the swift impact of an American film. The Comte de Camors comes home one summer's evening, writes an amoral testament to his son, and shoots himself. At that same moment the son is seducing the wife of a boyhood friend, tells her he now despises her in consequence, and finds himself remorseful at what he has done. He goes home to the tragedy, to his father's farewell letter, to his material and unspiritual inheritance. If anyone can read this first chapter and not go on, he or she must be blasé indeed. These episodes are, however little more than a setting of the scene; a kind of psychological prologue. Up to that night, Louis de Camors, uxorious but bored, had needed a motive force, a purpose, a faith. He now believed he had found it. For Louis de Camors had an inner pride and strength. He was, says Feuillet, a perverted soul but not a base one. He is in that line of deluded egocentrics that stretches from Julien Sorel to Raskolnikov. And even in such company he is never small change. He has, moreover, his Lady Macbeth. Charlotte de Luc d'Estrelles is one of the great women in French fiction. From the first moment when, at twenty-five, she offers herself in marriage to the ruined Louis de Camors to the climax when she suggests to him in later years of wealth and fame that he should murder his wife, she is always a strange, proud, passionate creature.

A foil to these two, and in the end the destroyer of them and their world, is Louis's wife, Marie. The marriage is an odd one, for Camors proposes to the mother, who answers by dedicating her daughter to him. Camors thinks nothing of the idea. Charlotte, however, has married a rich old general immediately after Camors has declined her offer. Later she becomes Camors's mistress. The general suspects and, in a magnificently contrived scene, Charlotte, like some Becky Sharp, with the general listening behind the curtain, tells Louis he must wed Marie. Thereafter, Marie discovers their secret; is brought to accept it. Finally the climax comes with two superb, related strokes of irony. Charlotte's husband dies through discovering her and Camors together. Free, she is no longer satisfied to share Louis with Marie. Camors, for his part, finds Marie believing he is trying to kill her at the moment he thinks he is saving her life from Charlotte.

With these two great hammer blows the story closes. The only true faith Louis de Camors had was his pride. It and he are mortally shattered. "Thus died," said Feuillet, "this man who was a great sinner, but who was nonetheless a man." I do not know the standing of *Monsieur de Camors* in France to-day but it is well worth reviving in English.

PEACOCK AS A POET

Mention Thomas Love Peacock as a poet and the likelihood is that at once someone will pipe up with

> The mountain sheep are sweeter
> But the valley sheep are fatter . . .

But that, it may be objected, is a song. Peacock himself declared it to be "The War Song of Dinas Vawr". While no one would wish to challenge Peacock as a writer of songs, above all of drinking songs, is not poetry another matter?

I would like to leave that issue on one side for the moment. We can get along without settling it because we can, I think, get along —for the purpose of the argument—almost without the songs; certainly without the drinking songs. This may surprise readers who know Peacock only in his novels, and for whom such rollicking affairs as "A heeltap! a heeltap! I never could bear it!" "If I drink water while this doth last" and the glorious "Hail to the Headlong!", falling naturally into the general fantastication of the plot and setting, have overshadowed the beauties of the quieter lyrics. The emphasis was strengthened some years ago by a pleasant little volume *Drinking Songs from Peacock's Novels.* Here was obviously a festive, jovial, jingling old gentleman, a bit of a genius in his queer way. But a poet? Or else, at the other extreme, people may have come across an equally slender volume *Rhododaphne.* That, they may have felt, settled Peacock's poetical pretensions once for all.

The fact is that *Poems* and *Poems and Plays* fill two volumes out of the 10 in the Halliford edition of Peacock's works. Much handier is the volume of Peacock's poetry Brimley Johnson compiled for Routledge's "Muses' Library" 50 years ago. The odd copy is still to be found in the second-hand shops and I commend it to anyone who comes across it there. Brimley Johnson was one of the Honest Dobbins of the book world. He had taste and judgment; he was careful and conscientious. In this companionable, pocketable—for those who have the right kind of bookmen's pockets—volume of over 400 pages, his work must have given pleasure here and there through two generations.

Sheer bulk cannot, of course, make a poet. Nor does one need to accompany Saintsbury all the way in the opposite direction when he chants:

> The laughing Queen that caught the world's great hands

and proclaims that, because of that one wonderful line and despite "volumes of triviality and vulgarity and sentimental gush", Leigh Hunt was indubitably a poet. Peacock has no need of either of these props. He has very few "jewels five-words-long". And, with one exception, his long poems can be left to the devoted. One has to have a real affection for Peacock to find enchantment in "Palmyra", "Rhododaphne", or "Fiolfar, King of Norway".

Peacock wrote poetry from boyhood on. By twenty-one he had produced a respectable amount of apprentice work. But it was two or three years later, some time after 1808, that he struck an assured note in "Remember Me".

> And what are life's enchanting dreams,
> That melt like morning mists away?
> And what are Fancy's golden beams,
> That glow with transitory day?
> While adverse stars my steps impel,
> To climes remote, my love, from thee,
> Will that dear breast with pity swell
> And wilt thou still remember me?

There are eight verses, and I wish I could recite them all.

It may be objected that even this is precious near a song. Listen, then, to "The Grave of Love", which Earle Welby found so "inexplicably beautiful".

> I dug, beneath the cypress shade,
> What well might seem an elfin's grave;
> And every pledge in earth I laid,
> That erst thy false affection gave.
>
> I pressed them down the sod beneath;
> I placed one mossy stone above;
> And twined the rose's fading wreath
> Around the sepulchre of love.
>
> Frail as thy love, the flowers were dead
> 'Ere yet the evening sun was set;
> But years shall see the cypress spread,
> Immutable as my regret.

Or read that lovely lament, "Long night succeeds thy little day", which Peacock wrote on the death of his three-year-old child, Margaret. Or pick up *Gryll Grange*—pick it up in any case—turn to chapter XV and find "Youth and Age".

> I played with you 'mid cowslips blowing
> When I was six and you were four;
> When garlands weaving, flower-bells throwing,
> Were pleasures soon to please no more.
> Through groves and meads, o'er grass and heather,
> With little playmates, to and fro,
> We wandered hand in hand together
> But that was sixty years ago.

If you do not read on, then I have failed to make my case.

The Devil's advocate never suffering unemployment, there may still be objections that these are small cargo for immortality. I would not agree, but, as the lawyers say, even if I did, I would claim that many of the songs in the novels *are* poetry. (If songs are not poetry what becomes of Robert Burns?) Were this not enough I would summon up the one exception among the longer poems. "The Genius of the Thames" is, to me, one of the best things that majestic stream has inspired. Starting with the description of an autumn night on its banks, Peacock tells the story of its long history, takes the reader along its course, and then, hearing music at Richmond, reflects on those once great empires through which the Euphrates and the Tiber flowed.

> Time, the foe of man's dominion,
> Wheels around in ceaseless flight,
> Scattering from his hoary pinion
> Shades of everlasting night.
> Still, beneath his frown appalling,
> Man and all his works decay:
> Still, before him, swiftly-falling,
> Kings and kingdoms pass away.
>
> Cannot the hand of patriot zeal,
> The heart that seeks the public weal,
> The comprehensive mind
> Retard awhile the storms of fate,
> That, swift or slow, or soon or late,
> Shall hurl to ruin every state,
> And leave no trace behind?

The first time I heard those lines was in the school chapel when, instead of the usual sermon, the closing verses of "The Genius of the Thames" were read to us. I was at an impressionable age and they moved me deeply. But I do not think it is merely recollected emotion that convinces me Peacock was a poet.

MASK AND SLIPPERS

Many were the good works of Joseph Dent, and I have always regretted that he died during the general strike of 1926 and so did not get his due. Among them were three memorable editions after the First World War: *Modern English Essays* (five volumes, 1922); *The Collected Essays and Addresses of Augustine Birrell* (three volumes, 1922); and *The Collected Essays and Papers of George Saintsbury* (four volumes, 1923). To many young men coming out of that ordeal they were both a beacon and a sorcery. The gusto of Saintsbury, the urbanity of Birrell, the variety of that cavalcade of other writers from Mark Pattison to J. C. Squire, and the lure of them all towards the great books of the past—these things were irresistible. If any man asks me what songs the sirens sang in those days I can tell him; also that their number was 12.

Recently I have been re-reading the whole of Birrell and it is of him I want to write to-day, because I was struck with something which I missed 30 years ago. It is that, contrary to the accepted view, Birrell as a writer was best when he was dealing with politics. Let us get the accepted view out of the way first. It would be nonsense, of course, to deny the avuncular Birrell, easily and slipperedly introducing us to his multitude of friends, not only such famous ones as Dr. Johnson, Borrow, Lamb, Sterne, Richardson, Cowper, and Pope; but also the lesser known Roger North, Richard Cumberland, and that good man Dr. Brocklesby. He had, moreover, in his own long life seen Carlyle calm; had known Browning, Tennyson, and Matthew Arnold; had gossiped in libraries, out of libraries, and about libraries endlessly and to our delight. Some of his sayings, such as the number of books a man should have before he begins to talk about them, are now standard. (But the effort to make him famous for his "Birrellisms" was a mistake; he was never a writer of apophthegms.) As for his style, he himself described it best.

> My sentences, so they say, go slithering along, half down a page, and then end up with a cracker tied to their tails; and it also appears that I am guilty of horse-play. . . .

That is true, so long as we picture a nice, gentle Dobbin of a horse, kicking out from joy of life and never vicious. Also one can echo him—and how refreshing the candour of the octogenarian is—when he says:

> At intervals, say of five years, I can re-read all my books with pleasure, and when I do so I am quite taken aback to discover how good little bits of them are. Again and again, I hear myself laughing out loud over passages in my own writings. I am also sometimes quite startled at the amount of learning displayed.

To complete the triptych one can take what he said about Matthew Arnold and apply it to himself.

> Most critics are such savages—or, if they are not savages, they are full of fantasies, and are capable at any moment of calling *Tom Jones* dull, or Sydney Smith a bore. Mr. Arnold was not a savage, and could no more have called *Tom Jones* dull or Sydney Smith a bore, than Homer heavy or Milton vulgar. He was no gloomy specialist. He knew it took all sorts to make a world. He was alive to life. Its great movement fascinated him, even as it had done Burke, even as it did Cardinal Newman.

Taken together, these passages give you the author of *Obiter Dicta* and *Res Judicatae* as well as he can be given. He had little to offer in literary criticism. He had few purple passages to get into anthologies. He made no discoveries. But he is always a pleasant companion, easy, and sane, and sure; and with a most engagingly individual tone of voice.

It seems to me now, however, that you meet another, and more vital, man when you read Augustine Birrell on Sir Robert Peel, on Bright, on Disraeli, on Gladstone. Here is the man who could write of the wording of an Opposition amendment to the Queen's Speech, "Such language moved my bile." And if you want to see some kicking that is not in fun watch him whenever he approaches the subject of Wellington. I now have a suspicion that Birrell studied and knew the three volumes of C. S. Parker's *Sir Robert Peel from his Private Papers* more thoroughly than he did *The Ring and the Book*, and I do not believe he will turn in his grave if he knows I have said so. After all, the only two appendices he attached to his autobiography were a half-page bibliography and the text of a speech he made on Church and State in the House of Commons in 1899.

The Easter Rising of 1916 engulfed not only Birrell's ministerial career but also his political reputation. He wrote himself off as a politician, and in so far as, in the better days of politics, that was the price of the disastrous wreck of a policy, we must do the same. But the man who matched Balfour over the 1906 Education Bill until the Lords took a hand, and lasted out nine years in Ireland, had a feeling for political life which we should not write off also. Unfortunately his manner obscured and nullified it. The famous tone of voice which had charmed thousands in the library failed to impress most of the six hundred in the House of Commons. All too often he spoke of *res judicatae* as if they were mere *obiter dicta*. He talked about politics as he wrote about books, and it was misplaced. But when he wrote about politics that was another matter. Then the feeling came through. If only he had had the application he might have given us a great political biography instead of so many trifles, memorable as they are.

Birrell himself complained that his legal side was completely overlooked and that in spite of his half a lifetime of devotion to and affection for the law, his silk gown, and his lectures on comparative law from the chair of University College, he was never once in all his twenty-one years in the House of Commons referred to as "the honourable and learned member". He seemed also surprised that no one had ever called him Professor Birrell. The trouble was that he never had the energy to take off his mask and so it was accepted as face value.

HENRY, NOT CHARLES

Fame—particularly journalistic fame—being what it is, there is already a generation which does not know Clement K. Shorter. A great reviver and "discoverer" himself, he would not have been in the least dismayed by this. Some day, he would have been sure, someone will re-establish him. The noble Norwich edition of George Borrow is there as one kind of memorial, but it is rather monumental. A far better life-line to Posterity will probably be his *Life of George Borrow* or *The Brontës and their Circle*. Both have, by now, been largely superseded, but I—and many others must also—owe them much and remember them with affection. They had the good fortune to come out in the Wayfarer's Library, and copies of them are still to be seen.

I am sorry that amidst all the celebrations of Everyman's jubilee no one put in a word for this younger, and physically more attractive in some indefinable way, brother among Dent's "libraries". That, however, is the common fate of younger brothers—who knows the names of Methuselah's? All the more, therefore, does Shorter's devotion to one of them place us still further in his debt. He was a keen admirer of Henry Kingsley. Some people might say an immoderate one. In a biography he wrote for a late Victorian edition of *The Recollections of Geoffry Hamlyn*, he put forward the view that interest in Henry would outlast that in Charles. At first, this may seem absurd. Who can believe the day will ever come when anything that Henry Kingsley wrote will be mentioned in the same breath as *Westward Ho*, or *Alton Locke*? Yet Shorter's precise words may prove to be true. We know quite enough about Charles Kingsley and, as Quiller-Couch said when discussing this prophecy of Shorter's some 60 years ago, most of what we know we do not like. With Henry it is different. Whether we look at the weak, amiable face as it gazes at us from the frontispiece of *Geoffry Hamlyn*, or read about his life, which Shorter had to confess "was on the whole a failure", we have an instinctive desire to get closer to the man. We feel he would have been a companionable acquaintance. We hope someone will fill in the "blank years" when he was out of England. For all I know, some eager Australian student may have already done so for a thesis. Or an enterprising Sydney publisher may decide, while there is still time, to bring out a centenary volume on Kingsley's stay (1853–58) in Australia. Judging by the Australian chapters in Kingsley's stories, parts of which have an autobiographical ring, he had some exciting adventures. The times were rough and cruel. Every now and again in *Geoffry Hamlyn* and *The Hillyars and the Burtons* he feels compelled to justify some outlandish or outrageous episode with a footnote: "A fact", or "This happened in —."

Australia should certainly take Henry Kingsley to her heart as much as she has done Adam Lindsay Gordon. He never wrote anything as durable as *The Sick Stockrider*. He could not so vividly put the brave, fiery, independent Australian spirit into a quatrain or an epigram. But his novels have the same temper. Much is forgiven even to the most villainous man, provided he *is* a man. In a new society without inherited ranks or distinctions, it was up to each individual to make his own place. The books to-day have a curious fascination a hundred years on. They show us the great mingling of English and Australian life in its beginnings. The aborigines were still an unknown quantity to be feared. The bushrangers were a known one as terrible as anything that scourged the Far West.

But Henry Kingsley would not have survived so far—and, sad though it is to relate, would have little future in England to-day—if he were no more than an early romancer about Australia. He was a good teller of tales about almost anywhere. Lest, however, this be too large a claim for his works as a whole, most of which will never be revived, I will confine myself to the "big four": *Geoffry*

Hamlyn, *The Hillyars and the Burtons*, *Austin Elliot*, *Ravenshoe*. They all have certain things in common: indifferent writing, crude melodrama, plots which come and go through the story with disconcerting alternations (Kingsley had not Trollope's superb gift for driving such pairs in hand). But he had a wonderful eye for character, that queer gift to make his stories come alive, a warm humanity, the Ancient Mariner's power of holding his audience, and a point of view very much his own. He could see heroes and scoundrels, strong men and craven, foolish women and wise ones as all smaller in the eye of eternity than their exaggerations would have us believe them to be. Henry Kingsley may have been a weak man; he was a serene one.

Of the two "Australian" novels—large parts of both take place in England—*The Hillyars and the Burtons* is the simpler and more attractive tale. It gives a fascinating picture of old Chelsea and mid-nineteenth-century life on the Thames. *Geoffry Hamlyn* is a much more powerful work. In George Hawker, Kingsley gave us a Victorian villain of the first water. *Austin Elliot*, albeit a good story and in the World's Classics, is the weakest of the quartet.

The strongest is surely *Ravenshoe*. It is Henry Kingsley's masterpiece. A wholly English book—the Boat Race and the Derby are both in it for good measure—it is crammed with authentic people and exciting incidents. The plot has never seemed to me to be as far-fetched as has been made out. The studies of Lord Welter and his wife Adelaide, of Father Mackworth, Lord Saltire, old Lady Ascot, the various Ravenshoes, are unforgettable. *Ravenshoe* is a book one lives in to the point that every new contrivance of the author seems merely one of the usual quirks of everyday life, the only setting in which, as we know, anything can happen.

PHOENIX GONE

Most of the signposts in Vence now lead you to the Matisse chapel, and the talk on our crowded bus as we swung through St. Paul du Var showed that most of the passengers were going there. But my own purpose was, being close by, to make a pilgrimage to D. H. Lawrence's grave. It is many years since I read him last; yet the great impression he made on me in my youth remains. To come to him in those days immediately after the First World War was to be plunged into strange emotions and thoughts untold. One read, but was disheartened by, the mass of hysterical nonsense that was written about him after his death. The heightened interest seemed only to lower the real man. Much of it made nonsense of his books. Yet something perdurable remained.

As the years have gone by, the shelf of books about Lawrence has grown longer than that of his works. Of them all, I still think the most intimately revealing is *D. H. Lawrence*, by "E. T.", whom he took for the Miriam in *Sons and Lovers*. "E. T.'s" story closes with the writing of that book. It marked the end of their friendship. But its insight, its detail, its revelations of Lawrence's reading as a youth make it, for the understanding, the key to the later man. We see the adolescent couple trying out the "deeper waters" of George Eliot. "Lawrence adored *The Mill on the Floss*, but always declared that George Eliot had 'gone and spoilt it half-way through.' He could not forgive the marriage of the vital Maggie Tulliver to the cripple Philip." And "E. T." tells us that:

> While Lawrence was at College Sarah Bernhardt came to our Theatre at Nottingham, and he went to see her in *La Dame aux Camélias*. The next day he wrote to me that the play had so upset him that at the end he rushed

from his place and found himself battering at the doors until an attendant came and let him out. He ran to the station to find the last train gone, and had to walk home. He added: "I feel frightened. I realize that I, too, might become enslaved to a woman."

One other book I would put alongside "E. T.'s." It is Catherine Carswell's *The Savage Pilgrimage.*

Two things need to be said to correct false impressions of Lawrence. The first is that, on the whole, he had a happy life. I know this begs the question of what happiness is; but this miner's son who painted even before he wrote, and who seemed destined to become a suburban schoolteacher, managed to break away and fulfil himself, to travel extensively to Italy, Sicily, Germany, France, San Francisco, Ceylon, Australia, and Mexico. He loved using his hands and had a way of life which enabled him to do so. He saw himself acknowledged as well as vilified in his lifetime. And if some of the adulation was nauseating and some of the abuse cruel, he at least had the artist's satisfaction of knowing that the world was not indifferent to what he was saying. He died while still finding life capable of surprise and wonder.

The second is that although he was a sick man, seemingly perpetually involved in quarrels and perpetually on the move, and died at the age of forty-five, his output was considerable. The novels, stories, travel sketches, essays, and poems form a larger body of work than that of many a greater writer. And, as if to show they occupied only a part of his time, there are all the other activities related in the 850-page volume of letters. The idea of a thwarted, embittered, railing, agonized genius denied recognition till after his death should have long since vanished.

Of this output, what will endure? Twenty-five years have passed since Lawrence's death in Vence and for the kind of writer he was, and for the ideas he put forward, that is a short span. No doubt our grandfathers (and even more our grandmothers) would think we are galloping along so far as psychology and morals are concerned. But in reality progress is slow. We wisely tread the new ground warily; all too often there are nothing but quicksands beneath our feet. Lawrence had something to say that may make more sense to a succeeding generation than it does to ours. They may understand better even the way he said it.

All the same, I think that Lawrence will last as an artist rather than as a prophet. As his credentials I would put forward *The White Peacock*, *Sons and Lovers*, *The Trespasser*, and *The Rainbow* among the novels; *Look, We Have Come Through*, some of the *Birds, Beasts, and Flowers*, and *Ship of Death* among the poems; *Sea and Sardinia* and *Etruscan Places* among the non-fiction prose works; and, of course, the *Collected Letters* for the man himself. It is no inconsiderable baggage with which to go to Posterity.

At the cemetery gates I asked the *portière* if she could tell me in what part lay the remains of "l'écrivain anglais, Lawrence". She was a pleasant, friendly woman, and looked as if she had been asked the question before. "On l'a enlevé, il y a longtemps," she said. I asked if the stone with the famous Lawrence symbol, the phoenix, "done in local stones by a peasant who loved him" (as Aldous Huxley tells us) was not still there. She told me that had been transported also. As I looked around the small enclosed graveyard, with its mingled French and Italian names, and the blue of the sea on the distant horizon catching the eye, I could not help feeling sorry. Here was something simple, beautiful, ages-old, appropriate. For among all Lawrence's strange gifts the greatest was integrity.

THE AFFRIGHTED DON

Reports of the latest film based on *Moby Dick* say it is a huge success. That is bound to mean that, like some major constellation, the saga of the Great Whale will wheel into the orbit of a new world of readers. I am not among those who despise "the book of the film" technique. Anything that can induce any body of new readers to take up a masterpiece is valuable. The introduction once made, the masterpiece will do the rest.

I hope, at the same time, the good work will not stop there, and that some of the newcomers will be led on to other of Melville's works. Melville can hardly, of course, be regarded as a one-book man. The success of *Billy Budd* in yet another medium has seen to that. But on Melville's tombstone neither work is mentioned. There, if I remember rightly, he is described merely as the author of *Typee*. Of all South Sea island books I know, it is the most enchanting. And *Omoo*, its sequel, is equally irresistible once it has been embarked upon. Melville had lived what he was writing about. Having deserted from the grim Acushnet he spent four months among the Marquesas islanders, never quite sure whether he would eventually be eaten or not. Yet he presents the islands, his stay among the cannibals, and his various adventures as almost an arcadian tale. If the excitements of the Pequod and the hunt of the great white whale cause any reader to make landfall with *Typee* and *Omoo* he will not be disappointed. And thence he may go on to *White Jacket* and *Mardi* before he feels it time to call "enough".

If there is any such revival of interest in Herman Melville, there is one work of his, above all others except *Moby Dick*, which should be brought back into the limelight. For it is a masterpiece—to my mind one of the finest pieces of literary art we have—and will bear, a hundred years after its birth (for it was first published in 1856) any amount of glare or scrutiny. "Benito Cereno" is a long short story, some 30,000 words or so; it is to be found in the volume called *The Piazza Tales* (published in Constable's Miscellany between the wars, and still to be encountered from time to time).

It is difficult to say whether the force of the tale is greater when its *dénouement* comes as a complete surprise or when its outline is known. Personally I think the latter. Then, like a piece of classical music, one can appreciate every touch. Not a line, not a phrase, not a turn of the head in it is irrelevant. Seemingly artless in its profusion of incident—something is happening every moment of the time—it has the economy of great art.

Mr. John Freeman, in his volume on Melville in the English Men of Letters series, has pointed out that in this tale Melville is to a most astonishing degree the forerunner of Joseph Conrad. Captain Delano, the American skipper in "Benito Cereno" might certainly have been one of Conrad's captains. He has the same practical obtuseness that comes from goodness, just enough imagination to suspect every solution but the right one, an integrity which excludes the capacity to sense evil. His ship is lying at an island off the coast of Chile. The year is 1799. There comes into sight a rather battered Spanish ship, the San Dominick, obviously in need of help. Delano goes aboard her to see what he can do.

Almost at once things strike him as odd. There seem to be more blacks aboard than whites; the behaviour of each lot is peculiar; episodes occur, any one explicable in itself, but together making him uneasy. All the time he feels an air of "dreamy inquietude". Most peculiar of all is the demeanour of the captain, Don Benito Cereno. Clearly he is ailing; at times he seems half-dead; every moment he has to be supported by a devoted black servant. " 'Faithful fellow!' cried Captain Delano. 'Don Benito, I envy you such a friend; slave I cannot call him.' " Of Cereno's own faithfulness Delano has no such certainty. At moments he seems to be plotting Delano's destruction; at others to be hiding some secret from a presumably disreputable past. Captain Delano goes through every possible phase of pity, indignation, suspicion, apprehension, at the extraordinary behaviour of the coughing, near-fainting, seemingly cruel and arrogant Don. He conjectures every fantastic possibility except the right one. The mystery, the suspense, the oddness, the unease, the feeling that wickedness is all about not only the good Captain Delano but the reader mounts and mounts.

Then, as Delano leaves the San Dominick, the veil is shattered with one frenzied leap. At the end of it Benito Cereno is cowering in the long-boat with the American; the faithful Negro slave Babo is frenziedly swimming after the Don intent on stabbing him. The other Negroes "with mask torn away, flourishing hatchets and knives" show themselves to be what they are, "in ferocious piratical revolt". The rest of the story is a deposition by the dying Don Benito explaining exactly what had happened. It is like the last chapter in the best detective stories, in which every loose end is tied up, every mystery solved, every episode made obvious, all conjecture swept away. It is pure matter-of-fact.

Then the superb horror and irony of all that has gone before can be admired. The fact that Cereno was saving Delano's life, not seeking to destroy it; that the touchingly faithful slave Babo, for whom Delano offered fifty doubloons to have him as his own private servant, is really a scheming, murderous, black-hearted villain and the true master of the San Dominick. There is an episode, in which when Delano is asking Cereno some awkward questions the obsequious Babo insists on shaving his master, that is in the best Grand Guignol tradition. There is the fact that, looking back on it all, Captain Delano could see that he was walking closest to his own death when he had felt himself most safe; what he thought was ominous was in truth the efforts of the remaining Spaniards to warn him. But Captain Delano "took to negroes, not philanthropically, but genially, just as other men to Newfoundland dogs." And even had the pirates been white it would have made no difference. He was "incapable of sounding such wickedness".

There is passage after passage in the story one would like to quote. They are unforgettable. But it is the quivering, nervous tension of the whole that counts. There is the opening sunshine, the gathering clouds of the slow, sinister development, the crash of thunder with the Don's leap, and then the storm and flurry of the fight; followed by the calm explanatory clearing up of the close. "Benito Cereno" is one of the great short stories of the world, and lest I be accused of going over old ground let me acknowledge that Arnold Bennett long ago proclaimed this in one of his articles. But, so far as I know, it was never put between permanent covers, and there is now a new generation to whom the joyful news must be again proclaimed.

PUTTING IT DOWN

"With the artist," says Lessing, "execution appears to be more difficult than invention. With the poet, on the other hand, the case seems to be reversed, and his execution appears to be an easier achievement than his invention." Not merely the Sunday painters know this; even the most accomplished professional can become infuriated as time and time again his hand fails to reproduce what his eye is seeing. A whole phase of art criticism seemed at one time to be building up on the physical details of how painters paint. Probably it went too far. But I am sure all too little attention has been given to how writers write.

The thought came back to me when re-reading Mr. G. M. Young's *Gibbon* the other day. (One of the abiding pleasures of Mr. Young's work is that one can invariably be stimulated in a new way by even its most familiar passages.) On the technical side of his craft, says Mr. Young, Gibbon established a standard of workmanship for English historians once for all.

> His method was to make notes, on cards, as he read: compose a paragraph at a time, walking up and down his room: commit it to writing, add the references, and then proceed to the next. I think this ambulatory habit may have helped his accuracy; Hume, who wrote with feet on the sofa, found it "unco-fashious" to get up and verify his facts.

When he spoke of execution, Lessing was, of course, thinking of words being the poet's instrument rather than his quill or his ball-point. Nonetheless, two widely different poets did not consider these lesser things trivial. "As I enter upon this part of my work," wrote Baudelaire when he came to discuss Delacroix's pictures in the Salon of 1846, "my heart is full of a serene joy, and I am purposely selecting my newest pens, so great is my desire to be clear and limpid, so happy do I feel to be addressing my dearest and most sympathetic subject." And no chapter in Kipling's *Something of Myself* is more fascinating, and written with more warmth, than that headed "Working-Tools". "Mercifully," says Kipling, "the mere act of writing was, and always has been, a physical pleasure to me", and he strikes a responsive chord at once. He was "choice, not to say coquettish" about his implements; his pens (including "a slim, smooth black treasure" called Jael), his ink, and his writing blocks all had to be just so. They were almost as important as his daemon.

Beyond the tools, there is the way they are used. At one end of the scale (I will not say which) is Trollope with his carefully compiled daily schedule of words for a whole novel before he ever set pen to paper. At the other there is Flaubert, arranging certain key words on the blank page, as an artist might rough in one or two tone values, and then spending days endeavouring satisfactorily to fill in the space in between. There is the extraordinary manuscript of *The Dynasts* which shows that Hardy wrote out on alternate lines certain key descriptions by acknowledged authorities, and then transmuted them into the blank verse of his masterpiece, crossing out the leaden original as he went along. There are the secret Brontë Angrian writings, often with over a thousand words on a foolscap page. There is Charles Reade, with his innumerable drawers of card indexes, ready to provide him with verisimilitude on every possible subject, but often sinking his novels instead. There is Bernard Shaw writing the original manuscript of *Pygmalion* in shorthand; and now the ever-increasing modern hordes who hammer out their inventions on typewriters. (Have they yet, one wonders, wrung the neck of the old gibe that with a pen one composes, but on a typewriter one can only improvise?) Any student looking around for new ground to explore for a thesis could do worse than analyse the consequences of some of these things.

Dictation would need a separate thesis—perhaps several—all to itself. Personally I think almost every artistic composition is the worse for it. At once Milton will be quoted against me. But I am ready to draw a distinction between poetry and prose. Take authors as far apart in both time and manner as Sir Walter Scott and Henry James; in both cases I will argue that their written novels are better than their dictated ones. There are many reasons for this. I will quote Lockhart for the simplest:

> The *copy* (as MS for the press is technically called) which Scott was thus dictating, was that of *The Bride of Lammermoor*; and his amanuenses were William Laidlaw and John Ballantyne; of whom he preferred the latter, when he could be at Abbotsford, on account of the superior rapidity of his pen; and also because John kept his pen to the paper without interruption, and though with many an arch twinkle in his eyes, and now and then an audible smack of his lips, had resolution to work on like a well-trained clerk; whereas good Laidlaw entered with such zest into the interest of the story as it flowed from the author's lips, that he could not suppress exclamations of surprise and delight—"Gude keep us a'!—the like o' that!—eh sirs!—eh sirs!—and so forth—which did not promote dispatch.

Modern secretaries are admittedly much speedier (no good thing in itself for the author) and far more self-effacing. Perhaps some highly efficient and expert young woman will write to tell me so. And no doubt the public relations officers of the dictating machine companies will soon be dictating letters to explain how their contrivances are less obtrusive still. I am old-fashioned enough to believe, however, that the page of paper is for the writer what the canvas is to the painter; he will be far more likely to achieve composition, and avoid repetition and solecism, if what he has already done is immediately and continually in front of him, and if there is no expectant human or waiting machine to get him into the state of desperately feeling he must say *something*. Inspiration, unlike business, is a private matter. I am sure that when Musset's muse uttered her famous invitation

> Poète, prends ton luth et me donne un baiser

she did not expect either audience or microphone to be present.

WHAT HAPPENED TO MYERS?

Sir Edward Cook, who wrote a very good single-volume life of Delane in the place of Dasent's two meandering tomes, himself once wrote a meandering essay on "The Second Thoughts of Poets". *Love in the Valley* came into it, of course, though rather cursorily, and so did the works of Coleridge, Keats, Tennyson, Rossetti, Matthew Arnold, FitzGerald, Myers, and Wordsworth. To-day's readers, if ever they come across it, the only thing that can command even momentary attention is the name of Myers. Who was Myers? What did he write? How can he be so forgotten if he was once fit to be enrolled in such company? *Que diable allait-il faire dans cette galère?* Is it we who are wrong or Sir Edward Cook?

Almost as if he foresaw the day when Posterity would ask that question, Cook presents Myers's credentials.

> A poem which has vied with FitzGerald's *Omar* in popularity is Myers's *St. Paul.* It appeals to a different audience; but, apart from its religious address, the distinctive stanza employed by Myers, the faultless rhythmical cadence, and the sonorous verbal melody have for fifty years [Cook was writing in 1918] attracted lovers of poetry. The very defects of the piece, as they may be deemed by a severe taste—its sometimes metallic ring, its over-elaboration of phrase—have perhaps assisted its vogue. Between its appearance in 1867 and the poet's death in 1901 there were six later editions, and as soon as it passed out of copyright, the book mart was flooded, as in the case of *Omar,* with cheap reprints of the first edition.

But even in those days it did not sweep quite everybody off their feet. Prince Leopold urged Ruskin to read it. "*St. Paul*," said that Biblical purist, "is not according to my thought."

It is doubtful, however, whether most readers who loved to recite its verses were much concerned with the thought embodied in *St. Paul*. The rhythm was the thing. Now the astonishing thing about it is the categoric assertion that Myers got it from a leading article in *The Times*. Freaks like that do sometimes happen. Did not Lord Dunsany once write a poem using the phrase from an Eton-Winchester cricket match report, "when umpire Lee was hit on the knee by a very fast ball from Faber"? But the metre of *St. Paul* is altogether different mettle.

> Lo as some ship, outworn and overladen,
> Strains for the harbour where her sails are furled:
> Lo as some innocent and eager maiden
> Leans o'er the wistful limit of the world,
> Dreams of the glow and glory of the distance,
> Wonderful wooing and the grace of tears,
> Dreams with what eyes and what a sweet insistance
> Lovers are waiting in the hidden years.

One would like to know which of Delane's or Dasent's leaders could possibly have set off such a tune as that.

Great as the fame of *St. Paul* became, Frederick William Henry Myers was considered, even at the height of its success, as something more than its author. For one thing, he was a fairly prolific poet. His *Collected Poems* run to over 400 pages. For another, he was a classical scholar, and a writer of prose that has comfortably outlasted his poetry. His two volumes *Essays Classical* and *Essays Modern* are still well worth reading. The essay on Virgil in the former was long regarded as the best short study of its subject. For myself, the essay on "Greek Oracles" has always seemed even more fascinating and exciting. Among the *Essays Modern* are studies of Mazzini, Renan, George Sand, George Eliot, and Victor Hugo. That on George Eliot is one of the best things Myers ever wrote, and contains the passage for which he is now most quoted:

> I remember how, at Cambridge, I walked with her once in the Fellows' Garden of Trinity, on an evening of rainy May; and she, stirred somewhat beyond her wont, and taking as her text the three words which have been used so often as the inspiring trumpet calls of men,—the words *God, Immortality, Duty*—pronounced, with terrible earnestness, how inconceivable was the *first*, how unbelievable the *second*, and yet how peremptory and absolute the *third*. Never, perhaps, have sterner accents affirmed the sovereignty of impersonal and unrecompensing Law. I listened, and night fell; her grave, majestic countenance turned toward me like a Sibyl's in the gloom; it was as though she withdrew from my grasp, one by one, the two scrolls of promise, and left me the third scroll only, awful with inevitable fates.

In two other fields you may encounter Myers. He contributed *Wordsworth* to the English Men of Letters series, not one of its more notable volumes, and he spent the later part of his life in founding, with his friends Henry Sidgwick and Edmund Gurney among others, the Society for Psychical Research. To this he gave untiring, disinterested, and, indeed, noble devotion. There was, in fact, a strong streak of nobility in him, or, at least, a strain of simple goodness. It was warm, emotional, rather blurred; but it had its appeal for the men and women of his day. We are the poorer for the loss of it in ours. A harder, more sophisticated age, facing with unexpected suddenness unyielding problems, has found his poetry a mass of verbiage. Thus there was almost an air of impatience, in *The Times* and elsewhere, when efforts were made to revive his work in the nineteen-twenties. Not even the fact that he was the father of L. H. Myers, who wrote *The Orissers*, could save him. But when one looks at those photographs of him, gentle, benevolent, and somewhat ineffectual, taken by his wife—who was one of the finest of Victorian photographers—and reads his fragments of autobiography and other prose pieces, one feels he was a man one would like to have known. And, whether it has any vital meaning or not, *St. Paul* is still fine stuff to declaim.

WREYLAND GOSSIP

As soon as I saw the back page of *The Times* on Monday morning I said, "Cecil Torr." For there, making one's heart gay and taking one's thoughts into the West Country, were pictures of May Day at Lustleigh, in Devon.

> There is a May-day festival here, for which I am responsible. There used to be dancing round the May-pole at the flower show and other festivals, but none upon May-day itself; and I put an end to that anomaly. The children at Lustleigh school—boys and girls—elect one of the girls as Queen, and her name is carved upon a rock on the hill behind this house. Then on May-day the Queen walks in procession under a canopy of flowers carried by four of the boys, her crown and sceptre being carried by two others; then come her maids of honour; and then all the other children of the school, most of them carrying flowers in garlands or on staves. The procession winds along through Lustleigh and through Wreyland, halting at certain places to sing the customary songs, and at last ascends the hill behind here. The Queen is enthroned upon a rock looking down upon the May-pole: the crown of flowers is placed on her head, and the arum-lily sceptre in her hand: the maids of honour do their homage, laying their bouquets at her feet; and the four-and-twenty dancers perform their dance before her. Then comes the serious business of the day—the children's tea. This year, 1917, there was a shortage of cereals; but I saved the situation with two hundred hard-boiled eggs.

That comes from *Small Talk at Wreyland*, one of the most enchanting books ever written. I have quoted it because it is a good example of Cecil Torr's love of detail and tradition; his exactness comfortably cloaked in an easy style.

Few books with such lasting power as *Small Talk at Wreyland* have opened with less flourish.

> Down here, when any of the older natives die, I hear people lamenting that so much local knowledge has died with them, and saying that they should have written things down. Fearing that this might soon be said of me, I got a book at Christmas-time 1916, and began to write things down. I meant to keep to local matters, but have gone much further than I meant.

Thousands of readers must have become thoroughly grateful that he did. One of the many charms of *Small Talk at Wreyland* is that for subject matter it wanders through the ages and all over the world. One moment we are being entertained with local weather lore, the next with the reflection that "Tiberius must have been the Mrs. Grundy of his generation." We learn in detail how a Devon woman was convinced she had seen the Devil when in fact she had met the Rural Dean. We take part in a discussion on Goethe's, Petrarch's, Homer's, and Toplady's sources of inspiration. "A good many of the people here are of the opinion that the Earth is flat," says Cecil Torr, "and I do not know of any simple and decisive way of proving it to be a globe." They easily demolished Aristotle's argument (*De Coelo*, II. 14.13). A few pages later we have a small girl on Good Friday "fasting" with a hot-cross-bun on his doorstep; sailors flogging Judas Iscariot on that day in the Mediterranean; a procession at Thebes; and the scrubbing of the high altar at St. Peter's on Maundy Thursday. "As I was in Rome, 14 April 1892, I went to see it done."

Seeing and writing were two of the main hobbies of the Torrs. (Cecil Torr's grandfather even got on board the Bellerophon to have a look at Boney.) They had been in Wreyland a long time; "there was an Inquiry here on 22 December 1276—William de Torr was on the jury"; but they also were men of the world, and travelled. The instinct must have been hereditary. It was strong in each generation. Cecil Torr's own writings we have. But the charm of his book is that it also gives us some of the writings of his father and grandfather, or at least the results of their observations. Cecil Torr's father kept a diary from 1833 to 1878. His grandfather and grandmother wrote over 1,000 letters to his father which were all preserved. Cecil Torr himself was born in 1857 and could remember incidents back to 1860. An ability to remember, however, is of little use without the power of selection. For years the painter had the advantage of the photographer precisely because of what he could reject. Not an anecdote of Cecil Torr's is superfluous or boring; not a reference or an allusion is there that is not made, either by comparison or relation, interesting. He can make even the weather of a hundred years ago have a sudden attraction for us.

Behind every page, moreover, there is the man himself, civilized, learned, humorous, crotchety, never conventional. Take this on elections:

> Barefaced bribery is not a bad thing, in its way. The voter got hard cash and the candidate provided it; whereas the voter only gets wild promises now, and these always cost the country a good deal, even if they do no good to anybody. Moreover, when the voter could be bought, there was not the same necessity for cramming him with lies. With his pocket full of money and no illusions in his mind, he went gaily to the poll, feeling that it was all a festival at which he was an honoured guest. And in very many places it was little else.

Torr was a man who "degenerated with the times" to two glasses of port instead of two bottles, and attributed any subsequent ill-health to this. He saw Garibaldi and Boulanger, and the Sultan Abdul-Aziz. He planned a musical instrument on Pythagorean principles (and decided the only name for it was the Cacophone). He writes of a cat that ran up a clock, of dogs and vipers, of the practice (as recently as 1902) of passing a child through a split ash tree to cure it of a rupture, of Parson Davy, who in his sermons "denounced the vices of his congregation in such terms that the people fled from the church and complained to the Bishop"; and of his grandfather's observations on the apparent extinction of "the old barn-door or dung-hill cock".

He had been at a real table d'hôte, "mine host sitting at the head of the table", and his father before him at Blinzler's in Godesberg on August 25, 1852, was faced with "1, soup; 2, roast beef and potatoes; 3, mutton cutlets and vegetables; 4, fish and sauces; 5, ducks and salads; 6, hare and stewed fruits; 7, roast veal and salads; 8, shell-fish and puddings; 9, fruits, sweetmeats and cheese." The queerest table d'hôte Cecil Torr himself ever experienced was at Tournai on Good Friday in 1875: a first-class dinner lasting three hours, of 15 fish courses, and dozens of champagne.

Torr died in 1928. He modestly wrote: "I find the things I have remembered best have seldom been the things best worth remembering." All one can say is that few people who ever set their memories down have given their readers a more varied or more entertaining bedside book. The only other one I would put in the same class is Aulus Gellius. *Small Talk at Wreyland* was originally published in three volumes. They are rather hard to come by. The handiest edition is the slightly dumpy but very convenient single volume published by the Cambridge University Press in 1926. Torr would have liked the thought of its winning new readers as a result of those pictures in *The Times*.

REPEAT PERFORMANCE

There must be as many reasons for re-reading books as for reading them in the first place. With some kinds of literature—history, biography, and so on—it may be a form of mild study. Probably our reading, and almost certainly our experience, have become wider since we first took the book up, and we want to see how it fits into the pattern of what we now know. In the case of essays—perhaps the most popular material for re-reading; goodness knows how many times, for instance, I have been through the five volumes of Dent's *Modern English Essays* or the various collections of "Alpha of the Plough"—there is the same joy that one gets from hearing once again any short and well-loved tune. Poetry *has* to be re-read and re-read if it is to be fully savoured. But it is the habit of re-reading novels that is perhaps the most interesting of all.

Why do people re-read novels? The question once engaged the subtlety of Virginia Woolf. She suggested that they did so "to find some other form of pleasure to take the place of that careless rapture which floated us so triumphantly along in the first instance." It had to be sought below the surface. It was "the lasting quality" in a novel that the second-timer was after.

There are those, of course, who read certain books through again and again till they can almost recite them by heart. It is a strange form of relaxation and, for some reason I have never been able to understand, it is particularly associated with the works of Dickens. (There was a time when the same could be said to a lesser degree of Sir Walter Scott; now it seems to take most people all their time to get through anything of his once.) Thackeray has never been very prone to this kind of mania. There must be a hundred people who can repeat the sayings of Mr. Micawber or Sam Weller for each one who can quote anything by Captain Costigan or Jeames de la Pluche.

Some people read a novel a second time "to see how it was done". Like most spectators of a conjuring trick they do not feel satisfied until they believe they understand the mechanics of the illusion. This kind of re-reading was set in some spate in the early 1920s by Mr. Percy Lubbock's fascinating book *The Craft of Fiction*. (It was the inspiration of Virginia Woolf's essay.) The number of readers *Madame Bovary* and *Vanity Fair* must have had who, with Mr. Lubbock for a guide, were really on a tour of dissection must have been many. Flaubert and Thackeray are fair game. I cannot feel the searchers can have got much satisfaction out of Turgenev and Henry James; the one so simple and the other so complicated as to defy all analysis. (*War and Peace* is yet another, and altogether more formidable, matter.) I hope there was a new generation of these enthusiasts when *The Craft of Fiction* was republished two years ago. It is a good thing for readers to realize that writing novels involves honest workmanship as well as art. Much pleasure can be gained by getting behind an author's pen, becoming aware of his skill in construction or subtlety in characterization; seeking the touches that cannot possibly be seen in the course of a first reading.

It can be argued that all these are specialist or exceptional classes of re-readers. There are plenty of ordinary readers who simply take up some book they have liked in the past and decide they would enjoy settling down with it again. The inclination is as natural as that of keeping one's friendships in repair. Life is full enough of surprises as it is; there is much to be said for merely renewing acquaintances and retreading old ground. It is inevitable that what are loosely called "the English classics" should be favourites for this kind of thing; as often as not the description "classic" merely denotes lasting power. But many modern novels can prove equally rewarding. I re-read some time ago Hemingway's *A Farewell to Arms* and found it as moving as ever. Mention of Hemingway, however, brings a reminder that there is one kind of fiction that will not stand re-reading. This is the once "ultra-modern", highly mannered novel that proclaimed almost a new use of language. Such works do not wear well. Like some of our futuristic architecture they merely become shabby with age. The day may dawn when they will have value as period oddities, but that time is not yet. There are quite a number of British and American "explosive forces" of the inter-war years who are unreadable to-day. *A Farewell to Arms* escaped this. Not only its subject but also its style had a timeless quality.

I said earlier that the earnest dissectors of *War and Peace* were not likely to be numerous. One might as well take a scalpel to a whale. *War and Peace* is one of that small number of titanic works which the ordinary reader just cannot take all in at one, or even two or three, readings. One must come back to them again and again; concentrating on one occasion on some single strand or set of characters in the vast story; on another occasion on another strand; and even then at the end of one's days there will probably be the feeling that a final re-reading is still needed to see the work whole. Fortunately the number of writers who have been capable of creating on this scale is small. Balzac is disqualified because, in spite of all he said, and even had he finished it, *La Comédie Humaine* could never have been an organic or artistic whole. *The Tale of Genji* is. So is Proust's great work. We can read *A la Recherche du Temps Perdu* endlessly, find each time something that has hitherto escaped us, and yet never be in any doubt that we are confronted by so completely integrated a work that we are the poorer for any detail we miss.

Proust, moreover, gives us the clue to one of the secrets of the pleasure of re-reading. The man or woman who comes to a book a second time is never quite the same person as he or she was when it was read first. The characters in it seem to change because we ourselves are constantly changing. The Eustacia Vye we meet as a boy is a different creature from the woman we encounter when we read *The Return of the Native* in our middle age. The sympathies aroused by *The Way of All Flesh* or even *Paradise Lost* veer through the years from one character to another. When they stand on our shelves books seem static, unchanging, inert things. We have only to open them to realize that they have their own lives, even if it is merely as mirrors of ourselves.

THE HYPNOTIST

Mind and memory are curious instruments. Visiting Venice this year, the sound of a gondolier's song heard on the Piazzeta suddenly brought home to me the fact that I was in the city not only of Marco Polo but of Dr. Nikola. Had anyone through the years asked me about Dr. Nikola, I could have conjured up a number of things about him—his black hair and burning eyes, his hypnotic powers, his implacable will, his sinister cat Apollyon. Yet I doubt if it would have occurred to me that he was a Venetian. But the whole of *Farewell Nikola* is based on this. In some ways it is the least compelling of the Nikola stories; at the same time it was for me a child's introduction to Venice.

Doubtless the books that will be pushed into the stockings—and pillow-cases—next Monday night will be more high-powered and sophisticated affairs than they were 50 years ago. But no young reader thwarting atomic spies or voyaging with spacemen on Christmas afternoon will have a more authentic thrill than that which came to his grandfather when at the same age he first encountered Dr. Nikola. The turn of the century was a vintage time for villains. But even the great Moriarty was a minor misdemeanant compared with the searcher after the secret of immortality. Do not misunderstand me. I would not for one moment class Guy Boothby with Conan Doyle. But Doyle's great character is Holmes. Again, Boothby was not as accomplished a story-teller as Hornung in the Raffles books. Yet Nikola made a quite different impact from these others. They excited and mystified; Boothby's Nikola caused a genuine *frisson d'horreur*.

Looking back on the books now, I can see it was because Dr. Nikola, the most mysterious character of them all, was to his boyish readers no mystery. Or, at least, all his mysterious powers were connected with familiar things. Many of us who first met him in *Dr. Nikola* came upon him at billiards "practising losing hazards of extraordinary difficulty". Again, when in a tight corner in the monastery on the road to Tibet he worked out Euclid's forty-third problem on the floor of his cell in charcoal, that was something we all understood. We could not do it ourselves, but we knew what it was about. (And we *could* copy his habit of drawing 8's in the dust endlessly one inside the other.) Similarly, his "patent American fountain pen" was a marvel we had heard about and hankered after. The new anaesthetic he had discovered that made the subject impervious to all pain but did not deprive him of his senses had, like catalepsy, often been among our morbid imaginings. The voltmeters and smell of ozone in the rejuvenation experiment were masterpieces of the familiar. As for Nikola's most mysterious power of all, hypnotism, had we not often attempted it upon each other in the dormitory?

The other attractive thing about Dr. Nikola was his cosmopolitanism. He could be met in the Strand, in Peking, in Brussels, Kabul, Nagasaki, Nijni Novgorod, or the South Sea islands. In these days when travel has become a mere matter of hops, and children fly home for their Christmas holidays from London to Burma, this may not seem impressive. Then each name was still a romance. To recite them had the same clarion effect as the horn of Roland at Roncesvaux. The Dalai Lama did not go on propaganda tours and Lhasa was still "the forbidden city". Even one-eared Chinese like the evil Quong Ma were not as well known as Mr. Chou En-lai. Nevertheless, at first Boothby made too much of travel. Everybody in *A Bid for a Fortune* is so continually on the move that it is a restless book. Boothby, himself an eager traveller, an Australian who wanted to see as much of the world as possible before he settled in England, seemed to want to pack every possible place between his covers.

Guy Boothby wrote between fifty and sixty novels and not

having read them all I cannot say whether some Nikola tales have gone uncounted. But the four that have survived are *A Bid for a Fortune*, *Dr. Nikola*, *Dr. Nikola's Experiment*, and *Farewell Nikola*. Read in that order, they tell a connected story. In *A Bid for a Fortune* (mostly adventure: character not yet fully developed) Nikola possesses himself of the Chinese stick that can lead him to the secret monastery. *Dr. Nikola* (far and away the best) tells the story of how he got there but was exposed. In *Dr. Nikola's Experiment* (too much padding) he applies the knowledge of rejuvenation he brought away with him to an aged Spaniard, the results being disastrous for the patient. *Farewell Nikola* is a kind of *coda*, bringing the characters of *A Bid for a Fortune* together once again, allowing Nikola to tell his life story, showing him robbed of his just vengenace, and leaving him finally back in Tibet.

When the wind howls round the house at night and the world seems very lonely (says Hatteras) I sometimes try to picture a monastery on a mountain-side, and then, in my fancy, I see a yellow-robed, mysterious figure, whose dark searching eyes look into mine with a light that is no longer of this world. To him I cry—"Farewell, Nikola!"

Fustian? Certainly. Yet I can still recite those closing words. Poor junk to carry around all these years? I am afraid so. But to all those moralists who try to improve children's reading I would say that it was from Dr. Nikola I first got the idea that the success people have in attaining their ends depends as often as not on how single-mindedly they want them, and that whatever is worth doing is worth doing well.

MINE OWN ACCOUNTANT

For as long as one can remember, occasional writers have been playing the game of choosing the six best, or the three best, biographies in the English language. It is a nice comfortable game to play, reminding one very much of a choir competition at the Eisteddfod. For, inevitably, there are, to begin with, two set pieces; and as we know them well we settle down to see what the latest comer will make of them. The variations on the theme of appreciating Boswell's *Life of Johnson* and Lockhart's *Life of Scott* are not yet exhausted. Even the most perfunctory ones lead us into pleasant ways. But it is when we come to the third, and optional, piece that we really sit up and take notice. What is the writer going to choose? Trevelyan's *Macaulay*? Forster's *Dickens*? Carlyle's *Sterling*? Southey's *Nelson*? Morley's *Gladstone*? A good time can be had with any of them. All I would myself say about the whole business is that if John Gibson Lockhart really does come second to Boswell a mile measure would not fill the distance between them.

When we turn to autobiographies it is altogether another matter. Rousseau and Cellini run a much closer race. (They have now been put into so many standard editions as to be almost English classics.) But in autobiographies by Englishmen (and, of course, Scotsmen and Welshmen too) the field is surprisingly poor. Is there really something in the traditional picture of the plain, blunt, taciturn, unimaginative Englishman, feeling abashed under his own gaze? Kiss me, Hardy; we would rather die upon the beaches than admit it. But the record, or the lack of one, is there.

It is obviously necessary to be clear what we mean by autobiography. It is not compilations of letters, or diaries, or journals. (That rules out, curiously enough, three preachers: Fox, Wesley, and Woolman.) It is not, no matter how brilliantly done, either a personal record of one side only of a man's life, like Newman's *Apologia pro Vita Sua*, or one period of his activity, such as Ruskin's *Praeterita*. (Without that disqualification *Praeterita* would walk away with the prize so far as I am concerned: truly did Frederic Harrison describe it as "one of the most pathetic and exquisite Confessions in the language.") The autobiographer must be presenting his life as a whole, both in time and character. He must be giving us the full man, as far as he can see him. We should close the book feeling "that is all ye need to know".

It is all a matter of degree, of course. If every one of these conditions was absolute both Rousseau and Cellini themselves would be disqualified. As it is, I must confess that Trollope's *Autobiography* only just scrapes over both hurdles. Can it be placed in the first three? I doubt it. For one thing, it is necessary to have read a good many of his novels to appreciate his own judgments on them. For another, honest, forthright, and manly as he is, he is unconsciously falsifying himself, as Mrs. Oliphant did in her melancholy story. There was another and even better person, larger than the book.

I think one must also put lower down the list Thomas Hardy's Life, written by his wife, which is now increasingly acknowledged to be largely autobiography. Colley Cibber was neither a clever enough man nor a foolish enough one to make his *Apology* first-class. Carlyle's *Reminiscences* can now be seen in better perspective than when Froude originally published them, but they are still among his lesser works. Lord Herbert of Cherbury's self-portrait is more fascinating than any of these. It remains, however, caviare to the general public. But it is all too easy to go on discarding. It is time to make a choice.

Surely Gibbon's must be included in any list of the three best autobiographies. It is one of the few such works worth reading in its varying versions. In them we can still see Gibbon, not only the historian, but the youth, the militiaman, the lover, the man of affairs, and the man of the world, better than anyone else has yet seen him. Almost everyone since has perforce had to see him through his own eyes. And how worth while contemplating he is.

Second place I would give to John Stuart Mill. It is true that later revelations, notably Professor Hayek's and Mr. Packe's researches, have not allowed him to bask in the same unvaryingly amiable light. But even with his waspishness and his womanishness Mill was a good and noble man and his *Autobiography* is a good and noble book. It is an example to all others of the serenity and fine temper in which a man's own life can be written.

My third and final choice would go to *An Autobiography* by Sir Arthur Keith. This is not because an eighteenth-century historian and a nineteenth-century political economist are thus joined by a twentieth-century scientist, though this has its point. But I have read few books which made me feel I was nearer to the man; a man of great gifts and fine character, who looked back over a long life without rancour, or regret that it had inexorably come to its end. It will, I believe, grow in stature with the years.

A TRAVELLER IN BIG THINGS ALSO

W. H. Hudson was described to me as "a half-neglected author nowadays". The truth is that he always was. The story of the years of poverty in London, eventually relieved by a Civil List pension, has been told often enough (too often, for it makes him appear a defeated and melancholy man, which he never was). But even in the last years of his life, when fame came to him, success was only relative. It became the fashion to talk of Conrad and Hudson as twin peaks of English writing, the men who had more or less taken over from Hardy and Meredith. But Hudson's popularity never approached Conrad's, and though both went into a probably equally low trough after their deaths, time brought Conrad the expected revival. So far this has been denied to Hudson. When Dent's brought out a new collected edition of Conrad after the Second World War it went well. There was a new flow of critical appraisal of Conrad and a new generation found he had something for them. But although five years have gone by since the cheap uniform edition of Hudson was launched, Dent's, who have never wavered in their belief in Hudson, have brought out only seven volumes.

Perhaps like people in another place I should at this stage declare my interest. I bought them all as they came out, and long for the series to be continued. The limited edition of Hudson now fetches a high price, beyond my (and most people's) means. It is unthinkable that the remaining 17 volumes should slowly go into desuetude, the more so as they include *El Ombu*, *Dead Man's Plack*, *A Crystal Age*, and *A Traveller in Little Things*—some of the best and most characteristic things Hudson ever wrote. There have, too, been few books about Hudson; far fewer than about Conrad.

Youth rightly is prepared to take little on trust. One must explain why Hudson is worth reviving. What has he to offer this day and age? As often as not, when his name is mentioned, the response is "Oh, the man who wrote about birds." Write about birds—and many other animals—Hudson did. That is no qualification in itself. Many other people have done the same. Birds, to my mind, are not very rewarding studies; from what little I have seen of them they are quarrelsome, selfish, vindictive creatures. Naturalists may delight in them; most of the things written about them seem poetic high-falutin to ordinary folk. Now Hudson certainly called himself a naturalist. But he was also four other things—a story-teller, a philosopher, a shrewd observer of his fellow-men, and a writer of the most deceptively simple and enchanting prose. (Some people would also add that he was essentially a poet; which I would not deny; but it is on these four things his claim to last must rest.)

I put story-telling first. Almost everything Hudson wrote was a story. Take his very first book, *The Purple Land*, or his last, *A Hind in Richmond Park*; take even such a volume of essays as *A Traveller in Little Things;* Hudson cannot stop recruiting his memories, experiences, observations, and reflections into tales. No writer of his quality has poured out a greater stream of real or imagined anecdote. And whether he is doing it in the space of little more than a couple of pages, as in his humorous description of his encounter with the "commercial" who mistook his calling and so gave his book its title, or in such middle-length works as *El Ombu* and *Marta Riquelme*, or in his finest romance *Green Mansions*, he is the deliberate artist, conscious of exactly what scale he is working upon, reading easily because he worked hard that it should be so, personally unobtrusive but ever present in a vicarious way.

This is said in the belief that Hudson was an artist even about himself. I never met him, but the picture one gets of the man from his contemporaries, and particularly in his letters, is not that which his writings have left to posterity. Either his true self could hardly ever come through in the traffic of daily life or he put most superbly on to paper the man he would like to have been. Such a hypothesis is not sentimental. Other great writers have faced us with the same conundrum. And lest anyone who has not read Hudson should think that in his works he is a warm, woolly, and wishy-washy creature (as are all too many minor nature writers) it should be said that his writings are clear and sharp, as were his observations on wild life, which he knew was a perpetual battle to keep alive; and his real or imagined tales of men and women can be unsparing. But in all these there is a certain largeness and nobility in the narrator which he does not seem to have carried about with him day by day.

What the truth was it does not matter now. We have been left with the best of whatever bargain there was. Maybe if we ponder *Far Away and Long Ago* sufficiently we shall find the answer. But that wonderful piece of narration leaves us little volition to think. It sweeps us along. Read it, and the two tales in *El Ombu*, and *A Hind in Richmond Park* (in that order), if you want to know whether Hudson has anything to say to you or not. Or, if you object that these are too substantial to act as mere samplings, there are the thirty-seven *hors d'oeuvres* in *A Traveller in Little Things*. Do not, however, let Hudson's modest dissembling deceive you. He was a traveller in big things also.

THE SHORTER CERVANTES

In the turbulent year of 1640, while the English were beating the Dutch on Long Island, Portugal was revolting against Spain, the Archduke Leopold was driving the Swedes under Field-Marshal Banér into Thuringia, the French were taking Turin, Montrose was occupying Northumberland, and the London apprentices were scandalously and riotously mobbing Archbishop Laud, Master Laurence Blaicklocke, at his shop at the Sugar-Loafe next Temple Bar in Fleet Street, was offering such of his customers as had either time or equanimity left to read a new and most handsome volume.

I had it in my hands at the British Museum the other day. It can be described as a small folio. The title page, elegantly decorated and laid out, announces six tales "full of various accidents both delightfull and Profitable". In the Epistle Dedicatory the worthie Mrs Susanna Strangewayes (and presumably every undecided customer) is promised "matters of harmlesse Merriment, and Disports . . . The Sceane is so often varied, the Passages so pretty, the Accidents so strange, and in the end brought to so happy a Conclusion." The author is declared to be "one of the Prime Wits of Spaine, for his rare Fancies, and wittie Inventions" (not till the second edition 14 years later was he also identified as "the same that wrote *Don Quixot*)".

Thus was launched upon the English reading world Cervantes's *Exemplary Novels*. It is, indeed, one of the most engaging assemblages of short stories ever written. Reading them again recently I was struck by the goodness and serenity lighting them all. There is war, there is violence, there are pirates, there is deception, attempted cuckoldry, and one solitary case of rape. But the translator chose his encomiums justly. It is the delight, and the profit, and the wit that take up permanent residence in the reader's mind. Honour is unscathed, justice is done, true love wins through, virtue prevails. What would even five years in the galleys be, compared with the first subsequent five minutes in Leonisa's arms? Let Leocadia be ravished, shall not she and everyone rejoice when Rodolfo's grand-parents recognize his son, and the couple are married in the end? Did the Duke of Ferrara seem to betray and abandon the Lady Cornelia? It was only to spare her until the time when she should no longer have an unwelcoming mother-in-law. Does the selfish-ness of Queen Bess of England keep Ricardo and his Isabella cruelly long apart? That even her hard heart will turn out to have one or two streaks of at least nine-carat gold.

I have mentioned the translator in passing. But he is worth a steady glance to himself. In the great and noble, but alas very brief, line of England's master translators from Florio and Urquhart and Motteux to Scott-Moncrieff, I would firmly insert James Mabbe. Being a scholar he could not avoid a wretched pun on his name and announced himself to the world as Don Diego Puede-Ser (that is, Maybe), although there is good evidence that he and everyone else pronounced it Mab. But his claim on memory now is fourfold. He was bursar of Magdalen College, Oxford, in six separate years. He wrote some verses in the first folio Shakespeare. He gave us our chance to read the *Exemplary Novels.* He was a master of English prose. This last may not be obvious. Ever since Macaulay (and increasingly of late years) we have given primacy to the single-syllable word and the short sentence. But this came about mainly because the early Victorians (and again increasingly the neo-Georgians) had lost the art of handling the long ones. Yet when they are done by a master how attractive they still can be. All virtuosity is enthralling and the modern reader can find the same fascination in watching Mabbe weave his way (aim unerring, rally sustained, and variations of pace perfect) as Hazlitt did in watching John Cavanagh at fives. Drop in upon him at random; at the moment for instance—and no great moment it is—when Leocadia, misled, as well she might be, by the behaviour of her lover, has stolen away from Don Rafael.

> But scarce had she got into the street but Don Rafael began to miss her, and as if he had lost his soul he inquired after her; but nobody could tell him which way she was gone. And so, without any longer tarrying, like one that was desperate, he went out to seek her, and hied him with all the haste he could thither where he was told that Calvete lodged, lest she might happily have gone thither to procure a mule to ride away; and not finding her there, he went like a madman through the streets, searching after her, one while here, and another while there; and imagining that she might peradventure return back to the galley, he came to the seaside, and a little before he came thither, he might hear one call aloud from the shore for the boat of the captain galley, and he knew that the voice that called for it was that of Leocadia, who, being jealous of some ill intention towards her, hearing one coming behind at her heels, she laid her hand upon her sword, and stood upon her guard until that Don Rafael drew nearer to her; whom she presently knew, and it grieved her to the very heart that he had found her, and more particularly all alone in a place so far from all company; for she had perceived by more shows than one which Don Rafael had made her, that he did not wish her ill, but so well that she would have taken it for a good recompense that Marco Antonio had loved her half so well.

We do not hold our breath. There is no need to do so. Not for a moment are we in any danger of losing our way. There seems no reason why the sentence should not go on for ever. But when the full stop does come we cannot restrain the exultant bravo due to any *tour de force*.

Cervantes wrote twelve "exemplary novels" in all, publishing them together in 1613, between the appearances of the first and second parts of *Don Quixote*. The full course of Mabbe's version I do not know, but it was issued in two neat and handy volumes in 1900, with some illustrations by Frank Brangwyn. It is those volumes one sees from time to time in the second-hand shops today. One set in the Charing Cross Road the other day announced the edition had been limited to 1,500 copies. It does not seem that kind of production. There is nothing *de luxe* about it except its language. But the books are well worth the few shillings generally asked. I have had mine many years, and they have given me endless pleasure. The work is well worth reviving. The six tales omitted from this edition should be translated. The whole would make a most admirable publishing venture which should give Cervantes a new audience, for, let it be confessed, *Don Quixote* is heavy going. Should this some day come about, however, I hope the original six will be left in the words of the incomparable Mabbe.

TRUTHFUL JAMES

Treasure is to be found in the most unexpected places. A friend recently asked me whether I had seen William Roughead's *Tales of the Criminous*, adding that he did so because he knew of my interest in Henry James. I obtained the volume and there, as an appendix to such diversions as "Enjoyment of Murder", "Death in Cuddies Strip", "The Trial of Mary Blandy", and "The Riddle of the Ruthvens", were some 16 pages of "The Letters of Henry James".

That the great novelist and the Scottish historian of crime had corresponded was known. Mr. Percy Lubbock and Mr. Leon Edel have between them published five of the letters. But there were 14 from James to Roughead in all, and Mr. W. N. Roughead, in editing *Tales of the Criminous*, has done a great service by publishing them entire. The origin of the correspondence is disclosed in James's first sentence: "You obeyed too many days ago a very generous impulse in sending me your admirable volume on those strange Scots Trials . . ." But though the first move came from Roughead, the novelist was by no means reluctant to become involved. Oscar Slater, Deacon Brodie, Seddon, the Arran murder, Braxfield, they all interested him. "Mr. Smith's is a very pretty tale, always with your fine light touch and worth re-telling; yet would have been more worth it, one reflects, if he had only been more of a hand at his noble craft." But although there is a hint in a footnote that the letters have a special significance in revealing James's concern with personality rather than with plot, they stayed in my mind for a different reason.

They are in James's most florid style. "I succumbed to your Witchery." "I devoured the tender Blandy in a single feast." "Had I not been long ago supremely enlightened as to editorial ineptitude in general, the illustration of it given me by your news of the *Juridical's* failure to follow the course of its indicated highest interest" (it had temporarily dropped Roughead) "would be more vividly illuminating." "I rest my telescope on your shoulder and am yours all gratefully, Henry James." Now James was 70 when the correspondence began. It trickled through the last three years of his life. He was at the height of his fame and playing back each ball to a younger and obviously lesser man. What led him to write in this manner?

Mr. Leon Edel, than whom there is now, in my belief, no more percipient writer on Henry James, grappled with part of this problem in the introduction to his *Selected Letters of Henry James.* He quotes Harold Laski's general observation to Mr. Justice Holmes, "These letters make me vomit", and he goes on to describe James's "brilliant wall of words", his "elegant banter", his "verbal ambiguity and ironic shadings". James himself spoke of "the mere twaddle of graciousness". Have we here, then, yet another case of "after James the First and James the Second, the Old Pretender"? That can hardly be. James could have damped down the correspondence, indeed have ended it, at any time he wished. Yet he almost drew Roughead on. He clearly was fascinated by the crimes. Unlike so many of his other flowery epistles, these letters ring true.

There the puzzle lay and, so far as I am concerned, would have lain for ever if I had not had the good fortune to go to New England. There I saw in a drugstore a new compilation by Mr. Edel, *The American Essays of Henry James.* It occurred to me it might be a good thing to walk with James on his own home ground. (I have never forgotten the revelation it was to read Browning's Italian poems in Italy; suddenly they all came alive and made sense.) Mr Edel has collected "all of Henry James's essays on American letters together with certain of his miscellaneous writings on American subjects". Their dates of writing range from 1865 to 1915. The span of the subjects is equally large: W. D. Howells, Whitman (no wonder James hung his head in shame about that piece for ever after), Francis Parkman, the unknown Miss Woolson, and the slightly known Wolcott Balestier. But it was "Part One: The New England Voice" that particularly held me. To have James discoursing on Emerson, on Hawthorne, on Charles Eliot Norton, on Lowell, and on "The Correspondence of Carlyle and Emerson", and to be listening to him doing so in Cambridge, Massachusetts, was suddenly to glimpse a new James altogether.

We have become so used to Henry James the expatriate, the traveller from birth, the quasi-European, the man of the world, that we tend to discard his true origins. We know the famous essays on Flaubert, on Zola, on Trollope, on Turgenev. But here is altogether another man and, to my mind, a more sure and genuine one. James was 19 when he went to Harvard, and he lived at the parental home in Cambridge through his last really formative years. It was in that setting he began to write. It was from New England men that he received his first inspiration. Even to-day Cambridge is old-fashioned—age and venerableness seem to cling to much of Harvard in a way they hardly do to Oxford; to walk through parts of it at dusk is to be back in some of the ancient Inns of Court. What it must have been like 90 years ago can, I think, be imagined.

At any rate James's interest in Mr. Roughead's criminal studies—the attraction that every close community feels pulling at it from the horrible but fascinating world outside—his ornate flourishes, his excessive civilities, his euphemisms and euphuisms, all seemed to fall into place; into this place. The septuagenarian was being true to the stripling. There had, indeed, been only one James all through, with his spiritual home in these shades. Maybe all this was only another trick of the dusk. If so, I can only plead, "We have heard the chimes at midnight, Master Shallow." For was I not staying in Quincy Street?

COMMONPLACE BOOKS

Everyone knows what the Personal column of *The Times* meant to Sherlock Holmes; and since his day it has extended its place in English life. But I have always wanted to stake a modest claim for the social significance of To-day's Arrangements. Events such as the annual protest meeting against the contemplated closing down of the Pidlington Magna railway station or Professor Snook's lecture on the effects of atomic fall-out on the laying habits of the lesser-crested ptarmigan may never get reported, but the fact that they have taken place can tell future historians much about our transient troubles and enduring character. At least, so I had always thought. But my faith in the representativeness of To-day's Arrangements wavered when I saw the announcement that someone was to present a "Personal Anthology". For can a personal anthology which is to provide an hour's talk be anything but a commonplace book? And do many people keep commonplace books nowadays?

Not long after, as so often happens, I was in a house where my hostess showed me her commonplace books. They enticed; a neat, elegant little regiment, demure in some kind of linen covering, the right size, thick, dumpy, and of most excellent cream-laid paper. I labour these physical details because I believe that Kipling was right when he placed such loving emphasis on "working-tools". And many years before *Something of Myself* was published, another artist had first thrilled me with the same lesson. Edward Gordon Craig in *Nothing, or The Bookplate* had with great gusto described not only how bookplates should be commissioned, designed, and cut, but even how they should be pasted in. I can still remember the excitement of his injunction—after the book had been laid out (don't forget to discover which is the right end), the little bit of paper had been immersed, the extra-large sheet of blotting paper had been used, exactly the right amount of paste had been applied, and the paper-knife had been thrust under the plate—to throw all caution to the winds and to "Let her go, Mr. Asher." (Only those who went to the Tivoli Music Hall in Mr. Gordon Craig's young days will appreciate the allusion.)

These things *are* important. Commonplace books should have one item on a page. (Only a very rare collocation or contrast is permissible.) Let the page be too large, and the extracts become too long. If the books are not really thick, the collection grows scrappy. Cohesion is lost; too many volumes have to be hunted through. The better the paper on which the extracts are written the greater the physical and even the mental pleasure in transcribing them. I am all against typed extracts in a loose-leaf binder. Personality is lost; what should be a retreat looks more like an office.

Of course that raises the question what use should be made of commonplace books. Some eminent fortunates—Maurice Baring supreme among them—can declare them to the world. But how often do the rest of us go back to our collections? To verify a quotation, perhaps? To share with a friend some remembered piece of wisdom or beauty? To recapture a mood? Then, as often as not, it is the spirit in which we wrote the extract down that most strongly comes back to us, and this can be the best reward of all. For to have read so actively that one was stimulated to copy the passage was to have once been ardent. There are few more grateful recollections in life than that.

Commonplace books might be expected to reveal character. But not at a casual reading. For even the most constant man or woman is a creature of moods. The strongest of immediate reactions can subsequently prove misleading. Of course, if you do not mind repetition and, as Matthew Arnold did in his *Notebooks*, are happy to put the same quotations down again and again, then the result can become important for the biographer or student. But few of us are ever going to be studied, thank goodness.

The ideal commonplace book is the residue of much reading. The jewels and the aphorisms should have been dug out of the solid prose (or verse). If they have been merely picked up because they were already lying about, they can never have the same personal value. We might just as well have set about copying a Book of Quotations.

The essence of a commonplace book, moreover, is that it should not be commonplace. The fringed plot God Wottery can surely be left to the school anthologies. We do not want to strive after novelty, it is true, or to collect for effect. To do so would kill the commonplace book by making it self-conscious. And obviously even the most hackneyed passages will continue to make their impress on each generation. But we shall, in the course of a lifetime, meet most of them in many different places. It is the rarer acquaintances that give greater reward for being enrolled. Here, from a very small corner of the field, are a few I myself have treasured.

The learning of suspended judgment.

Bertrand Russell.

The mark of a truly civilized man is confidence in the strength and security derived from an inquiring mind.

Mr. Justice Frankfurter.

Earnestness of conviction is compatible with a sense of liability to error.

John Morley.

Change is not made without inconvenience, even from worse to better.

Richard Hooker.

Whenever a separation is made between liberty and justice, neither is in my opinion safe.

Edmund Burke.

And, from another corner of the field, there is this wise and consoling piece of observation, whose truth only grows with experience:

It is the crowning virtue of all great art that however little is left of it by the injuries of time, that little will be lovely.

John Ruskin.

Is there any better test of the ideal commonplace book?

THE BETTER MAN

My eye was caught the other day by a headline in a Paris newspaper announcing that this autumn we are to celebrate the centenary of Auguste Comte. I have never had any great interest in the founder of the Religion of Humanity. But for some reason, the origin of which I cannot trace, the men who tussled together in the tail of that strange comet have always had a fascination for me. Lewes, Mill, Herbert Spencer, Huxley, Morley, Leslie Stephen, Frederic Harrison—what grand men they were. Hating shams, intellectually honest, muscular with the pen, they fought lustily for the things they cared about. And though each one of them has been superseded and is in something of a trough to-day, they fought about things that mattered. Then, as Morley said in another context, "for a season, literature was a weapon and an arm, not merely a liberal art."

It is about Morley I want to write to-day—about the man of letters, not the politician. He would have winced at that epithet, have been hurt that the reference was not to the statesman. He would also probably have been surprised at the choice. In the two volumes of *Recollections* he wrote in his eighth decade, he got his literary life more or less out of the way in the first 150 pages. But though there is plenty to fascinate us in the Cabinet Minister, the Irish Secretary (the Foreign Secretary *manqué*), and the Secretary of State for India; though there is much to be disclosed of his strange and contradictory character during these later years; it is the author of the books *On Compromise*, *Burke*, *Cobden*, *Diderot*, *Rousseau*, *Voltaire*, the writer of the studies on Turgot, Robespierre, Condorcet, Vauvenargues, De Maistre, who will live, and to whom we are indebted. As between young John the journalist and "Honest

John" the politician I have no doubt which was the better man.

If appreciation is to be just, it is as well to say at the outset what Morley was not. He was not a first-class literary critic. It is true we owe to him the admirable English Men of Letters series. His collected works include essays on Emerson, Byron, Wordsworth, George Eliot, and *The Ring and the Book*. But our understanding of these writers would not have been less had the essays stayed unwritten. Nor was he a profound or original writer on politics. Two volumes are rather solemnly titled *Oracles on Man and Government* and *Politics and History*. They contain some sound sense. But Morley was no Burke or Bagehot. We must go to his other fields to find what is memorable.

H. A. L. Fisher, speaking of Morley on the centenary of his birth, in 1938, said:

> Morley began life as a free-lance journalist with very little money or backing, and raised himself by character and nobility of soul to a position of great intellectual authority in his generation. His many excellences led him naturally into the field of historical biography. His five English and three French biographies opened up to his fellow-countrymen a wide panorama of helpful and at that time unfamiliar knowledge, which was the more impressive since it was the vehicle of the author's deepest reflections on the problems of life and mind. Some biographies were written to amuse. Morley's were written to edify. Many a young reader of Morley's biographical work has been affected in his whole attitude to life by these well-balanced volumes.

The same is true of his writings around the French Revolution. Yet he remained strangely sensitive for close on thirty years to an attack based on his connexion with this subject. He could *not* forget Goschen. In the heat of the political fray that ebullient opponent, referring to Morley's French studies, called him "the St. Just of our revolution". Looking back on it now dispassionately we can be glad he did so, for it caused Morley to write "A Few Words on French Models", one of the most autobiographical and moving of his essays. Twenty-nine years later, in the *Recollections*, he was still seeking to rebut the charge.

Burke, Austin, Mill, Turgot, Comte—these, Morley declared in 1888, had been his preceptors. In the *Recollections* an old man's memory wanders farther afield. Meredith is the first great figure presented—the sixteen pages are among the best there are about the poet—and tribute is also paid to such influences as Spencer, Huxley, Mazzini, George Sand, Victor Hugo, and Matthew Arnold. Moving in the past or present Morley chose noble company. Dealing with a Rousseau or a Robespierre he can treat them in the same high fashion. Admittedly, his approach is that of Diderot rather than of Carlyle. But passion was not beyond him. And for sentiment one needs only to go to his writings on Mill. There is, too, the tender episode of the week's walking tour on which he took Leslie Stephen after Minny Stephen's death.

In "Memorials of a Man of Letters", reviewing the correspondence of Macvey Napier, who followed Jeffrey in the chair of the *Edinburgh Review*, Morley muses aloud on his own experiences as an editor. His 15 years in charge of the *Fortnightly Review* were, I am sure, the span of his best and most enduring labours. He not only set the arena for some of the best controversial writing in the second half of the nineteenth century; he himself was one of the *Fortnightly*'s most frequent and rewarding-to-read contributors. From 1867 to 1882 periodical-writing enjoyed its last great reign.

Almost exactly midway through the period Morley wrote *On Compromise*. It was his best book, allying him for as long as his fame shall last to Whateley's dictum, "It makes all the difference in the world whether we put Truth in the first place or in the second place." Morley was worthy of that conjunction. So he was of his own words at the end of his life:

> The oracle of to-day drops from his tripod on the morrow. In common lines of human thought and act, as in the business of the elements, winds shift, tides ebb and flow, the boat swings. Only let the anchor hold.

That of the John Morley from 1838 to 1883 has.

THE WICKED LORD

Macaulay's New Zealander, "in the midst of a vast solitude" sketching from a broken arch of London Bridge the ruins of St. Paul's, is now a venerable figure. Everybody has heard of him and since the triumphant survival in the last war of that heart of London he has become perhaps an even greater object of derisive affection. Not so generally well known is the fact that he had a predecessor; and when, in a bookseller's catalogue recently, I came across "*POEMS by A YOUNG NOBLEMAN, of distinguished abilities, lately deceased; particularly THE STATE OF ENGLAND, and the once flourishing City of London, in a LETTER from an AMERICAN TRAVELLER, Dated from the Ruinous Portico of St. Paul's in the Year* 2199, *to A Friend settled in Boston, the Metropolis of the Western Empire: London* 1780," I could not withhold my shillings.

Frankly, the poem is no great shakes. The title is the best thing about it. Lines such as:

> A poor emaciate Briton led me on
> Through streets, and squares, and falling palaces
> (Where here and there a habitant was seen),
> To where stood once amongst the peopled town
> Th' Exchange of London . . .
>
> Now onward we proceed into a field
> O'ergrown with rank and noisome weeds, and here
> The honest Briton wiping from his eye
> The starting tear, in broken sobs of grief,
> And mingled indignation thus exclaim'd—
> "In this unwholesome fen, by the foul toad,
> And eyeless newt inhabited, *once* stood
> The Bank and Treasury of England . . ."

are among the better samples. After more of this kind of stuff, and hazy references to Britain's downfall, some of which have a topical ring,

> "The fall of public credit, that had long
> Tottered upon her airy base, involved
> In sudden and promiscuous ruin all
> The great commercial world . . ."

there is the usual premonitory disturbance of the elements, after which

> Before my astonish'd eyes a phantom stood.

In his right hand the apparition holds a broken spear, in his left a mouldered Magna Carta. He proceeds to deliver himself of historical references more appropriate to the eighteenth than to the twenty-first century, and ends with a rousing exhortation to Britain, America, and Russia to unite.

The joy of all reading is that even third-rate literature is part of the vast web of history and life. Happy the reader who continually finds one thing leading him to another. The author of the poem is nowhere mentioned in the volume, even though he was well known in his lifetime and famous in his death. He was Thomas, Lord Lyttelton, "commonly called"—as the Dictionary of National Biography hastens to say before even mentioning his parentage—"the wicked Lord Lyttelton". Wicked he certainly was, and there is a touching ineffectuality in the prefatory Sketch of the noble Lord's character for which the publisher of my volume "is indebted to a Gentleman, who had been his intimate Companion for many Years, and now mourns his Loss."

> His love of women, it has been said, has led him to seduce and debauch the artless virgin and inexperienced wife, while his passion for play has been attributed to avarice and to poverty. In the pursuit of the one no arts have

been left unattempted to obtain the confidence and affection of the unsuspecting female; in the other it has been asserted that fraud and meanness have both been practised to ensure success.

This is a pretty damning indictment, but most gentlemanfully does the friend stand up to it. The noble lord, he says, was "less cautious in his amours than a more *prudent*, though not a *less guilty* man would be" and he goes on, "without entering into the wide field of ethics," to exclaim that "we may surely venture to affirm that men do not consider themselves obliged to observe the laws of chastity." As for the allegations of sharp practice at gambling, it just was "not possible to practise tricks at the clubs and in the societies which his Lordship frequented". Such things belonged only "to the inferior class of gamblers, pursuing play as a *means of subsistence*".

Skipping all the more exciting details of his life, except perhaps to say in passing that our author would have enjoyed himself hugely in the upper House recently and their Lordships would certainly have heard from him, for he regarded himself as an authority on copyright and made his maiden speech to them on this subject in 1774, we must come to his apotheosis—his last seventy-two hours on earth. On the night of the 24th of November, 1779, Lyttelton, 35, hale, vigorous, and buoyant, dreamed he would be dead in three days. A woman in the form of a bird came to warn him. It was a good joke and he made much of it. (Still, there is evidence that it shook him.) But he went about as usual, the hours slipped by, nothing untoward occurred, he felt as well as ever, and on the evening of November 27, 1779, he got into his nightgown satisfied that he had beaten the banshee. With half an hour to go to midnight he was dead.

In the small circle of "the Town" the effect was not unlike that of the Lisbon earthquake. Here was a portent. You meet references to it everywhere. Mrs. Piozzi records it in full; Mrs. Delany puts it in her autobiography; Boswell relates that five years later Dr. Johnson observed:

"It is the most extraordinary thing that has happened in my day. I heard it with my own ears, from his uncle, Lord Westcote. I am so glad to have every evidence of the spiritual world, that I am willing to believe it."

So it is that in the literature of that time one comes across Thomas, Lord Lyttelton with a frequency that neither his sins nor his speeches nor his writings could have assured. Famous because of a ghost, he is a shadowy figure. Now, for me at any rate, this volume fills him in.

The last word is best left, as so often, with Horace Walpole. He observed that: "It seems a little odd that an apparition should despair of being able to get access to his Lordship's bed in the shape of a young woman, without being forced to use the disguise of a robin-redbreast." It would be odder if Macaulay did not know his poem.

RICHARD YEA AND NAY

I was sorry that the first review I saw of Richard Aldington's *Introduction to Mistral* treated it a trifle sourly. Ever since the days of *Death of a Hero* Aldington has had the power to make some people cross—which is no bad thing—but lately a new note has made itself heard. Both *Pinorman* and *Lawrence of Arabia* aroused bitterness as well as anger. And, as usually happens in such cases, there was a desire to write Aldington off altogether, to make out that he was not only a writer whose opinions did not matter but one whose work had never amounted to anything anyway.

This is a view with which I shall always be ready to quarrel. I have little to say in favour of *Pinorman*, and nothing in defence of the book about Lawrence. But Aldington wrote a book about the other Lawrence which is first-class. *Death of a Hero* was not the first of the books proclaiming the disillusion of the generation which fought the First World War but it was in the vanguard. And a man who has written such other novels as *All Men are Enemies* and *Women Must Work*; whose poems include *A Fool i' the Forest* and *A Dream in the Luxembourg*; who has one of the best single volumes on Voltaire to his credit; and whose other work ranges from *French Studies and Reviews* to translations of *Alcestis* and *Fifty Romance Lyric Poems* cannot be dismissed so easily.

Neither range, nor bulk, nor persistence are, of course, enough to make a writer significant. Even when all three are added together something is still required. My belief is that in some degree Aldington has it. Perhaps the first thing to remark about him is the length of time he has been before the public notice. Although now only sixty-four he was already known as a poet—one of the Imagists—before 1914. He himself has told us that he began *Death of a Hero* almost immediately after the armistice; that is, when he was twenty-six. But, like so many other men who attempted there and then to put down their searing thoughts on all that had happened, he found the effort premature. The manuscript was jettisoned. Then ten years later he began all over again. The one decade of hope we have had in this century was ending. The 1920s have been most maligned. They were a notable, a gay, and a good time. They produced things in literature, music, drama, and life that are not to be despised. But suddenly, as if with some premonition that Hitler and all that he presaged was on the threshold, came the angry hammer blows of protest against both the beastliness of war and the folly of a generation that had let itself drift into war. *Journey's End* was first produced in December, 1928, *All Quiet on the Western Front* in April, 1929, *Death of a Hero* in September, 1929. The spate of war books was soon at the full.

It can be held that among them all Aldington's book was the most bitter so far as "the civilians" were concerned. This was the more surprising in that the ten intervening years had been passed by him in the contemplation of such literary figures as Ronsard, Proust, Rémy de Gourmont, Saint-Evremond, Eliot, Joyce, Landor, and others. He was also writing poetry. There was, however, the hope that *Death of a Hero* was a kind of catharsis. *Roads to Glory*, *The Colonel's Daughter*, *All Men are Enemies* seemed to confirm it. Anger there still was but it had not quite the same bitter edge. The story of Tony and Katha in *All Men are Enemies* had scenes of great tenderness and beauty. It looked as if a new Aldington was emerging and would develop. *Women Must Work* did not carry the process noticeably further, but it seemed to mark time. That was in 1934. In 1935 came the essays *Artifex* and the long poem *Life Quest*.

One must at this point go back, again ten years, to another poem, *A Fool i' the Forest*, published in 1925. Here Aldington presented the modern man, one who is still "by temperament more fitted for an art than a scientific civilization". He showed him poised between Mezzetin, symbolizing the imaginative faculties, and the Conjuror, who is science and intellect. He took a position:

Praise and a crown of glory to the race
Which first shall say: "We have enough
Bread, olives, meat, a little wine,
Rough wool dyed purple for our robes;
Now let us live as men.

A Fool i' the Forest was a turning point in Aldington's development as a writer. Increasingly he proclaimed the idea that an art impulse exists in all men, has been recognized in all preceding generations, but denied in our industrial civilization with grave results. He returned to it in the main essay in *Artifex*, taking as his starting point the cave drawings in Altamira. He was more urgent in *Life Quest*.

But men and women
Before it is too late
Will you not draw back from greed and destruction
Ere the earth becomes a cruel desert
And the sea a sterile pollution
And the sun black with anger against you?

And, declaring that "in myself I feel exquisitely alive", asking only that "my life quest go on until I die", he proclaimed:

But there is a deep and delicate life
If you can seek in patience
For the moment, and let it come to you
From Sun, Earth and Sea.

Aldington seemed to be reaching towards a new world, or at least an old world re-born. We confidently looked forward to a more satisfied, less frustrated stage.

Then something happened. Maybe its culmination was the shattering blow of the Second World War. But whatever it was had set in before that. Neither *Very Heaven* (1937) nor *Seven Against Reeves* (1938) were major works. And since then, to my mind at least, there is nothing to put against his best. But that best is good. My admiration of it and gratefulness to Richard Aldington for it remain. He has a firm place among the writers of the inter-war years. His message was less striking and less dynamic than D. H. Lawrence's but it was healthier. He pioneered the work of other writers, both English and French, as a generous and perceptive critic. He has two novels (*Death of a Hero* and *All Men are Enemies*), two books of poems (*A Dream in the Luxembourg* and *Life Quest*), and two biographies (*Voltaire* and *Portrait of a Genius, But*...) that will stand. It is to them we must look if we wish to get Aldington's true measure.

REVOLUTIONARY

The war of numbers between Napoleon and the French Revolution never ends. In my own case, the man, at the moment, comfortably outdistances the movement. I do not think this is altogether due to predilection. The full Napoleonic bibliography would make almost a small library in itself. And what a diversity of writers have been attracted to Bonaparte, from Walter Scott and Hazlitt to Holland Rose, Bainville, Rosebery, and Belloc, not forgetting A. G. Macdonell, who in *Napoleon and his Marshals* wrote one of the most entrancing books of them all.

But after a time a certain feeling of sameness creeps in. However many ways there may be of writing tribal lays, the variations on the saga of 1793–1815 are not infinite. Also, as we get older we return to the passions and the enthusiasms of our youth. Once again the French Revolution becomes so many-faceted as to seem inexhaustible. Stirring, mysterious, ennobling, heartrending; how much there is about it that we find we do not know. Here is a subject that need never flag and, taken in judicious spells, really will see us through our days.

An attempt to make any survey of the books about the French Revolution in the course of an article is only to be paralleled by the young person who asked Proust if he would epitomize *A la Recherche du Temps Perdu* in a couple of sentences. No one can have read them all. Figuratively speaking, I know only a handful of them. Nevertheless, it is warming to look along the shelves and to recall old pleasures. At one end of the scale there is Albert Sorel's *L'Europe et la révolution française*. Although it once absorbed me for a long and memorable period I mention it only as an act of piety; a Grand National of a book, hardly for the ordinary reader. At the other end, there are the host of volumes on Marie Antoinette, the Du Barry, Charlotte Corday, and all the various figures who lend themselves to large type, handsome plates, and a suitable amount of sentiment.

What of the volumes in between? Many young people come to Burke, pay all too little attention to the words *Reflections on* in his title, and are disappointed. To my mind, if you want the issues as seen through English eyes a better book to begin with is Alfred Cobban's *The Debate on the French Revolution* in "The British Political Tradition" series. But, of course, most people are after the story. The first thing is to get a firm hold of the outlines. For these there may by now be something better than Louis Madelin's *The French Revolution* in the National History of France, but I do not know it. There is, too, of course, Hilaire Belloc's *The French Revolution* in the Home University Library. But I prefer Madelin. Indeed, I am heretical enough to believe that, so far as writing on the French Revolution is concerned, Belloc has been surpassed by his *fidus Achates*. If you wish to follow one readable, modern writer on the subject, I wholeheartedly recommend J. B. Morton. As a test of his quality read the chapter on the death of the Dauphin (*The Dauphin*, ch. viii, pp. 175–199). There was once a day when I could recite its closing pages by heart. (As Conrad said: "Oh youth! Pass the bottle." Well, comparative youth, anyway.)

Morton sees the French Revolution largely as a series of dramatic or character studies. His two volumes *The Bastille Falls* and *Camille Desmoulins* are both of this nature. A writer who has quarried the period even more extensively, possibly more thoroughly than any-one else, is G. Lenotre (the pen name of the historian, Gosselin). His volumes on the by-ways of the Revolution are legion. As readable as any are the five volumes of *Vieilles Maisons, Vieux Papiers*. (One occasionally comes across second-hand copies of *Episodes of the French Revolution in Brittany* by him in the old Nelson series.) Many of Lenotre's pieces are slight, some almost trivial, but he does build up a remarkable picture of revolutionary Paris. So did the American,

Gouverneur Morris, who was Minister to France during the Terror. Morris's *Diary of the French Revolution*, edited by Beatrix Davenport, was published in England in two handsome volumes just before the last war, and is a vivid day-to-day record by a foreign eyewitness. A book of altogether another order, fiction this time, but which remains in my memory after many years as a powerful and vivid piece of reconstruction is the novel *The Ninth Thermidor* by the Russian, Aldanov. I would dare to put the scene in which the young hero, Staal, cannot keep awake during the famous sitting of the Convention when Robespierre unsuccessfully fights for his life alongside the famous battle of Waterloo chapter in *La Chartreuse de Parme*.

The reader may ask how he can have been brought so far without a word about Carlyle. Badly overdue, indeed, is the sage of Chelsea's coming into his own. Both as a writer and as a philosopher he has been out of favour for a long time now; most of his 30 volumes stay unread. But in *The French Revolution* he cannot be denied. Modern scholarship may have detected some inaccuracies here and there. They do not matter. This may be history seen in lightning flashes; how else match the grandeur of a cataclysm? Time has left Carlyle's masterpiece unapproached and unimpaired; as G. M. Trevelyan said, a "flame-picture of what was in very fact a conflagration". It is one of the most dramatic stories ever told; a great prose poem for all time; and still the book on the French Revolution that outclasses all the rest.

GEORGE DARLEY

Artistic genius is the urge for self-expression. This has been dissected and romanticized, admired and deplored many times. It is also the desire to be remembered. This has never been given half as much prominence. Yet sometimes may it not be the greater force of the two? Clearly a wish for lasting fame is not enough in itself. Otherwise even the approaches to Valhalla would be much more crammed than they are. There must be gifts behind it. But if those gifts are there, it is difficult to disentangle a man's motives in composing, or painting, or writing. Even a writer with so austere an integrity as Joseph Conrad could be found stepping aside to wonder aloud how Posterity would look at him.

The urge being so great, it becomes a nice point whether an author would prefer to be remembered even for the wrong reason rather than not to be remembered at all. False fame or oblivion? It is no easy choice. On the one hand, vicarious appreciation, or appreciation of irrelevant qualities, must be a constant turning of the knife in the wound done to self-expression. On the other, if only memory can be kept alive at all, does there not remain the chance that some day re-examination will lead to re-appraisal, and that appreciation will then be accorded justly?

This question has been in my mind many times during the past 12 months, the outcome of a nagging half-suspicion that when I wrote about Meredith's *Love in the Valley* I did less than justice to George Darley. His incoherent, reproachful image seemed to dog me, until I banished it by making a fairly constant companion of his poems. Poor Darley, he deserved at least this much justice. Minor misfortunes can make those who have pretensions to fame look merely ridiculous. But when they are multiplied to the extent they were in Darley's case they assume the proportions of tragedy. One can ignore the fact that a man of wit, bonhomie, and conviviality, born for society, should have had a stammer so extreme that he was forced to become a recluse. It can, as I have indicated, have been a good, as much as a bad, thing for him that he is now mainly remembered because the metre of *Love in the Valley* is reputed to have come from his *Serenade of a Loyal Martyr*. But, according to R. A. Streatfeild, who did noble work in trying to revive interest in Darley 60 years ago, his most popular song "I've been roaming" was for years included in Hatton's *Songs of England* as the work of George Soane, while Palgrave printed "It is not beauty I demand" in the *Golden Treasury* as a genuine Cavalier song and promptly took it out of the later editions when he found that Darley had written it. The shade of Darley, who was born in Dublin, may well believe the bad fairies have always been at him.

But how stands the real reckoning? Was he a true poet or not? Does he deserve to last in his own right? Here Meredith should help him. For those who care about poetry intrinsically, and are not deafened by the clamours of renown, it can be only to Darley's advantage that their first contact with him should be *Serenade of a Loyal Martyr*. It is a short poem, little known compared with its mighty successor, and well worth printing in full.

> Sweet in her green cell the Flower of Beauty slumbers,
> Lulled by the faint breezes sighing thro' her hair;
> Sleeps she, and hears not the melancholy numbers
> Breathed to my sad lute amid the lonely air?
>
> Down from the high cliffs the rivulet is teeming,
> To wind round the willow banks that lure him from above:
> O that in tears from my rocky prison streaming,
> I too could glide to the bower of my love!
>
> Ah! where the woodbines with sleepy arms have wound her,
> Opes she her eyelids at the dream of my lay,
> Listening like the dove, while the fountains echo round her,
> To her lost mate's call in the forests far away?

Come then, my Bird!—for the peace thou ever bearest,
Still heaven's messenger of comfort to me,
Come!—this fond bosom, my faithfullest, my fairest!
Bleeds with its death-wound, but deeper yet for thee.

A year of living with that, having got it by heart, has made me see its own beauties more and more. But the most assiduous devotion to his supposed *magnum opus*, *Nepenthe*, reveals no beauties at all. Such lines as

I crept me to a promontory
Where it had fallen from earth's top storey

and

My burning soul one drop did quaff—
Heaven reeled and gave a thunder laugh!

make the reader reel also, in despair. And lest it be said Darley was one of those, superbly good in short lyrics, who just could not do the "big bow-wow stuff", one has to disclose such a lamentable *gaffe* as this:

But now, alas! that Love is old,
Beauty may e'en lay down her lute,
His wings are stiff, his heart is cold,
He will not come and warble to 't.

The truth is, I think, that Darley was the most uneven of poets, and his best just missed that vital magic to carry him and the rest of his work along. Yet he had *something*. It is 111 years since he died; he is still a name; there have been three efforts to revive him. I doubt if any future one is likely to have better luck than its predecessors. But the anthologists should never come to neglect him entirely. Let the last quotation put on these small scales be one of his most exquisite things:

I sat with one I love last night,
She sang to me an olden strain;
In former times it woke delight,
Last night—but pain.

Last night we saw the stars arise,
But clouds soon dimm'd the ether blue:
And when we sought each other's eyes
Tear dimm'd them too!

We paced alone our fav'rite walk
But paced in silence broken-hearted:
Of old we used to smile and talk.
Last night—we parted.

Darley's friends during his lifetime said there had been rare moments of intense feeling when, intimately, he had suddenly lost all his disabilities. That, too, can be the claim of his friends after death.

MASONRY

For some years I read a detective novel every week. It was in what I still regard as the heyday of the detective story, when such masters as Connington, Christie, Sayers, Berkeley, and Rhode were all putting forth their conundrums more or less together. And every now and again one would also come across some authentic thriller such as Dan Billany's *The Opera House Murders* or, from the past, Israel Zangwill's *The Big Bow Mystery*.

One result was that in due course I had long shelves given over to the crime department. The time came, alas—as it always must in the case of expanding collections of books and unexpanding homes—when something had to go. At such anguished moments two courses are possible. Either one can pick volumes here and there for the sacrifice, some bad poetry, indifferent history, and the weakest of the novels—in which case one invariably wants the volumes later and laments the day of folly when they were jettisoned—or, draconically, a whole section can be removed. I chose the latter. Crime had to go.

Searching around for a suitable recipient we thought of the boys' school house library. So we bundled the books into sacks, loaded them into the car, and went off feeling not unlike Father Christmas. We were, quite frankly, rather dashed when the house librarian, with the aloof imperturbability which at the age of 15 one has to well-meaning but misguided adults, accepted the sacks without any sign of enthusiasm, albeit politely—and we thought it could only be politeness which prevented his opening them. Every bit of self-satisfaction had oozed away by the time we reached home again. However, all was well a few days later when there arrived an ecstatic letter, thanking us for our "magnificent gift" and adding:

"It has not escaped our notice that all the books are detective stories, a branch of English literature in which the house library has hitherto been very deficient."

Now although one can absorb more crime and detection than probably any other kind of reading matter without becoming surfeited, the point does come, even in its case, where satiety is reached. I had far passed the graduate stage of being able to spot the murderer in the opening pages; the Honours course was to detect the victim. Since then the detective novel has branched out and out. A whole younger generation of writers has arisen. I know them not. The great stream of poison, rain of bullets, swish of blunt instruments, and gentle rustle of nocturnal pushings overboard passes me by.

There is one exception, however. I do not try to resist the lures of Mr. Erle Stanley Gardner. And because it is obvious I am not alone in this I have been pondering the reason. What is Mr. Gardner's secret? He is no supreme practitioner, o'ertopping all the rest. Lures his titles certainly are: *The Case of the Stuttering Bishop*, *The Case of the Borrowed Brunette*, *The Case of the Sleepwalker's Niece*, *The Case of the Lame Canary*, *The Case of the Drowsy Mosquito*, *The Case of the Drowning Duck*. His invention seems to be endless. Each new title makes us curious. How can *it* possibly be relevant? Mr. Gardner's second strong point is that it always is. Ingenuity is perhaps his greatest gift. Yet complicated as his plots are they are never impossible. And his language is never complicated. He has a plain business-like style that proclaims "No nonsense." Often even the dialogue—and there is plenty of it—is action. He briskly bustles the reader along. But while he wastes no time on literary graces, he never forgets the machinery of living. Arnold Bennett once damned a detective story because no one in it ever seemed to have a meal. Mr. Gardner's characters are human. They get hungry; they eat; they become tired; they shave; they have Turkish baths. One of the most attractive things about Perry Mason, Mr. Gardner's attorney-detective, is what a Turkish bath can do for him. Della Street, his secretary-heroine, can even write shorthand.

Skilful deployment of the law is another of Mr. Gardner's arts. It is Perry Mason's real battleground. (An Erle Stanley Gardner novel without a courtroom scene would be like a Rachmaninov recital without the C sharp minor Prelude.) Of course, it is American law. It is strange. Yet we are made to believe we understand it. Nor are we spared the arcana. A judicious sprinkling of *corpus delicti* and other highly technical phrases gives us a seat beside the judge. We join in his pleasure when once again Hamilton Burger, the rather uncouth District Attorney, gets the worse of the encounter with the learned and astute Perry Mason.

Perry Mason, Hamilton Burger, Della Street, Paul Drake, Lieutenant Tragg—these are the heart of Mr. Gardner's strange attraction. The constants in every new Gardner variation, they are boldly drawn, in few strong, simple outlines. Every one always runs true to form. *They* are no mysteries. The murderers, the victims, the complicating characters, the onlookers come, do their little charades, and go. (Charades they are, for while there is violence there is no evil. They hold our attention but engage no emotions.) The old guard of known quantities remains. They say the same things, react in the same way, perform the same actions. In a world whose whole essence is that it should be bizarre and strange, they are the most ordinary, homely folk. Confronted by abnormality they refuse to be anything but normal. Unchanged by time or circumstance, living in a kind of eternal Californian spring, they meet every hazard and go on to their next rendezvous. Long may they do so. For is there not waiting for them just round the corner "The Case of the —— ——"? I wonder what it will be next.

THE OTHER LANGUAGE

It is a joy to see Miss Rebecca West's new novel so generally praised. Virtuosity can still overcome the natural atrabiliousness of critics. But virtuosity is, in its true sense, no more than skill in the mechanical part of a fine art, and there is, to my mind, one quality of *The Fountain Overflows* in which Miss West has gone far beyond this. It is the way in which she has portrayed the musical daemon, or genius. Obviously many writers have felt it in the past; they have failed when they sought to convey it. Henry Handel Richardson could, in our own day, and so can Richard Church. But even they have never attempted so major and so sustained a presentation as Claire Aubrey and her family. Miss West's daring is superb. Had she failed, not merely to carry conviction of their musical genius, but also to make us enter into it and feel we understand it, the fountain, far from overflowing, would not have played at all.

We have been given many credible artistic temperaments in fiction and a few convincing geniuses. But in this matter music seems to stand rather apart from the other arts. Neither Proust nor Romain Rolland pulled it off, and not all the words yet written have managed to give us a Beethoven as true as even his Fourth Symphony. Words, perhaps, are at the root of the matter. Most arts can be sensed and discussed in more or less everyday terms. Music really is another language. This baffled me and frustrated me in my youth. How eagerly one went from book to book seeking to have this or that work *explained*. Always one was disappointed. I remember quite early coming across Barbellion's description in *The Journal of a Disappointed Man* of the images Beethoven's Fifth Symphony conjured up for him. The whole entry seemed gibberish. Death sentence, wounded bird, pale youth, greyhound and thrush

. . . clearly I would never have any musical sensibility for I could not even begin to discern the faintest glimmer of any of these things. To my great good fortune I very soon afterwards came across another subjective interpretation of the same work. No two things could have been more different. Mr. Priestley did much better with Brahms's First Symphony in *Angel Pavement*, but that was description rather than interpretation.

Almost simultaneously Aldous Huxley settled the matter, for me at any rate, once for all:

> Music "says" things about the world, but in specifically musical terms. Any attempt to reproduce these musical statements "in our own words" is necessarily doomed to failure. We cannot isolate the truth contained in a piece of music; for it is a beauty-truth and inseparable from its partner. The best we can do is to indicate in the most general terms the nature of the musical beauty-truth under consideration and to refer curious truth-seekers to the original. Thus, the introduction to the *Benedictus* in the *Missa Solemnis* is a statement about the blessedness that is at the heart of things. But this is about as far as "own words" will take us. If we were to start describing in our "own words" exactly what Beethoven felt about this blessedness, how he conceived it, what he thought its nature to be, we should very soon find ourselves writing lyrical nonsense in the style of the analytical programme makers. Only music, and only Beethoven's music, and only this particular music of Beethoven, can tell us with any precision what Beethoven's conception of the blessedness at the heart of things actually was.

Because of that passage, and the reassurance it brought to me, *Music at Night* has always been my favourite among the Huxley volumes.

Only music can tell us. And did not Sir Walford Davies open one of his books with the terse statement "Music is a sensible and reasonable pursuit"? I have the book *The Pursuit of Music* with me still, and I have to confess I do not understand it. Still, it is the least of the impedimenta I owe to Sir Walford Davies. For in those halcyon days when he talked on music for the B.B.C., just before the lunch hour on Sundays, as nobody had ever talked about music before or has done since, I came to listen to him regularly. He told us to be not only listeners but doers. I bought his book. He told us that to read it without any attempt to hear the musical illustrations given would be almost useless. I bought a baby grand piano. He made us eager to be picking out these themes and motives ourselves. I started to do it. But, alas, I had to come to the conclusion that after a certain age it is no longer possible to teach the right hand and the left hand to do different things at the same time. The brain, or whatever controls such actions, is set. So the piano and the book have remained as monuments of a double failure. The piano has stayed unplayed, the illustrations have stayed unheard, large stretches of the book have stayed unread.

All this without sense of loss, however. The will to listen remained. It came to be sufficient in itself. The mark of the Philistine is supposed to be "I know what I like", yet one can trace through the years how liking has deepened or lessened, what kind of works have not stayed the course, the power of the greatest composers to go on *compelling*, even if one never attains the slightest idea of what they are trying to say or to mean. They have their moods and their timbres—no one else can make quite the same kind of noise as Beethoven or Sibelius—just as the great painters have their individual palettes (only the composers are more constant). That is enough. One even dares to ask whether—to go back to Huxley—"in our own words" they are saying or meaning anything. Why should they? Theirs is another language and it is waste of time to look for a Rosetta stone.

Not that I would decry books about music. They have their uses. They are excellent exercises in enthusiasm. They tell us about the tools, the mechanics, the mathematics, the mobilities of music. Music itself stays secret, in its hiding places of the heart and mind, unrevealed by them, and untouched. So when we come across a book like Miss West's that for a few brief seconds seems to twitch aside the veil of the mystery we are excited passing comprehension.

She tells us implicitly what all the programme notes ever written have failed to tell us explicitly. Groping, even though not understanding, it is with a grateful warmth we switch on the gramophone again.

LITTLE-TONEY

The Devil, as General Booth said, should not have all the best tunes. Ever since I wrote about the wicked Lord Lyttelton, the gambler and rake, whose death after seeing an apparition made him famous, the sad story of his earnest, assiduous, and strangely ill-treated father has asked to be told. He tried so hard to be so many things, and was buffeted in all of them. Statesman, man of the world, philosopher, poet, he is mainly known for the rude things famous writers said about him in each of these roles. Horace Walpole made fun of him as the Chancellor of the Exchequer who did not know what he was talking about. Lord Chesterfield cited him as a horrible example in deportment and manners. Smollett put an unkind caricature of him in *Peregrine Pickle*, and Dr. Johnson was decidedly cool in his study of him in *Lives of the Poets*.

Yet he *was* "the good Lord Lyttelton" and so came to be known. Pope did not despise the complimentary verses George Lyttelton sent from Rome. Thomson gratefully wrote of him as one

> of sense refined,
> Who felt each worth, for every worth he had;
> Serene yet warm, humane yet firm his mind,
> As little touch'd as any man's with bad.

And he was immortalized by Fielding, who said of him in the dedication to *Tom Jones*, "To you, Sir, it is owing that this history was ever begun." Lastly there is the tribute of the devastatingly learned and highly moral Mrs. Elizabeth Carter. When Lord Lyttelton died she consoled Mrs. Vesey.

> Endeavour to raise your spirits from the melancholy chambers of the grave, to those glad regions of immortality and happiness, where I trust our

excellent friend is rejoicing in his escape from the sufferings of a probationary life. It would be selfish to wish him back to a world where his trials derived their most painful acuteness from the sensibility of his virtue.

George, Lord Lyttelton, has, in fact, had the worst of both worlds. Distressing as were such adversities as the wickedness of his son and the unkindness of his contemporaries, the scales have continued to be weighted against him since. *The Castle of Indolence*, in which Thomson extolled his virtues, is hardly a popular poem. Even the most enthusiastic devotees of *Tom Jones* cannot tell you whether it has a dedication or not. And I doubt if the *Memoirs of the Life of Mrs. Elizabeth Carter, with a new edition of her Poems; to which are added some Miscellaneous Essays in Prose, together with her Notes on the Bible, and Answers to Objections concerning the Christian Religion* has any readers at all.

No. It is only in one mighty penumbra that Lord Lyttelton is nowadays found. No reader of Boswell's *Life of Johnson* can fail to be aware of him. And thanks to the ever-to-be-enjoyed efforts of Birkbeck Hill and Powell we now know even more. On hearing of Lyttelton's end Dr. Johnson wrote to Mrs. Thrale from Auchinleck that he suspected that it had been hastened by the vexation which his son had given him. Yet, paradoxically, it was the death of that son, the rake and profligate, which inspired Johnson with pious thoughts, while mention of the father as often as not threw him into a temper. Readers of Fanny Burney's *Diary* will remember the violent passion he got into with Mr. Pepys on the subject. Even the youthful and admiring Fanny thought that "this great but *mortal* man, to own the truth, appear(ed) unreasonably furious and grossly severe." Moreover, he was unjust. At one point he called out "The more my Lord Lyttelton is inquired after, the worse he will appear." And on and on he went, the evening becoming more and more unpleasant, till in the end Mrs. Thrale put her foot down.

The cause of the trouble was Dr. Johnson's *Life of Lyttelton*, which had offended Mrs. Montague and what Fanny Burney described as "a whole tribe of blues". Johnson had not particularly wanted to write it. "My desire is to avoid offence, and to be totally out of danger." But when he did so, he did not spare his subject. On both man and works he was severe. Then what Fanny Burney herself calls "the hostilities" commenced.

The strangest thing about the whole business—if Mrs. Thrale is to be believed—is that the real cause of Johnson's dislike was the fact that the grave Miss Hill Boothby had shown more favours to Lyttelton than to him. In her *Anecdotes of the late Samuel Johnson*—Mr. S. C. Roberts edited a comely edition of it for the Cambridge University Press some thirty years ago—she quotes Johnson as telling her that

> Lord Lyttelton and he used to strive for her preference with an emulation that occasioned hourly disgust, and ended in lasting animosity. "You may see (said he to me when the Poets Lives were printed) that dear B—thby is at my heart still. She *would* delight in that fellow Lyttelton's company though, for all I could do; and I cannot forgive even his memory the preference given by a mind like her's."

Poor Lyttelton! Posterity has tried to diminish even this triumph. For Abraham Hayward in his edition of the *Autobiography and Letters of Mrs. Piozzi* acidly commented "In point of personal advantages the man of rank and fashion and the scholar were almost on a par", and revived the cruel lines on Lyttelton of 120 years earlier:

> Who's dat who ride astride de Poney,
> So long, so lank, so lean, and bony,
> O he be de great Orator Little-Toney.

I see the volumes of his collected works on my shelves—the *Poems*, the *Speeches*, the *Life of Cicero*, the *Observations on the Conversion of St. Paul*, the *Dialogues of the Dead*, the *Persian Letters*—reproaching me that I have not said more about them, for they have given me pleasure in their time. I open one of them. Lyttelton is sternly lecturing the Government through "A Letter to a Member of Parliament".

> We shall judge all your other virtues now by your frugality.

To-day more than ever that is no bad epitaph for an ex-Chancellor of the Exchequer.

SI MONUMENTUM . . .

First editions have never interested me. For one thing, the cult—or, more important, the market—has become so esoteric that I long ago lost all confidence in my ability to say what is a first edition or not. Even if I had that ability, the whole business is so subject to fashion and lacking in intrinsic values that it is impossible to know whether one's money has been well or foolishly spent. More important still, I have never been able to see that any particular virtue attaches to a volume because it happened to come off the press in the first run rather than in the second.

Association copies are another matter. There surely is a thrill in possessing and handling a book which was once in far greater hands. There is endless interest in trying to trace how the association came about, what were the circumstances that led to the volume being given; why a Flaubert should have been moved to send a signed copy of *Madame Bovary* to Nadar "avec une forte poignée de main". Because a friend some years ago gave me Christina Rossetti's copy of *My Beautiful Lady* inscribed "from the author. April, 1864", I daily pass John Stuart Mill's statue in Embankment Gardens with an active awareness, can look at it for possibly the 5,001st time with an intimate personal eye.

For a man whose works are all around us, Thomas Woolner, the creator of both, is little known. Palmerston (now next door to Smuts) in Parliament Square, Tennyson, Keble, and Cobden in Westminster Abbey, Macaulay in marble at Trinity College, Cambridge, are all his. So was Gladstone in Guildhall until a German bomb destroyed it. So are many other effigies, not only in the United Kingdom, but in Australia and other parts of the Commonwealth. He was, perhaps, the favourite portrait sculptor of the eminent Victorians. Darwin, Kingsley, Wordsworth, Browning, Newman, Carlyle, Clough, Coventry Patmore, Disraeli, the Prince Consort, and the Queen herself all sat for him. And added to the thousands who have seen his marbles or bronzes and have never realized he existed, there are the hundreds of thousands who must have many times glanced at the frontispiece to Palgrave's *Golden Treasury* without knowing this was his work also.

But it is Woolner the poet and friend of poets who has become interesting to me. To read *Pygmalion*, *Silenus*, and *Tiresias* is to be struck by their conscious craft and honesty. They are now dead, but they once had life. "Equally with his more concrete creations in marble," wrote *The Times*, reviewing one of them on its first appearance, "the verse is evidently the outcome of a highly organized and sensitive mind." Richard Garnett said: "Woolner's poetry is that of a sculptor; he works, as it were, by little chipping strokes." Garnett also spoke of his "effects highly truthful and original, though scarcely to be termed captivating or inspiring".

This is fair enough, but *My Beautiful Lady*, at any rate, is better than this. For one thing, most of it is in rhyme, giving an effect of grace in the place of his blank verse's sinew. For another, the subject and the tone are intimate and personal. The tale is appropriately pre-Raphaelitish, for Woolner was one of the early members of the Brotherhood. The lady is encountered, is fallen in love with, languishes, dies. The lover is in despair. She speaks to him from Heaven. Ten years later he revisits her tomb and muses. But, in fact, the story is little. It is the mood that counts. And while Woolner is no Tennyson or Rossetti, he rings true. Genuine sentiments bridge the century gap in our feelings and habits, not rant. The verse is pleasantly varied, moving from rhapsody to elegy and on to near-epic; the diction is not too highly mannered. A lesser work, undoubtedly, but a true work none the less.

It could hardly be other, for Woolner, in poverty and prosperity, was all of a piece and a sterling character. A child prodigy, he was in a sculptor's studio at the age of twelve, exhibited his first work five years later, joined the pre-Raphaelites, emigrated to Australia in despair at his lack of success, and returned, still disappointed, after two years. By this time he was in his thirtieth year and thereafter the rest of his life story was twenty-eight years of commissions, hard work, fame, and friendship. Above all, friendship. Woolner seems to have been one of those rare souls, a successful artist with more friends than enemies. His daughter belatedly produced a "life in letters" of him in 1917 and although much of it is humdrum it is one of the pleasanter of the Victorian sagas. His friendships, moreover, have their place in literature. He gave Tennyson the stories of *Enoch Arden* and *Aylmer's Field.* And in art, also. Ford Madox Brown's painting "The Last of England" was inspired by seeing Woolner off as an emigrant.

To look at the portrait of Woolner in middle age, with his serene brow, his candid eyes, his mane of hair, and his still-schoolboyish face under a positively massive beard, is to understand his influence. And that he was loved in humbler circles is shown by a delightful picnic photograph of "The sculptor among his men". Best of all, I like the story of Carlyle and Woolner visiting Dickens at interval-time during one of the famous readings. Carlyle was full of praises and toasted Dickens in brandy: "Charley, you carry a whole company of actors under your hat." But Woolner's reaction was to be "filled with doleful forebodings as to the effect of these readings upon the writer's health".

Should you ever see *My Beautiful Lady* in the twopenny box it is worth reading. But I hope it will not prove to be Christina Rossetti's copy.

CARRIED AWAY

Somebody should write a history of emotion as a social habit. Why is it people will weep easily in one generation, be reserved in another, and be continually losing consciousness in a third? As we read of those Georgian and Victorian heroines who were so constantly swooning at the slightest shock or setback, who had to take a firm grip of the nearest chair and themselves if some *faux pas* was not to carry them away, we cannot help wondering what kind of people they were. Nor was it only the ladies who were thus out of control. Sir George Trevelyan in his *Life and Letters of Lord Macaulay* tells us how Macaulay made on the last page of Mrs. Cuthbertson's *San Sebastiano* "an elaborate computation of fainting fits that occur in the five volumes". They are

Julia de Clifford	11
Lady Delamore	4
Lady Theodosia	4
Lord Glenbrook	2
Lord Delamore	2
Lady Earderfield	1
Lord Ashgrove	1
Lord St. Orville	1
Henry Mildmay	1

Lord St. Orville's solo was particularly wholehearted and dramatic.

> One of the sweetest smiles that ever animated the face of mortal now diffused itself over the countenance of Lord St. Orville, as he fell at the feet of Julia in a death-like swoon.

Sensibility was largely an eighteenth-century innovation. The word itself was not, according to the Oxford English Dictionary, used before 1751 in this particular sense. We must, I suppose, regard it as yet one more manifestation of the power and influence of Jean-Jacques. Given the preceding temper and harshness of the age the fact that Rousseauism spread itself far and wide is not, perhaps, surprising. It is the speed with which it did so that is remarkable. When, for instance, Henry Mackenzie's *A Man of Feeling* was first published in 1771 it was at once, in the public mind, affiliated to *La Nouvelle Héloïse*. Fifteen years may seem a long time for one work to inspire another, but it is not sources we are dealing with but a whole mood of society in two countries separated by the Channel. I should, of course, write Society. Sensibility at once became and largely remained strictly a matter of class. While a feather was enough to knock Lady Angela time and again off her emotional perch Mary Barton naturally was expected to stand up to the sledge-hammer of Fate bloody but unbowed.

There was more to it, however, than Rousseau and race. Not accidentally or fortuitously did sensibility reach its apogee in the Victorian age. There is a passage in G. M. Young's *Victorian England: Portrait of an Age* describing how

> Once at Bowood, when Tom Moore was singing, one by one the audience slipped away in sobs; finally, the poet himself broke down and bolted, and the old Marquis was left alone. We are in an age when, if brides sometimes swooned at the altar, Ministers sometimes wept at the Table; when the sight of an infant school could reduce a civil servant to a passion of tears . . .

Mr. Young—he has never been sufficiently praised—sees the early Victorian mind "anchored to its twofold faith in goodness and progress . . . Poised and convinced, they could indulge, too, in a licence of feeling impossible to a generation bred in doubt." If that is so, no one can wonder that in these days people of feeling seem to think it embarrassing, and therefore unmannerly, if any emotion is shown at all.

Sensibility is, of course, one of the signs of artistic temperament. It would be fun to know what Dr. Johnson would have retorted if anyone had told him he had one. Yet he, too, could break down in public and Augustine Birrell has told us how, whenever he recited his own poem *The Vanity of Human Wishes*, he usually had to give up when he came to the lines beginning

> Proceed, illustrious youth,
> And virtue guard thee to the throne of truth!

I have read that on the first two occasions Rossetti heard the third stanza of *Love in the Valley* he swooned. So did Musset once at the theatre. And did not Tchaikovsky have the exquisite satisfaction of seeing Tolstoy weep during the playing of the Andante in his Quartet in D major? Among the figures of our own day, too, there can come the most surprising revelations. I was pulled up short recently when reading Bertrand Russell's *Portraits from Memory*. Recalling some Cambridge contemporaries he suddenly says:

> One of my earliest memories of Compton is of meeting him in the darkest part of a winding College staircase and his suddenly quoting, without any previous word, the whole of "Tyger, Tyger, burning bright." I had never, till that moment, heard of Blake and the poem affected me so much that I became dizzy and had to lean against the wall.

Even though, with his encyclopaedic mind, his passion for inquiry, his voice, and his lucidity, Bertrand Russell is the last of the eighteenth-century figures, let it be put to the eternal credit of Blake in this his centenary year that he once carried away the author of the *Principles of Mathematics*.

It is easy to trace the onset and rise of sensibility. It is hard to chart its fall. At exactly what stage in Victoria's reign swooning went out of fashion would be interesting to determine. It was probably earlier than one imagines. Trollope's heroines, for instance, often seem to be making a great deal of fuss about little, and to take a long time doing it, but they usually manage to keep their wits about them. Among the lesser lights, both Mrs. Steel's and Mrs. Spender's heroines invariably keep a stiff upper lip. Pinero's and other Edwardian heroines could take a good deal of punishment before giving in. Mrs. Miniver never gave in at all.

TO KILL THE COUNT

For the greater part of one's lifetime some books can be like ships that pass in the night. We meet them casually from time to time. Either because their appearance is so distinctive, or their name so striking, we get to know their outward selves quite well. The time comes when no more than a glance, even from a distance, is necessary to tell us what volume it is. Closer examination confirms our guess. The thrill of recognition becomes in time a friendly hail. We acquire quite a lot of information about our chance acquaintance while still remaining aloof. At last the day arrives when opportunity and inclination lead us to go on board.

One such book is *Mademoiselle Ixe*. An odd shape can fix a book in one's mind as much as anything else, and never was there an odder—or a more convenient—shape for a book than Mr. Fisher Unwin's Pseudonym Library. I have come across its long, slim, narrow volumes in many parts of the world. They must have been well made, for although more than sixty years have gone by since most of them were first published (forty since the re-issue), yet they are still invariably sound and whole. Among the better known members of the family are John Oliver Hobbes's *Some Emotions and a Moral*, Korolenko's *The Saghalien Convict*, Lile Rebeck's studies of life in Tonquin, *The House of the Dragon*, and *John Sherman and Dhoya* by W. B. Yeats. "The Pseudonym Library is a veritable Academy of New Reputations" it was enthusiastically declared in 1894, after the new venture had been going only three years. It had as a poster one of the very finest of all Aubrey Beardsley's drawings. It ran to something like sixty volumes and it all started with *Mademoiselle Ixe*.

I wrote a few weeks ago about the way in which, more and more in our day, art and aesthetics are being governed by material and physical considerations. But so they were being also in the 1880s and 1890s. The three-decker had come to an end but readers still wanted quantity for their money. Or, at least, publishers believed they did. Seventy, eighty, ninety thousand words was considered the right length for a novel. A 25,000–30,000 word tale such as *Mademoiselle Ixe* went the rounds of the publishers and always came home again. All this had been in accord with the views of Mr. Fisher Unwin until Mary Hawker's manuscript landed on his desk. The length was all wrong, but he just could not bear to forgo publishing it. All his flair and resourcefulness was challenged. The $6\frac{3}{4} \times 3\frac{1}{4}$ inches format was chosen; a fine type was found, not too large for such a layout, yet enabling the book to run to 185 pages. With a nice feeling for publicity pseudonyms were decided upon. Mary Hawker's was Lanoe Falconer. Ernest Radford was moved to verse in the *Pall Mall Gazette*:

> Fisher Unwin publishes,
> Price one-and-six,
> In the "Pseudonym Library"
> "Mam'selle Ixe."
>
> Publishers are constantly
> Up to new tricks;
> This is their latest—
> "Mam-selle Ixe."

and so on for three more verses. The first edition came out in October, 1890, new ones followed in February, March, April, June, August, October, December, 1891. The astonishing and indefatigable Mr. Gladstone read it and sent a word of praise on one of his famous postcards. In France Taine declared its virtues. Stepniak commended it from Russia. Mr. Fisher Unwin had, indeed, found a winner.

It would be wrong, of course, to think that the tricks did it.

Artistic values can be helped by material aids; they cannot be made by them. *Mademoiselle Ixe* was good in itself. One critic at the time of its first appearance declared it to be one of the finest short stories in the English language. This is too high praise; but it is certainly one of the most beautifully poised and cleverly written. The scenes in which efforts are made to discover Mademoiselle Ixe's religion are comedy worthy of Barchester. The way in which the mysterious governess gets everyone dancing to her will, and sets the stage generally for her *coup de feu*, is a masterly display of the author's craft. The relationship between the Nihilist intruder into an English household and the young girl Evelyn is delicately done. And Mademoiselle Ixe herself—would-be assassin yet noble, schemer yet self-sacrificing, passionate yet drained of almost all other feeling except the affection that slowly grows in her for her charges—is a woman we do not forget. The plot itself is ordinary: a bungled attempt to kill a tyrannical Russian count while he is on a visit to an English country home. Maybe the idea was both shocking and appealing to our late-Victorian great-grandparents. It is the artistry and skill of its development that has made it last.

Mary Hawker was herself very much a country-house product. Most of her life was spent in Hampshire. She wrote from girlhood onwards, but she was forty before she had anything substantial published. She was an accomplished musician, and her biographer, Mrs. March-Phillipps, revealed that it was hearing a Russian air which first sent her to the works of Turgenev and Stepniak. Then she read in *The Times* of February 28, 1890, a terrible recital of cruelty and brutality in a Siberian prison. She was moved through her whole being. She wrote *Mademoiselle Ixe*.

She wrote other tales also. Mr. Fisher Unwin, obviously wishing to cash in on his success, rushed out *The Hotel d'Angleterre and Other Stories* as No. 6 of the Pseudonym Library in 1891. It had a modest success. I am told the curious fact that recently there has been some demand from the public libraries for her ghost story, *Cecilia de Noël*, also published in that year. Indeed, although she lived sixty years in all, the bulk of her work was published in 18 months. It is mostly lightweight. She could accomplish only one *Mademoiselle Ixe*. As for the ever-ingenious Mr. Fisher Unwin, he promptly went on to the Autonym Library. It was, alas, a failure.

A SHADE FAMILIARLY

I am, by nature, sceptical. A great deal of my life has been spent in imploring associates and colleagues not to overlook the virtues of honest doubt. With Mr. Justice Frankfurter—if I may dare to join even the tail of such august company—I believe "The mark of a truly civilized man is confidence in the strength and security derived from the inquiring mind." And in my own, admittedly limited, experience inquiry has never led the most unnatural phenomena to have anything but perfectly natural explanations. I have never seen a ghost or read of one I believed in.

Yet all of this is subject to one magnificent exception. I am ready, against all reason, to accept the word of that great and good man, William Blake. *There* was a man of visions, if ever there was one; and every one of them rings true. Their extreme matter-of-factness to him heightens the effect. As Crabb Robinson noted: "The wildest of his assertions was made with the veriest indifference of tone as if altogether insignificant." And it is to Crabb Robinson, or rather to him and to Professor Edith Morley, that I owe what for me is one of the most delightful scenes in all the long and varied tapestry of our literature. But before we come to it, let me put on record this generation's debt to Professor Morley. Her labours on the Crabb Robinson papers started in 1912. She devoted—among other activities—a working lifetime to them. She has given at least some readers endless joy and pleasure. And when she announced a few years ago that she had at last had to abandon the task owing to lack of public support, it was good to know privately her conviction that she had not left anything of importance unquarried.

In *Blake, Coleridge, Wordsworth, Lamb, &c.; being selections from the Remains of Henry Crabb Robinson* she brings out well the fact of

Milton being one of Blake's familiars. And she gives us this enchanting episode from Crabb Robinson's *Blake Reminiscences*:

> As he [Blake] spoke of frequently seeing Milton, I ventured to ask, half ashamed at the time, which of the three or four portraits in Hollis's Memoirs is the most like. He answered, "They are all like at different ages. I have seen him as a youth and as an old man with a long flowing beard. He came lately as an old man. He said he came to ask a favour of me. He said he had committed an error in his *Paradise Lost* which he wanted me to correct in a poem or picture; but I declined. I said I had my own duties to perform!

The scene is as charming in its innocence as it is grand in its truth. Granting that a century's reflection could have induced Milton to perceive one error in *Paradise Lost*, to whom of all Posterity could he have more reasonably appealed to correct it than to Blake? And though by that time Milton was immortal, and neither Thrones, Dominations, Princedoms, Vertues, nor Powers could withstand him, the one and only man who might truthfully retort that he was too busy was Blake.

The encounter is one which the mind plays with endlessly. The immediate reaction, of course, is to wonder what the error was. It is not a profitable pursuit. The answer is to be found in Gilchrist's *Life of William Blake*. I would not care myself to hazard an opinion on the particular point. But clearly possibilities range much farther afield. If even a Milton can have a *post-mortem* doubt about his masterpiece, what about the lesser immortals? The Elysian Fields have hitherto seemed abodes of serenity and bliss. But can there be anything more upsetting for the artistic spirit than to perceive flaws in one's work only when one is no longer able to do anything about them? Stendhal would not be likely to have—and, indeed, would not relish—a quiet time anywhere. But he was a perfectionist in his own way. Does he still want Mathilde de la Mole to carry her lover's head on her knees to all eternity or does he now realize it to be a silly business, almost the only false piece of theatricality in his works? Matthew Arnold, tired of all other finicking refinements in

"Dover Beach", must surely have got around to the far more important fact that its last two lines do not easily scan. (In that particular queue Tennyson should be prominent with an alternative closing two lines for "Enoch Arden".)

All these, it may be objected, are minor blemishes. Elysium is a place of limitless horizons. Tolstoy may well be wondering whether, in spite of the stimulation he has given to Mr. Isaiah Berlin and others, he was not wrong to let his theory of history nearly waterlog such an unsinkable work of art as *War and Peace*. Goethe is perhaps now convinced that the second part of *Faust* was a great mistake. Shakespeare may wish to rewrite *Troilus and Cressida*. But all of them are surely beyond worrying about trivialities? On this there can be two views. May it not possibly be the specks which are unlivable with to all eternity? "Out, damned spot!"—and knowing there is no way it ever will come out. Unless, hoping for better luck than Milton had with Blake, one applies, a shade familiarly, to Sir ——, or Professor ——, or Mr. ——. But that is the third, and best, part of the game, much too dangerous to play in public.

MON AMI PIERROT

"I intended an ode, and it turned to a sonnet." Why does an article in *Le Monde* on the appearance of yet another volume of the great edition of Sainte-Beuve's letters make me want to write about Taine? Certainly it is no wish to belittle M. Jean Bonnerot's noble effort. This massive collection of his is likely to be one of the great storehouses of our time so far as French literature in the middle of the nineteenth century is concerned. M. Bonnerot has been at work on it for over a quarter of a century. I started buying it when the first instalment came out in 1935. Three volumes were published before the war called a halt. In post-war years, I am afraid, I fell by the wayside. But I read that now, eight years after the sixth volume, a seventh has just appeared containing some 280 letters Sainte-Beuve wrote between the beginning of 1847 and August, 1849. As Sainte-Beuve's life has at this point still another twenty years to run—his most active years at that—and M. Bonnerot is now 75, I begin to fear for the completion of this masterpiece of editing. Every letter is fully documented, every volume has a wealth of critical apparatus; almost every reference is annotated. Thus is a happy hunting ground being made ready for generations to come.

Yet still I want to write about Taine. For while I look at the five feet or more of Sainte-Beuve's works with affection, I never pick up one of the much smaller platoon of Taine's works without an increasing respect. What a wealth of learning, and wisdom, and good sense there is in them. Yet for years it has remained largely untapped. From little causes great effects spring. It has long been a theory of mine that the true architect of Sainte-Beuve's staying-power was Charles Pierrot. He produced as volume 16 of the *Lundis* a *Table Générale et Analytique* which has been an inexhaustible quarry for later writers. How easy when one is getting together an essay on Pascal or Madame de Pompadour to look up this great index with its thousands of references and then bring in the spontaneous "aside": "As Sainte-Beuve says . . ." Victor Giraud added to Pierrot's good work by doing the same for the *Premiers Lundis*, the *Nouveaux Lundis*, and the *Portraits Contemporains*, and now M. Bonnerot is at work on the letters. Happy is the critic who has a good indexer.

Taine lacked his Pierrot. He also suffered from another defect. He was too much in advance of his time. Personally I have always had a soft spot for his *Histoire de la Littérature Anglaise* because a great part of it was written in the library of the Athenaeum. But when he died, *The Times*, while fully acknowledging him as the greatest French writer since the death of Renan a few months before, damned it as

> A book full of brilliant *aperçus*, of happy characterization, vivid word pictures; but a book which revealed in the author a magnificent capacity for riding a hobby to death. As every reader of it remembers, it is an elaborate exercise on the theme that every product of the mind is as much the effect of ascertainable causes as what we commonly call natural products; that man is a creature of his *milieu*; that his work, which is the expression of himself, is the result of his ancestry, his circumstances, the climate and the soil of his country, and the history of his time. The principle is applied throughout with brilliant ingenuity, and for a while the young reader is carried away by it. He has to go to Carlyle or Emerson for the other side; and gradually he comes to feel that M. Taine allows rather too much to the surroundings and too little to the man.

Saintsbury went further and called it a "positively and utterly worthless" work. Thus did the irrepressible spirit of poetry and romanticism squash nineteenth-century stirrings towards the social study of art. But to-day? Surely there is a whole school of sociologists and critics who should pay some tribute to Taine.

Not that I would suggest a republishing, or even a re-reading, of these particular volumes. They have been superseded not only by later works but by later events. But if anyone is looking around for a really long work to get to grips with they could do well with *Les Origines de la France Contemporaine*. Taine was moved to this great study by the disasters of 1870, and he devoted the last 20 years of his life to it. So honest and fundamental is it that it can provide us with clues to the discontents of France to-day. That conscientious craftsman Arnold Bennett made it one of his stand-bys during his Paris years. He became, indeed, a great reader of Taine. He found *Notes sur l'Angleterre* "a wonderful book"; the *Voyage en Italie* fired him to set down more of his own impressions; he noted in his *Journal*: "It is difficult to read *Graindorge* without thinking that the author was a first-class man." It is true he went on to reflect that it was just as difficult to think that the writer of Taine's letters could have been a first-class man. But this was only an ephemeral judgment. Three weeks later he has changed his opinion. Taine

> was undoubtedly a great and an austere man, with very high principles. He thought only of his work, which was the ascertainment of historical truth . . . The portrait of the man gradually grew clearer to me, and inspired me with ideals similar to his own: the doing simply of the work which one believes to be best, and the neglect of all gross and vain considerations.

Taine cannot rival Sainte-Beuve when it comes to commanding the ardour of translators, but more of his work has been published in English than is generally known. It is a pity that the volumes most often seen are those of the *History of English Literature* and the *Life and Letters*. *The Origins of Contemporary France* (six volumes), *Journeys through France*, *On Intelligence*, *Philosophy of Art*, and two volumes of the Italian travel sketches have also been done. And now comes the news that this summer we are to have a fresh and complete translation of the *Notes sur l'Angleterre* by Mr. Edward Hyams. May it lead to a renewed interest in Taine, to a selection of his literary criticism in English, and—who knows?—to an index of his works.

THE NEW HERO

Some weeks ago Mr. V .S. Pritchett wrote for *The New York Times Book Review* a most interesting article on the modern English novel. I have found myself silently arguing about it on a number of occasions since. Mr. Pritchett was not surveying present novel-writing as a whole but was concerned only with the new young group causing most stir. Naming Kingsley Amis, John Wain, Thomas Hinde, Peter Towry, and John Braine, Mr. Pritchett said:

> They have put forward a new kind of hero and they have a distinctly new attitude to life . . . They break sharply with the war and pre-war decades. They are unromantic, or at any rate they are not romantic in the manner of the Thirties. As people these novelists are products of the social revolution of 1940. What has annoyed their seniors is that, on the whole, this generation does not care a damn about the things their fathers fought for . . .
>
> The England of the new novelists is the ugly England of the industrial suburbs and the new building estates: the hero and his friends are half-working class. By state aid and the luck of the war they have gone from the grammar school to the university and from there to some anxious little job in the safe provincial civil service. They are still shut out from the world open to the richer public school boy—or so they think it necessary to believe; though in fact this is not so.

Mr. Pritchett develops two points. The first is that "low" writing is nothing new in English literature. "An aristocratic society like the English can only survive if it continuously draws from below and is continually broadening"; and Mr. Pritchett shows there is a long line going back through Wells, Bennett, D. H. Lawrence, and Gissing to Defoe. His second point is "the irony . . . that the successful diffusion of socialist or welfare ideas in the West has created a generation consumed by personal quirks, suspicion and self-interest and of people committed to themselves." But two other trains of thought have come uppermost in my mind. Why has the spreading of advantage so often created not only jealousy but resentment? Not resentment that others less fortunate should remain underprivileged, but resentment at the fact that the advantages now enjoyed should exist at all.

Mr. Pritchett says, "The impression is of a sour, resentful commonplace England of Julien Sorels who have failed to find their rich patron." In fact they have found him, in the State. That can hardly cause resentment. The "angry young men" cannot have it both ways—ready to rail against the private patron and ready to rail against his disappearance. In fairness to them it must be said that in the cases I am referring to they do not want to have it either way. What they resent is that there should be anything to have. There are undergraduates at Cambridge to-day who, having got where a generation ago it would have been impossible to enter, nurse inside themselves a peculiar kind of grievance that a place with such traditions should survive. Whether they ever rationalize this feeling I do not know, but it forms a bond between them, sometimes hiving them off from the rest. The matter is not merely social or political. If we do not recognize the existence of this sentiment we shall be without one of the keys to the pre-fab towers (ivory is a middle-class commodity) inhabited by this small but vocal fraction of the new generation.

That brings me to my second consideration. The really significant thing is not what is written in any decade but what gets printed. And more than ever to-day the hard facts of publishing mean that little can be printed unless there is a fairly firm assurance that it will be read. For all we know, the angry young men have been at their typewriters for quite a long time. Hundreds of war stories, protests, and recollections were written from 1918 onwards but few of them saw the light of day. The reception of those that did was not enough to encourage others. Then in 1929 came the spate. The public was ready to take any amount of such literature. Relief at the end of killing was exhausted and no longer an all-sufficing mood. Too many hopes deferred had made too many hearts sick. A generation that had set out for a brave new world had reached only the outposts of the great depression. There was a growing suspicion that the war to end war had done nothing of the sort. So came the outburst, heralded by *Journey's End*. It was almost as if men and women sensed that Hitler was in the wings, although they could not know it.

I have written about this before, and it is all hindsight, of course. But it has its direct application to the situation to-day. Once again, following a period of exhaustion and passivity, a public mood has expressed itself in roughly the eleventh year after another war. But this time the protest is not against the war, but its aftermath. It has expressed itself in a sort of horrified fascination for the kind of heroes Mr. Pritchett was writing about in his article. Unlike the 1929 outburst, it is not a protest against something that has happened, so much as a fear of something that may happen. Readers know from their own experience that, however much "the new hero" may posture, he is still too insignificant to be of consequence in to-day's community. But what of to-morrow's? Are these new writers showing us, and therefore warning us against, the new man? If this is not the public mood, what is? Why does one book after another in the category Mr. Pritchett describes find the critics eager to discuss it and the readers ready to take another dose of the same medicine? If we knew the answer to that—and almost certainly it is still hidden and unknowable—we might be better able to glimpse the way our society is heading.

There are those who will say that the whole matter is much simpler, being explained by the excellence of the books as literature. I am afraid this is not so. For one thing, public fashion always quickly outruns the ability to maintain high quality. For another, in this particular case I have yet to find the book that will stay memorable. One may talk about their heroes being Julien Sorels—that does not make any one of them a *Le Rouge et le Noir*. And, if this is too unfair a standard, I have yet to find a near *Bel-Ami*.

I saw them; I coveted them; and then for a week I left them on their shelf *outside* a Charing Cross Road bookshop, at the mercy of all-comers. One acquires a certain nerve in such things. There were, too, arguments to be put on the other side of the scale. Four volumes of almost anything for 10s. is in these days a bargain; at the same time I am old-fashioned enough to want to think twice before gambling a whole ten shillings. Prudence may have pricked conscience, for the next question that arose was whether such a minor classic as the *Mémoires de Marmontel* should not be first read in its own language. Lastly—and this was most powerful—I knew nothing of "The Author of *The Swiss Emigrants*", who had translated it.

In the end it was, I think, "Edinburgh 1808" that decided me. Each new generation likes to read foreign works converted to its own idiom. There must, moreover, be modern translations of masterpieces, if only to keep their memories alive. But long reading has given me a liking for versions made as soon after the original as possible. The *Mémoires d'un Père* of Marmontel were first published in 1804; here within four years was an intrepid Scottish gentleman—and I felt sure in my bones he was Scottish—producing an English edition, and Mundell, Doig, and Stevenson, aided by Lackington, Allen, John Murray, and J. Richardson (was there ever such a cohort of backers?) publishing it.

How right they were! It is at first an enchanting, and later an entrancing, work. Jean François Marmontel had been born to poor parents on a small country farm in 1723. He was therefore 66 when the French Revolution broke out. A protégé of Madame de Pompadour, the recipient of royal favours, secretary of the Academy, historiographer of France, fashionable author, member of the electoral assembly of Paris, Marmontel might have expected to share the fate of so many others. But even in his younger and most dissipated days Marmontel had always been finally ruled by a certain shrewdness. Those days were now far behind him. At the age of 54 he had married a young girl, Mademoiselle de Montigny. When the Terror came, Marmontel, who was no coward—Bailly cites one act of remarkable moral courage, decided the time had come to get as far into the depths of the country as possible. There, eventually in Normandy, he settled down with his wife and young children, and compiled for them his memories of the days that were gone.

The setting and the circumstances are important. The old man, once again in Arcadia, with Inferno not so very far away, conjured up one of the most moving pictures of childhood days, of a remarkable mother, of ambitious and headstrong youth, that French literature possesses. Tender and affecting scenes, full of simplicity and piety and goodness, follow one another. Then the young would-be priest turns dramatist, goes to Paris, meets Voltaire, becomes a gallant, is accused by the great Marshal de Saxe of stealing his mistresses from him, writes operas with Grétry which can still be heard, and in no time is in grace and disgrace at Versailles. But all the time there is the other side of Marmontel, the colleague of Diderot and d'Alembert, the disciple of Vauvenargues. It was this man who contributed to the *Encyclopaedia*, who became editor of the *Mercure*—and wrote as good a recipe for a modern newspaper as can be found to-day, who became a man of affairs, and who met, recorded, and survived the Revolution.

The greatest charm about Marmontel is his absence of humbug. Whether he was guilty of any during his active years we can never know. Writing in his closing days all is open, frank, of an absorbing candour. His children must have had to wait many years to understand some of the things he spoke and wrote about. But the ages gained a wonderful series of character studies done at first hand—Voltaire, Rousseau, d'Alembert, Massillon, Madame de Pompadour, Louis XV and XVI, Chamfort, Mirabeau, Necker. Marmontel is in these things a French Clarendon, but with the gift of being more judicial. The picture of the whole way of daily life at Court, with its nepotism, its rule by favourites, its struggle for perquisites (for which Marmontel fought as vigorously as the rest), its complete detachment from all reality so far as the life of the nation was concerned, is better than any formal history. Indeed, it is only when we come to the Revolution itself, and the *Mémoires* do become rather formal history, that the inner excitement flags.

I would not have it thought that Marmontel was a man devoid of strong feelings or antipathies. He hated Rousseau, worshipped Voltaire, esteemed Necker immoderately. He was a man, too, of extreme sensibility. But even when he was most a courtier he never ceased altogether to be a philosopher, and it is a clear-eyed, endearing old man who tells his tale of young actresses in the springtime of life and of the *tricoteuses* at its close. He died on December 31, 1799, and, whatever the calendar experts may bleat, his century ended with him.

And "The Author of *The Swiss Emigrants*"? He was Hugh Murray, Edinburgh excise clerk and later a formidable Scottish geographer. He was 29 when his translation of the *Mémoires* appeared. It was not the first, for someone, whom I have not been able to identify, brought out an anonymous translation in 1805. But Murray's version shows him to have been a born writer. Easy, flowing, with no unhappy word or uncouth phrase to halt the reader, it has the illusion of taking one into the cottage of Marmontel himself. There the old man sits and talks against the coming night, in a voice and manner we shall never forget, even though all he had to say is a tale that is long since done.

WOMAN INTO LEGEND

A small fame can be livelier than a great one. The names of the Rousseaus and the Swifts go on resounding down the centuries. How often are their more serious works read? No one can commiserate with a Shakespeare on being neglected, but do not some of his critics and commentators drag him perilously close to the abyss of absurdity? Coming nearer our own day, what is the roll-call of those who really know the complete works of Meredith? The Titans stand like some giant totem poles; or like those figures of great antiquity, worn and lichen-grown, six or seven times larger than life—the musical statues Samuel Butler's hero met on the way to Erewhon. Meanwhile lesser mortals such as Butler himself, or a Peacock, or a Borrow, or a Christopher Smart go on, in sprightly fashion, prancing among them; engaging affection instead of commanding awe, winning that live attention which is worth any amount of dead respect. So it is with Katherine Mansfield.

She seems to have escaped the trough into which go all the truly great. Thirty-four years have passed since she died at Fontainebleau—the anniversary was yesterday—yet new editions of her stories, letters, and Journal continue to appear. When Mr. Antony Alpers produced his book on her in 1954 it had three impressions in its first month. Katherine Mansfield is now in the World's Classics (a series badly misnamed but at least denoting quality and pulling power). In the latest *Cornhill* there is a study of her which Elizabeth Bowen has written as a preface to an American collection of the stories. "Her spirit," says Miss Bowen, "was of the kind which does not die down."

Out of the *Cornhill* pages there gazes at the reader a photograph of Katherine Mansfield which is now familiar. I remember vividly its first appearance. It was in June, 1923, in the first number of the *Adelphi*. That introduced many to the Samuel Josephs (the story was apparently an early version of an episode in "Prelude"). Later numbers gave us a few more stories, some poems, a drawing, and—most important—the first extracts from her Journal. For one reader at least the legend had begun.

Katherine Mansfield had, of course, published many of her best stories before then. The collection entitled *Bliss* had come out in 1920. But in those days people in their teens could not normally buy books of new short stories at 9s. A shilling magazine was another matter, especially when one had D. H. Lawrence, Arnold Bennett, H. G. Wells, Middleton Murry, all thrown in for good measure. A pun is pardonable because it is exact.

> Bliss was it in that dawn to be alive,
> But to be young was very Heaven!

As the years went by, on many of these paths we kept coming across Katherine Mansfield. Lawrence, it is true, was far too egocentric to reveal much in his letters to or about her. But even he, the pathological creator of shams, had to admit "she has a genuine side." How genuine it was is best seen—for all their repulsions and cruelties—in her letters and journal. Early on (in 1914) we meet her reading Goethe's *Poetry and Truth*. They remained her only goals to the end. Yet she never paraded false humility. Even when she had to confess "I long and long to write and the words just won't come", she could immediately add "Yet, when I read people like Gorky, for instance, I realize how streets ahead of them I be." She could privately note " 'The Aloe' is right. 'The Aloe' is lovely."

Among the stories themselves everyone has his or her favourites, "Prelude" and "At the Bay" standing as twin peaks, rather apart. (But, as Mr. Alpers pointed out, when *The Garden Party* collection was originally published only Miss Rebecca West linked "At the Bay" with its forerunner and dwelt on its genius.) Nevertheless just as Katherine Mansfield read Henry James for the flash, "that sudden sweet shock, that violent throb of delight", so it is moments in her other stories that stay most in my mind: Ma Parker finding there was nowhere to cry ("Life of Ma Parker"); Mouse suddenly "listening" for Dick Harmon and it bursting upon the reader that he is not going to return ("Je Ne Parle Pas Français"); Else's "I seen the little lamp" ("The Doll's House"). It is impossible to explain why. As Willa Cather, writing of Katherine Mansfield in that book of surprises *Not Under Forty*, has said: "The qualities of a second-rate writer can easily be defined, but a first-rate writer can only be experienced."

Time is likely to show, however, that Katherine Mansfield is more than her stories. Willa Cather, who had a sure instinct for such things, starts her essay on the works with a reminiscence about Katherine Mansfield herself. It is a revealing reminiscence, and more and more has been disclosed of late years. However perfect the literary artist, the human being was far from perfect. We who have grown up with her fame and had her person revealed to us piecemeal can never really see her whole. But eventually new generations will come to her, with all the materials for assessment complete. I doubt, however, if the judgment can ever be final. That will remain her power. They will find her complex, complicated, often unlikeable, an enduring enigma; but compelling and vital always.

The costs of publishing are now so great that it is not easy for new "classics" to be born. (By this I mean volumes that find their way into people's pockets in generation after generation.) All the more exciting, therefore, was the suggestion in *The Times* the other day that the Edinburgh University Press's fine venture with Goethe's letters will in due course have to be produced in a handy size.

Should that happen it will surely join Lewes's *Life* and Eckermann's *Conversations* to make a most companionable trilogy. For Goethe is one of that very small band of great writers who can be lived with for themselves alone. We like to visit them from time to time and are all the more pleased because their works do not get in the way. It would be absurd, of course, to say that they have no works. Dr. Johnson, Goethe, and Jefferson, for instance, were all voluminous men. Yet they have this one thing in common. While we know all about their writings we rarely go to their volumes now. *Rasselas* occasionally, perhaps. A few poems of Goethe's. The Declaration of Independence once a year. But it is the men themselves we like to visit. *They* are inexhaustible.

And of them all it is to Goethe I would give the palm. Dr. Johnson is a more lovable man. He is in many ways a greater character. But visits to him should not be for too long. He was such a tumultuous person, with few points of repose. We find, as Mrs. Boswell did, that a little of him can go a long way. Jefferson is another noble figure. Whether we meet him in Mr. Saul Padover's *A Jefferson Profile* or in *The Life and Selected Writings of Thomas Jefferson* in the Modern Library, we quickly find ourselves in the company of an endlessly interesting, kindly, urbane, and essentially wise being. A little fussy, maybe. All those gadgets in the house at Monticello come to denote a rather restless nature. But for pure goodness, and magnanimity, open manliness and disinterested benevolence towards his fellow-men (always excepting the English of George III's day) it is hard to name Jefferson's equal. He is a man to be visited for himself if ever there was one.

If one had to name a common factor in this curiously assorted trio it would surely be the readiness of their response to every approach. They are endlessly alive and alert; each in his own way tirelessly individual. In Jefferson there was more intellectual curiosity than in Johnson. In Goethe there was most of all. Mineralogy, aesthetics, optics, acting—he was ready to be ceaselessly interested, and interesting. "Come at six so that we can get *Macbeth* read and off" he writes in a note to Schiller (how much Posterity is losing by the telephone); "at seven, when the moon rises, you are invited to an astronomical party to observe the moon and Saturn, for there are three telescopes in my house this evening." You never know, when you call on this man, what his eager intelligence will draw you to next.

If Goethe does come to have his Life-Letters-Table Talk trilogy I believe they will rank in that order. My estimate of Eckermann's *Conversations* has gone down rather. Nietzsche may once have called it "the best German book there is", but the worthy and in himself romantic Eckermann had not quite that last ounce of genius that made Boswell immortal. And the new one-volume edition of the *Letters* to some extent undermines his ground. Lewes's *Life and Works of Goethe*, on the other hand, seems to me a finer book on each new reading. I would put it among the small handful of very best biographies in the English language. Not the least attractive character in it is Lewes himself. Forthright, sensible, manly, outspoken, he tells his story and delivers his judgments without ever becoming garrulous or tiresome. He knew Germany; he had a proper respect for his hero, a true sense of the period. He was a good literary critic. He could manage a large canvas. The man he presents is not a demi-god, but a very remarkable human being. The old Everyman "library edition"—of blessed memory!—of

Lewes's *Life of Goethe* is one I increasingly slip in my pocket for country weekends.

What is the secret of Goethe's fascination and charm? The centenary celebrations eight years ago were a sad disappointment. Even the B.B.C. did not manage to do him justice, and I know it was not for want of trying. Obviously one attraction is his vitality. The life force was strong in him from the first day to the last. Then there is the air of eternal Spring he creates. Always is he radiating ardour and freshness. Because of this his endless love affairs seem free from licentiousness. Lastly, there was always charity and greatness in him. Leaving the ill-starred episode of the poodle on one side, there is almost no record of Goethe having been petty or ignoble. As the foreword to the Edinburgh volume points out: "Among the thirteen thousand letters there are hardly more than a score or so with disparaging remarks about people, nor are there more frequent instances of complaints originating in gloom or despondency." "A perfect man lay in great beauty before me," said Eckermann as he gazed upon Goethe's corpse. Well, there are all kinds of human perfection and imperfection. But the sense of Goethe's beauty of nature is still with us in our anything but Spring-like world.

GOLD MEDAL

This is being written—to use a phrase first attributed to Charles Lamb, a fact which should delight our subject—*con amore*. It is appreciation, not criticism. No doubt both time and learning could do it much better, and so one day someone will do it. But the news that the Queen's gold medal for poetry has been given to Edmund Blunden is so splendid that I cannot withhold a short note of pleasure. I have not consulted thoroughly the now fairly long line of his works. Those I have by me are only the *Poems* up to 1940, *Undertones of War*, *The Bonadventure*, *The Mind's Eye*, and *Votive Tablets*. I shall therefore say nothing of his later work, or his devotion to Charles Lamb, Shelley, Keats, Vaughan, and Clare. It is no matter. I have cargo enough.

The first things that strike one about this little collection are its diversity and its quality. Nature and war poems; war book, travel book, literary and other essays—each is first-class in its kind. Each, too, has stayed the course. When recently I quoted a list of 1914–18 books I had compiled in the 1930s, more remonstrances were made about the omission of *Undertones of War* than of any other work. The men who knew remember. There is the honesty of the opening sentence: "I was not anxious to go." There are such things as this:

> Daytime was play in the Islands [a part of the front near Festubert] that summer; night was a perpetual tangle. If one went forward patrolling, it was almost inevitable that one would soon creep round some hole or suspect heap or stretch of wired posts, and then, suddenly one no longer knew which was the German line, which our own. Puzzling dazzling lights flew up, fell in the grass beside and flared like bonfires; one heard movements, saw figures, conjectured distances, and all in that state of dilemma. Willow

trees seemed moving men. Compasses responded to old iron and failed us. At last by luck or some stroke of recognition one found oneself; but there was danger of not doing so; and the battalion which relieved us sent a patrol out, only to lose it that way. The patrol came against wire, and bombed with all its skill; the men behind the wire fired their Lewis gun with no less determination; and, when the killed and wounded amounted to a dozen or more, it was found that the patrol and the defenders were of the same battalion. I knew the officer who led that patrol; he was by temperament suited for a quiet country parsonage, and would usually have mislaid his spectacles.

Or this from the poem "Third Ypres" which he included in the same volume.

> The hour is come; come, move to the relief!
> Dizzy we pass the mule-strewn track where once
> The ploughman whistled as he loosed his team;
> And where he turned home—hungry on the road,
> The leaning pollard marks us hungrier turning.
> We crawl to save the remnant who have torn
> Back from the tentacled wire, those whom no shell
> Has charred into black carcasses—Relief!
> They grate their teeth until we take their room
> And through the churn of moonless night and mud
> And flaming burst and sour gas we are huddled
> Into the ditches where they bawl sense awake,
> And in a frenzy that none could reason calm,
> (Whimpering some, and calling on the dead)
> They turn away: as in a dream they find
> Strength in their feet to bear back that strange whim
> Their body.

Blunden once complained of the "slight injustice" done to him by the assumption that because *The Shepherd* won the Hawthornden Prize he must be a rustic poet. We must avoid the other injustice of giving the impression he is predominantly a First-War writer, although—as he himself pointed out in the collected volume of his poems up to 1930—war became part of his experience so young as to "mould and colour the poetry almost throughout this book". He also reflected 10 years later that "those who saw that tremendous time will know that it does not easily give up its hold." But he has many other strains. Poems such as "The Covert" and "The Barn" take us into the heart of old England; and the last verse of "The May Day Garland" shows how beguilingly he wages his war with our old enemy.

> And for these courteous children,
> And Love that's ever a child,
> The May should never fade to-night
> Could Time but be beguiled,
> Could Time but see the beauty of
> These singing honied hours,
> And lie in the sun adream while we
> Hid up his scythe in flowers!

With most poets, perhaps, there is too great a readiness on their readers' part to believe they are speaking in person when really they are singing in character. Blunden has warned us that many of his pieces were written "not as elements of an autobiography but in the spirit of projection and daydream". Yet here and in many other poems I am sure we have the man.

We have him, too, in *The Bonadventure*, which is one of the truest pieces of reporting that has come from a tramp steamer. Then there are the essays. These reveal more by implication, however. *Votive Tablets* contains his best work; *The Mind's Eye*, ranging through Flanders, Japan, England, and literature, displays his many-sidedness better. Some of his essays have been written for special occasions, a centenary, a new book coming out, a cause to be supported. But it is the choice of these things that can tell us much. Edmund Blunden has rarely written on a subject that did not engage his interest. It is sometimes said that he has not fulfilled his earliest promise, that the flow of creative work has not been kept up. If this is so—and I do not know what he has unpublished—it may be because he has of late years been fully occupied in being a good citizen of the world of letters.

FRIEDA LAWRENCE

Repairing too long a neglect, I was reading *The Lost Girl* when the news of Frieda Lawrence's death came. A sentence by Virginia Woolf, describing the book as "a compact and seamanlike piece of work, stuffed with careful observation rather in the Bennett manner", had startled me and I had gone back to it to check up. The description is remarkably apt of the first part. The opening chapter on James Houghton, the romantic draper, and his unending but hopeless war against the vulgarity and mediocrity of the local mining community is not only perhaps the best comedy Lawrence ever wrote, but also a beautiful piece of social reporting. The tale, moreover, goes from strength to strength. Even the women characters, Alvina Houghton, Miss Frost, and Miss Pinnegar, are nearer to the Bennett norm than D. H. Lawrence's women usually are. But with the arrival on the scene of the "Red Indian troupe", and of Cicio, we realize we are setting out on the usual Lawrence hegira once again.

All Lawrence's darts, dashings, excursions, and journeyings were, in fact, flights. There is nothing derogatory in this. Always, for him, reality seemed banality, and it more than offended him. He found it insupportable. Hence not merely his physical restlessness (he was one of the most widely travelled novelists who have ever lived), but also his creative restlessness. It was part of his literary attraction and of his lasting value. And although in most cases he searched to the end without feeling he had surely found what he sought, I am convinced that in the most vital matter of all, his marriage, he had the supreme felicity to have done so from the outset.

This may seem surprising, but it ought in justice to be said, and at once, before any appraisal of Frieda Lawrence that there may be by this generation is finally crystallized. Writing some months ago about the Lawrence legend I said he had had a happy life. That struck some people as a puncturing statement. It was merely put forward as a matter of fact. Now, if there is any puncturing to be done, I would do it by saying that meeting Frieda was the greatest find Lawrence made in his perpetual search and that marrying her was the wisest and most happy thing he ever did.

I never met Frieda Lawrence, nor, for that matter, Lawrence either. There are still alive many who knew them intimately and this statement will find agreement from some. It has been implied in a number of the books about Lawrence that have cascaded out since his death. But legends die hard. They become stark and cruel with time. And the number of people who, on hearing of Frieda Lawrence's death and were interested at all, said "Weren't they always fighting?" or "Wasn't that a stormy affair?" were probably as great as those who believe Jane Welsh was always throwing plates at Thomas Carlyle. No one would pretend to put Lawrence and Carlyle in the same class, but justice is a classless affair. Lawrence was a not inconsiderable figure in the history of English writing in the first half of this century—admittedly a rather poor period—and he was one of those men with a daemon ,whose lives are going to be scrutinized as closely as their works. And no one can do this without coming to a decided view about Frieda Lawrence.

By some quirk, I find that on my shelves her own story of her life with Lawrence, *Not I, but the Wind* . . . stands next to Mr. Harry Moore's *The Intelligent Heart* (the best all-round book on Lawrence yet written). It is no bad description for the woman herself. (In passing it is worth noting how significantly she put on the title page under her name "*Geb. Freiin von Richtofen*" and had the Richtofen family arms in solitary glory facing it.) In the foreword, she herself went straight to the point;

> Do I want to blow my own trumpet? Yes, I do. But will it have a clear rousing sound or will it be a bit wheezy and out of tune? Can I hear the

real song of our life, the motifs gay, bold, sad, terrible, or can't I? . . .

It was a long fight for Lawrence and me to get some truth between us; it was a hard life with him, but a wonderful one. Stark and bare, without trimmings and frills. But a few realities remained, a lasting truth triumphed. . . .

We had so many battles to fight out, so much to get rid of, so much to surpass. We were both good fighters.

She goes on to speak of "the class war", of the fact that they came from different worlds. There was also the difference in race. There was further the fact that in the countries of the mind and heart they inhabited different territories. But "Lawrence and I were adventurers by nature, we explored." Lawrence put the matter in his own way in his poem "Both Sides of the Medal", one of the series *Look! We have Come Through!*

> But we will learn to submit
> each of us to the balanced, eternal orbit
> wherein we circle on our fate
> in strange conjunction.

They explored, in strange conjunction, and a lasting truth triumphed. That is not too grandiloquent an epitaph for Frieda Lawrence. Unlike the wives of many greater authors than Lawrence, she was not merely part of the domestic appurtenances, to be recorded and then either ignored or deplored. She was an essential part of his innermost life and therefore of his best work. Her name is on no title page besides that of her own book but she wrote herself on to Lawrence's consciousness and into much of what he wrote, whether he knew it or not. She was a noble, healthy, fertilizing influence. And if all this seems too vague and high-flown for the sceptics, I would present them with one small picture recorded by Earl and Achsah Brewster of Lawrence a year or two before his death, meeting train after train at Vevey because he expected Frieda back from Baden-Baden, and coming home disconsolate. "We tried to cheer him up, but in vain. He always looked forward so eagerly to her return."

THE OTHER ALICE

No doubt there will be some who during the next 10 days will settle down to a "nice quiet read" with Mill's *Logic*, Lecky's *History of England in the Eighteenth Century*, or, perhaps, *Romola*. But time and place have their part to play in reading, as well as the book, and may, indeed, determine the choice of it. I have read Caesar's *Commentaries* while endlessly waiting for an aeroplane in war-time Lisbon; Thucydides while doing a business deal with some really tough Australians (an admirable choice, this); and *War and Peace* has taken me across the Pacific. What these things indicate I do not know. But no subtle reasoning or deep argument is needed to claim that an ideal Christmas book is *Alice for Short*.

It opens with a fog and a hard frost, yet nonetheless it is a cosy book. From the moment—and that is on the first page—we, in company with Charles Heath and his friend, Mr. Jeffery Saunders Jerrythought, meet little Alicia Kavanagh bringing home the jug of beer too large for her from the Duke of Clarence's Head to the basement where her parents lead their nagging lives together, we are in a nice warm theatre, watching a jolly, full-blooded, unsophisticated pantomime. There is the Cinderella theme. There is the ghost. There is the harsh and uncomely life of the poor, and the pleasant, placid life of the well-to-do, with a generous slice of Bohemia in between; and, of course, there is the transformation scene.

That gifted and enchanting child author William De Morgan—for at the age of sixty-eight he was more of a child than he had ever been—loved transformation scenes. Whether he was transporting little Joey Vance from penury to riches, Lizerann Coupland (in *It Never Can Happen Again*) from her blind beggar father to great friends; or Alice-for-Short from below to above stairs (and from Soho to Hyde Park Gardens), he did it with relish and gusto. And like a child, his eye missed not a single incident or detail along the way. Street fights, life's odd quirks and creatures, a walk in the country, a mysterious *revenant*, an old gentleman who disappears for ever through a hidden trap-door: all such things are accepted in an equal, matter-of-fact way. They have their purpose and place in the pattern, but it is for you to see it as you listen to the child, rather than for him to explain.

Not that William De Morgan is a picaresque novelist. His stories may seem episodic, but in fact they are tightly knit. If anything, they have too much plot. The Victorian novelist—and De Morgan was a true Victorian even though all his books were written under Edward VII and George V—was curiously like the modern cinema. Each work had to be a kind of double-feature programme; plot and sub-plot. (Trollope was a master at handling these pairs-in-hand.) But in *Alice For Short* De Morgan has not two plots but three. The one about the Luttrell ghost I have never yet fully understood, and it doesn't really matter. But the thread running through the work that every now and again brings us to the rather mysterious Verrinder and his wife is golden. The pages wherein old Jane emerges from her 60 years of traumatic insanity, never realizing she is not still an eager young bride, Alice's tender companionship of her, and Jane's sudden awakening to the truth, are among the most moving pages I know in fiction. Yet so much warmth, tenderness, and loving-kindness has gone into them that they never harrow.

But, of course, it is by its main story that *Alice For Short* must stand or fall. Are the widely differing Kavanagh and Heath families puppets or flesh and blood? Do we care whether Charlie succumbs to the wiles of Miss Straker or marries Alicia in the end? Above all, can such a conjunction—with its need to bridge the gaps in both position and years—be made credible if it comes about? To all these questions, for me at least, De Morgan gives a triumphant answer. The two families and their settings are never deliberately put in juxtaposition or contrasted; they are just parts of a multifarious world. And family life was William De Morgan's *forte*. He could handle relations between parents and children, above all between brother and sister, with wonderful insight. (It has been said Charles Heath is really a self-portrait. That may be true but De Morgan did the same thing in other novels.) As for the "happy ending", it is not flung at the reader in a take-it-or-leave-it fashion. All through the book one of the two sub-plots is steadily working us towards it; with a baronet, a will, and the Statute of Mortmain all being thrown into the scales of justification for good measure. Much as one may admire the great verve of *Joseph Vance*, its ending has always seemed rather bathetic. But from the first page to the last *Alice for Short* grows in conviction.

Finally there is the tone of voice of it all; that is, William De Morgan himself. I have said he was a child, and so he was. But he was also a dear and good man, who loved almost all human beings, and who wanted to give them pleasure. Fortunately, so far as I know, no one has yet thought him worthy of the higher criticism; no one has unearthed any psychological or sociological implications in his novels. He is not likely ever to become a cult, and fond as I am of all his works, the later ones, where garrulity became uncontrolled, grow tedious. But *Joseph Vance* and *Alice for Short* will surely long survive to catch and delight new readers. And as I grow older I become more and more convinced that *Alice for Short* is the better work of the two.

MOBY THEO

During Christmas time, as usual, Theodore Dreiser came into my mind, and I have since been thinking on and off what place he should have there. But before considering this it is necessary to explain the "as usual". One December, many years ago, the newspaper I was on was coming to the end of its serialization of *An American Tragedy*. All had gone well. The venture had been a surprising success. Then suddenly it was discovered that, as the installments—planned a long time ahead—were working out, Clyde Griffiths would reach the electric chair on Christmas Eve. This, the editor declared, was impossible. The B.B.C.'s shock tactics with Grace Archer were then nearly half a lifetime away, but the same consequences were dimly foreseen. It fell to me so to rearrange matters that the hero survived till after Boxing Day.

It is perhaps inevitable—and does Dreiser no harm—that *An American Tragedy* is invariably the book his name conjures up. But he was a voluminous author. He started his writing career as a reporter in the lushest days of American journalism, and to the end of his life he loved to spread himself. Even within each volume he found it hard to have bounds. In *A Book About Myself* he takes 500 pages to cover four years of his early life. As one critic has put it, "Mr. Dreiser never uses one word where two will do." He "plods drearily on through his task," said another, "without the relief of a ray of humour, save that which at times he supplies unconsciously." One begins to recall Bernard Shaw's wonderful description of Brahms as "that maundering leviathan". For here is still a third critic: "Mr. Dreiser pads earnestly after things as they are, with mournful voice and hopeful eye."

At this point I protest. That last was written about *Sister Carrie*.

And while *Sister Carrie* is a saddening book it is not at all like that. Opposition once aroused, one begins to ask whether this whole business of the turgidity of Dreiser has not been grossly overdone. As I remember it, Mr. Trilling in *The Liberal Imagination* contrasted Dreiser severely with Henry James. Now James was certainly a great artist and Dreiser was not. James is important in a way Dreiser can never be. But I have not come across a book of Dreiser's I could not finish, and only about half of James's that I could.

The truth is something of a paradox. Dreiser's popularity was established in the 1920s in Britain (about the same time as we were also giving America a lead in restoring Melville's reputation). Dreiser had given the impetus by publishing his one masterpiece, but *Jennie Gerhardt*, *Sister Carrie*, and *The Financier* all found readers. They were, however, mostly ordinary readers who care nothing about style so long as they are given a story. Most writers who do this can be ignored by the critics. Dreiser was too massive for that. He meant something. He had to be read. This imperative infuriated the critics. They paid him back by attacking his weakest point. And in some of his works outside those I have mentioned there was no redeeming feature.

What then has Dreiser to offer? First, an absolute integrity. *Jennie Gerhardt* is, to my mind, a more sincere book than *Esther Waters*; the study of the decline and death of Hurstwood in *Sister Carrie* is as uncompromising as that of any French realist. Secondly, Dreiser could create real people. The blunders, the inanities, the grotesqueries of his style go unnoticed as we follow the fortunes of his men and women. Thirdly, he knew what he was writing about. As a Chicago newspaperman he had seen "the great American jungle". He had met the knaves, the crooks, the gamblers, the speculators, the political bosses, and their womenfolk. *The Financier* is an American version of *The Way We Live Now* with the advantage that Dreiser knew his Cowperwood in a way Trollope could never know Melmotte. Finally, length, with Dreiser, was not verbosity. It is his battering-ram. He was determined to depict every relevant fact or incident or characteristic. He could leave nothing out. He had not the artist's discarding eye. He included everything with the inexorableness of daily life itself.

Nowhere in this carried farther than in *An American Tragedy*. But here, as in the case of Bennett's solitary masterpiece, *The Old Wives' Tale*, some magic mysteriously took hold. When I first read the book I was still at it the next dawn. To this day I can remember even the names of the two counsel, Belknap and Jephson, and the whole trial of Clyde Griffiths remains as vivid as if one had had one of the uncomfortable seats in court. The best tribute to *An American Tragedy* as a story is the fascination it has from time to time exerted upon Hollywood. The best tribute to Dreiser is that each one of the efforts to film it has failed.

Because Dreiser was an uncouth writer, had no system, did not attempt to create a fictional world, was too pessimistic to believe in any 'isms, he has not had his due. He wrote some atrociously bad books. He could never have been a Balzac. He might have been a Zola. He was a far more significant American writer than some who have become world-famous since his day.

THE UNDYING FIRE

The old year dies. We look back; we look forward. We sum up. We remember; we forget. We forget too much. Familiarity can breed contempt even for pain; especially pain of the mind at the distresses of others. We have fought for liberty so long that we can become deadened to other people's loss of it. At such a time as this, when millions still enslaved are in danger of becoming merely a book-keeping entry in the annual accounts of the cold war, it is good to go back to a book where cruelty is ugly; oppression repulsive; and the spirit of man, though submitted to every outrage and indignity, struggles through to freedom in the end.

Not much has been heard of Charles de Coster's *The Legend of Ulenspiegel* during recent years. Coming from Belgium, it had a short vogue in English at the end of the First World War. After yet another despotic occupation of at least part of the Netherlands had been triumphantly ended, it then seemed topical and appropriate. Two different translations appeared (I propose to quote from Mr. Atkinson's). Articles about de Coster were published. Edmund Gosse reminded us that his masterpiece was the "Belgian National Epic". But it had, and has, a wider value. Charles de Coster, archaeologist, professor, journalist, Bohemian, when—in the middle of good Queen Victoria's reign—he took the old "Merry Pranks" of German legend and turned it into what was, in effect, a prose poem on the rise of the Dutch republic, knew what he was about. Tyl, he once said, "takes up arms for liberty of conscience . . . Lamme Goedzack walks straight on through life, as though to be good and upright was all that mattered in this world." Nele, Tyl's mate, is fidelity. De Coster packed his canvas with characters and incidents; he never let go of enduring values.

Tyl Ulenspiegel and his friend Lamme Goedzack have been called Rabelaisian figures. They are far removed from that. Rather they are a new and more urgent breed of Don Quixote and Sancho Panza. And they are encountering the terrible realities of life, not its phantasms. The tale is really the parallel lives of two men, born at the same moment; King Philip, child of the Emperor Charles V, and Ulenspiegel, the Flanders peasant's son—the oppressor and the oppressed. Tyl's adventures are described by de Coster in his subtitle as "heroical, joyous and glorious in the land of Flanders and elsewhere". But many of the events are terrible and sickening. There are revolting cruelties and tortures; executions are often, indeed, a release. Yet joy is the pervading spirit of the book. Its opening sentence strikes the chord:

> When May was unfolding the white-thorn blossom Ulenspiegel, son of Claes, was born at Damme in Flanders.

Flanders, that wonderful plain that all who come to know it can never forget, and its historic spirit, light the book all through. Tyl's "six baptisms" in the opening pages depict its lustiness and sedate good humour. No sooner is Tyl weaned than he grows "like a young poplar". And as quickly his adventures begin.

There is never much point in reciting the episodes in a picaresque novel, especially when it is part allegory. Tyl moves through a world of fairs and markets, tramps and beggars and vagabonds, monks and inquisitors, theologians, Princes and Fools, Dukes and Landgraves, townsmen and peasants. He has passages with the Emperor Charles from the scaffold (whence he escapes by his wit), and with the Pope in Rome. He and Lamme join the famous Beggarmen and partake in their glory and triumph. Both in spirit and in history de Coster's Tyl is very different from his sixteenth-century prototype. He is neither gross nor madcap. He has nobility of soul and purpose. He is the spirit, not of the countryman against the townsman, but of his whole land against tyranny.

When the English versions of *The Legend of Ulenspiegel* were originally published some nervousness was obvious. This was because part of the tyranny and much of the cruelty were under the aegis of the Roman Catholic Church. Pains were taken to deny that the book was a Protestant tract. They were unnecessary. De Coster was dealing with history, and although almost all his incidents are invented, their mainspring and their background are all too verifiable. De Coster's enemy was not the Church. It was oppression from wherever it came. Like Voltaire, he cried "Écrasez l'infâme." He had a passion for personal and national liberty. To his hate was allied pity. He wrote other works, but he put his soul into this one enduring, fascinating, and moving book.

The Legend of Ulenspiegel is worth reading at any time. It is particularly appropriate to-day. At a time when there is a tendency despairingly to write off the cause of freedom as lost for ever in various parts of the world, it is good to recall the end of the tale. As the States General, assembled at The Hague, indicts and deposes Philip, declares him a murderer, and breaks his seals, Tyl himself gives up the ghost. All are gathered for his funeral.

Then the peasant digged the grave and placed Ulenspiegel therein and covered him with sand.

And the *curé* said the prayers for the dead above the grave: all kneeled down around it. Suddenly there was a great upheaving under the soil and Ulenspiegel, sneezing and shaking the sand out of his hair, seized the *curé* by the throat.

"Inquisitor!" said he, "thou dost thrust me into the earth alive in my sleep. Where is Nele? Hast thou buried her too? Who art thou?"

The *curé* cried out: "The great Beggar returneth into this world. Lord God! receive my soul!"

And he took to flight like a stag before the hounds.

Nele came to Ulenspiegel. "Kiss me, my darling," said he.

Then he looked round him again; the two peasants had fled like the *curé*, and had flung down shovel and chair and sunshade to run the better; the burgomaster and the alderman, holding their ears with fright, were whimpering on the turf.

Ulenspiegel went up to them, and shaking them:

"Can any bury," said he, "Ulenspiegel the spirit and Nele the heart of Mother Flanders? She, too, may sleep, but not die. No! Come, Nele."

And he went forth with her, singing his sixth song, but no man knoweth where he sang the last one of all.

Whether the months to come will anywhere see freedom physically revived or not, four thousand years of history are there to prove its spirit cannot be extinguished.

THE RIGHT AGE

"This book should be read when one is 55." Clearly the writer intended to make his readers sit up, and this one did. The statement was so madly precise; surely nothing but a touch of madness, even if it were only spring madness, could have so firmly excluded the 54s and the 56s. One could not help wondering, too, how the writer knew, unless he were himself 55. Then a talk by Bertrand Russell, printed in *London Calling*, on books that had influenced him when he was young, took the idea still further. For Lord Russell said that he had never found in later years that books had been as important to him as they had been between the ages of 15 and 21.

Is there "a right age" at which to read any particular book? Clearly there is something in the idea. I doubt if Albert Sorel's great work *L'Europe et la Revolution Française* would have meant much to me if I had read it in youth or early manhood. It is assuredly a book for middle-age. On the other hand, Carlyle's *French Revolution* must be read in one's 'teens or not at all. With Macaulay it is a case of the younger the better; and the same is almost as true of Gibbon. But not of Burke. He was a sad disappointment to me as a young man, and I have known others share the same experience. One does not know where to get hold of him then. Boswell and Morley and others had given one such great expectations of Burke. But when one took up *Reflections on the French Revolution*, or the *Speech on the Nabob of Arcot's Debts*, or the *Vindication of Natural Society* it was like trudging across a ploughed field. There were no obvious tracks, few beauties along the way, and no clear destination. Only *The Sublime and the Beautiful* held one's interest. To appreciate Burke in youth it is necessary to be a natural politician; otherwise only experience and years can bring the required leaven.

Lamb was no good to me as a boy or even much later. I thought him an overrated bore. My diary shows me more and more impatient with every fresh effort to get to grips with him. Life was real; life was earnest; life was challenging and exciting; and here was an old gentleman maundering away about dream children, dead cronies, and an assortment of things which could not matter less. To Lamb can be equally appropriately applied what Andrew Lang said of Montaigne: "He is a tired man's author, not a fresh man's. We all come to him late indeed, but at last, and rest in his panelled library." Lamb had no panelled library, it is true, but I now find myself reading him with increasing pleasure. In those days when Lamb was being spurned, Bacon and Hume were the men for me. Saintsbury's gusto put me on to more "new authors" than any other man, while Quiller-Couch provided urbane perspective.

Boswell I came to know really well at 20. Such is his magic, and the magic of Johnson, that there has never been a year in which he could not be read. Pepys I just could not get on with; he is a blind spot still. Mill I have never wearied of reading in youth and middle-age. I no longer think him the saint of anything—he seems to have been a rather unpleasant man—but his manly common sense, his noble belief in the virtues of argument, and his passionate stand for the rights of even the smallest minority were the sparks to make young ardour catch fire. Liberty, as Mill understood it, has vanished from many parts of the world since those days—and has been put in jeopardy in others—but the magnificent rightness of all he proclaimed remains. (None of this has prevented my enjoying and admiring James FitzJames Stephen in later years. I believe he was wrong, but he was a worthy opponent for Mill, both in matter and in manner.)

Stendhal, I am sure, is an author to read in one's twenties; only then do the Juliens and the Fabrices not seem silly. The full splendour of Balzac, on the other hand, is reserved for older, wiser—and sadder?—men. The great Russians can be read at any time. Is any other writer a young man's and an old man's author so much as

Turgenev? To persevere with Goethe needs the stamina of youth. Heine is essentially an author for middle-age, Marlowe is for inexperience, Shakespeare for mellowness.

One of the surprising things is how much better so many "children's books" are if they are escaped in early life. *Alice in Wonderland* is an obvious example. I read no Merriman till I was 40 and could never have found the same savour in him as a boy. *Flotsam*, to mention only one work, needs experience of life to reveal its full poignancy. Merriman was a master of the failure and the might-have-been. These things mean little in early years. Wilkie Collins, however, is a boy's author if ever there was one. Of the poets Shelley is for youth, Wordsworth for old age. To wrestle with and understand Browning calls for the full equipment of one's middle years.

And so the game can go on; for its possibilities are endless. But it *is* a game. For few people map or plan their reading through life. Chance and circumstance play the largest part in almost all reading for pleasure. Happy should we be that it is so. The two greatest charms of this exciting hobby of reading are that for even the longest life the wealth is inexhaustible, and for even the most knowledgeable book-lover there is no knowing what may be just around the corner.

Index